THE ELOHIST AND NORTH ISRAELITE TRADITIONS

SOCIETY OF BIBLICAL LITERATURE
MONOGRAPH SERIES

edited by
Leander E. Keck

Associate Editor
James L. Crenshaw

Number 22

THE ELOHIST AND
NORTH ISRAELITE TRADITIONS
by
Alan W. Jenks

SCHOLARS PRESS
Missoula, Montana

THE ELOHIST AND NORTH ISRAELITE TRADITIONS

by

Alan W. Jenks

Published by
SCHOLARS PRESS
for
The Society of Biblical Literature

THE ELOHIST AND NORTH ISRAELITE TRADITIONS
by
Alan W. Jenks

Copyright © 1977
by
The Society of Biblical Literature

Library of Congress Cataloging in Publication Data

Jenks, Alan W.
   The Elohist and north Israelite traditions.

   (Monograph series — Society of Biblical Literature ; no. 22)
   A revision of the author's thesis, Harvard, 1965.
   Includes bibliographical references and indexes.
   1. E document (Biblical criticism) 2. Prophets.
I. Title. II. Series: Society of Biblical Literature. Monograph series ; no. 22.
BS1181.2.J46   1976   221.6   76-40189
ISBN 0-89130-088-0

Printed in the United States of America

To Denda, with gratitude

Preface

This book results from the thorough revision and rewriting of a doctoral dissertation which was presented at Harvard in 1965 under the primary direction of the late Professor G. Ernest Wright. Professor Wright suggested the subject to me, contributed many of the most important ideas, and encouraged me to work toward its eventual publication. I am one of the many people who will always be grateful for the life and work of this great man and scholar. I here express my deep thanks for all that he taught me, for the many ways he helped me, and for the example which he set.

I also thank Professor Frank M. Cross, Jr., for the many fundamental ideas which he contributed, both through his teaching and through his writings, and Professors Krister Stendahl and Paul Rieman whose criticisms of the original dissertation helped me to shape this book. I am of course responsible for any errors.

Some of the many people who have helped me during the revision process are Professor Leander Keck, editor of the Monograph Series, Professor William F. Stinespring of Duke Divinity School who read my manuscript and offered extremely helpful criticisms and suggestions for improvement, Professor and Mrs. Patrick D. Miller who arranged for me to live and work for a time at Union Theological Seminary in Richmond, Mrs. Martha Aycock of the Seminary library there who gave me indispensable aid in locating publications, and Rabbi Paul Reis of Morgantown who gave me very tangible assistance in the last stages of manuscript preparation.

Most of all I thank my wife for her patience, moral support and direct assistance in any number of ways during these years in which "the Elohist" has been almost a member of the family.

Morgantown, West Virginia

20 May 1975

Table of Contents

Chapter	Page
Preface	vii
Abbreviations	xiii
Introduction	1

I Toward a New View of E: Criticism since 1900 2

A. The Impact of Form Criticism 2
B. The Disappearance of Separate Sources 4
C. The Rejection of E as an Independent Source 9
   1. Mowinckel 9
   2. Volz and Rudolph 10
D. The Structure and Origin of the Hexateuch 12
E. Conclusions 15

II The Content and Scope of E 19

A. The Patriarchal Narratives, Genesis 12—50 19
   1. Texts Having Yahwist Parallels 21
   2. Texts Lacking Yahwist Parallels 24
   3. The Joseph Narratives, Genesis 37, 39—50 27
   4. Texts in which J and E are Mingled 33
   5. Summary 38
B. The Exodus and Sinai Covenant Traditions, Exodus 1—34 39
   1. The Mosaic Birth and Call Narratives, Exodus 1—3 40
   2. The Plague Narratives, Exodus 4—12 41

		3.	The Deliverance from Egypt, Exodus 13—17	42
		4.	Jethro's Visit to the Israelites, Exodus 18	44
		5.	The Sinai Pericope, Exodus 19—34	45
	C.	The Wilderness Wandering,	
		Numbers 10—Deuteronomy 34	54
		1.	Rebellion in the Wilderness, Numbers 11—12	54
		2.	The Balaam Pericope, Numbers 22—24	55
		3.	The Baal Peor Incident (Numbers 25) and Israel's Settlement of Transjordan	58
		4.	The Last Days of Moses, Deuteronomy 31—34	59
	D.	The Conquest, Joshua 1—24	60
	E.	The Primeval History, Genesis 1—11	63
	F.	Conclusions	66

III The E Traditions and Early Northern Prophecy 83

	A.	The Prophetic Traditions Concerning Samuel	83
		1.	History of Criticism	83
		2.	The Age and Character of the Samuel Source	85
		3.	Samuel and the Cult	86
		4.	E and the Prophetic Traditions of 1 Samuel	89
		5.	Conclusions	92
	B.	The Elijah-Elisha Traditions	93
		1.	Literary Criticism	93
		2.	Historical Background	95
	C.	Prophecy and the Prophet in the Elijah-Elisha Traditions and in the E Tradition	96
		1.	Relation to the Monarchy	96
		2.	Prophetic Revelation	97
		3.	The Prophet and the Cultus	98
		4.	The Prophet versus Israel	99
	D.	The Relation of E to the Elijah-Elisha Traditions	100
	E.	The Date and Provenance of E	101
		1.	The Political Context	101
		2.	The Cultus of Jeroboam I	103
		3.	E as a Tenth-Century Collection	105

IV E and Later North Israelite Traditions 112

	A.	Hosea	112
		1. Jacob, Hosea 12:3-7, 13	113
		2. Moses and the Exodus, Hosea 9:3; 11:5; 12:13	113
		3. The Covenant, Hosea 4:2; 8:12	114

	4.	The Golden Calf, Hosea 8:5-6; 10:5-6	115
	5.	The Wilderness, Hosea 9:10; 11:1-4; 13:4-6	115
	6.	Kingship Condemned, Hosea 3:4; 7:3-7; 8:4, 10; 10:7, 15; 13:10-11	116
	7.	Conclusions	116
B.	Deuteronomy	117
	1.	Deuteronomy and the Contents of J and E	118
	2.	E and Deuteronomic Theology	119
	3.	E and the Style of Deuteronomy	122
	4.	Conclusions	125

Index of Biblical Passages 131

Index of Modern Authors 145

Abbreviations

AJSL	*American Journal of Semitic Languages and Literatures*
AT	Altes Testament
ATD	Das Alte Testament Deutsch
BA	*Biblical Archaeologist*
BASOR	*Bulletin of the American Schools of Oriental Research*
BBB	Bonner biblische Beiträge
BJRL	*Bulletin of the John Rylands Library*
BKAT	*Biblischer Kommentar: Alten Testament*
BWANT	Beiträge zur Wissenschaft vom Alten und Neuen Testament
BZAW	Beihefte zur *ZAW*
CBQ	*Catholic Biblical Quarterly*
CQR	*Church Quarterly Review*
EV	English versions (when chapter and verse numbering differs from MT)
ExpT	*Expository Times*
FRLANT	Forschungen zur Religion und Literatur des Alten und Neuen Testaments
HAT	Handbuch zum Alten Testament
HKAT	Handkommentar zum Alten Testament
HTR	*Harvard Theological Review*
IB	*Interpreter's Bible*, G. A. Buttrick (ed.)
IDB	*Interpreter's Dictionary of the Bible*, G. A. Buttrick (ed.)
Int	*Interpretation*
JB	*The Jerusalem Bible*, A. Jones (ed.)
JBL	*Journal of Biblical Literature*
JBR	*Journal of Bible and Religion*
JNES	*Journal of Near Eastern Studies*
JSS	*Journal of Semitic Studies*
KHAT	*Kurzer Handkommentar zum Alten Testament*

KS	*Kleine Schriften zur Geschichte des Volkes Israel*, by Albrecht Alt (3 vols.; 2nd ed.; Munich: C. H. Beck, 1959).
LXX	Septuagint
MT	Masoretic Text
OLZ	*Orientalische Literaturzeitung*
OTS	*Oudtestamentische Studien*
RB	*Revue biblique*
ThGl	*Theologie und Glaube*
TLZ	*Theologische Literaturzeitung*
UGS	*Überlieferungsgeschichtliche Studien: Erster Teil: Die sammelnden und bearbeitenden Geschichtswerke im AT*, by Martin Noth (first pub. 1943; Darmstadt: Wissenschaftliche Buchgesellschaft, 1957).
VT	*Vetus Testamentum*
VTSup	Vetus Testamentum, Supplements
ZAW	*Zeitschrift für die alttestamentliche Wissenschaft*
ZDMG	*Zeitschrift der deutschen morgenländischen Gesellschaft*

Introduction

In the torrent of literature dealing with the history and composition of the Pentateuch, only a small trickle has been devoted to the Elohist tradition (E). Much of this small scholarly output has been produced with the aim of destroying the hypothesis that such a unitary and continuous body of traditions ever existed outside the minds of modern Western scholars. As a result, two of the three monographs examining E have attempted to show that the passages ascribed to the Elohist do not represent an ancient and independent epic tradition at all, but are simply supplements to the J tradition.[1]

Quite apart from the question of large-scale scholarly productions, it would not be hard to show that in most teaching and writing on the Pentateuch less attention is accorded the E tradition than J.[2] This is partly a result of the fact, to be sure, that E is much less fully and clearly represented in the Pentateuch than J; but it also results, we believe, from the tacit judgment that the E traditions are intrinsically less significant than J and were composed relatively late in Israel's history.

These considerations alone would justify a new treatment of E. The development of new methods and views in Pentateuchal criticism makes such a treatment even more desirable. In the following pages we shall attempt to answer those who would discard the hypothesis of an independent E tradition. We shall agree quite frequently that the methods and suppositions of the older critics were often pretentious or faulty, so that some of the modern attacks on their works have been justified. Nonetheless, we hope to show that there is a sizeable and significant body of traditions in the Pentateuch which can be assigned to E, even though the earlier critics exaggerated the certainty with which these traditions can be isolated and the number of stylistic features which can be detected in them.

Most important, we intend to show that the E traditions comprise the fragments of an originally continuous epic tradition. We shall show that there is good evidence for assigning a very early date to this Elohist epic and for connecting its formulation with the time of the division of the kingdom, *ca.* 922 B.C. Thus placed in history, E can be seen as an early expression of the religious views and emphases which are discernible in a whole stream of north Israelite literature, from the Samuel traditions to the Book of Deuteronomy.

---

[1]The two monographs rejecting E as an independent tradition are: Paul Volz and Wilhelm Rudolph, *Der Elohist als Erzähler, ein Irrweg der Pentateuchkritik?*, BZAW 63 (Giessen: A. Töpelmann, 1933); Wilhelm Rudolph, *Der 'Elohist' von Exodus bis Josua*, BZAW 68 (Berlin: A. Töpelmann, 1938). The only other monograph on E is Otto Procksch's *Das nordhebräische Sagenbuch: Die Elohimquelle* (Leipzig: J. C. Hinrichs, 1906).

[2]Cf. H. W. Wolff's forthright comment in "The Elohistic Fragments in the Pentateuch," *Int* 26:2 (1972) 158: "There are still among us those who sit at their desks and murder the Elohist with their pens."

CHAPTER I

Toward a New View of E: Criticism Since 1900

First identified by Hupfeld in 1853, the E strand was characterized by the literary critics of the nineteenth century as an independent epic narrative reaching from the Patriarchal stories in Genesis to the account of the Conquest in Joshua. According to critical consensus, this source was marked by the use of *Elohim* as the divine name, by a more advanced theological outlook than J's, and by a peculiar interest in prophecy. These characteristics led the majority of critics to date E to the era of the first classical prophets, *ca.* 750 B.C.[1]

Wellhausen himself, in picturing the composition of the Pentateuch, had allowed for a long process of writing, rewriting, expansion, and even for the continuing influence of oral tradition.[2] But later followers of the great master had tended more and more to view the sources as true written documents produced by one author at one time. Any later additions which were perceived were commonly attributed to the shadowy "JE redactor."[3]

(A) The Impact of Form Criticism

The most significant break with this rather academically oriented view of the growth of Israelite literature came with the publication, in 1902, of Hermann Gunkel's brilliant commentary on Genesis.[4] Gunkel grasped the central importance of the relation of ancient literature to the life of the people, and in so doing laid the groundwork for many of the most creative achievements of twentieth-century Biblical criticism. The traditional history of Israel's beginnings, Gunkel saw, had not emerged full-blown from the pen of an author or even a group of tradition-collectors, but had first grown up in a natural fashion in the life of the people. For centuries the traditions now woven together in the Pentateuch had been transmitted orally, whether in the cultus or around the campfire.[5]

The key to the unravelling of the earlier stages of the traditions, according to Gunkel, was a close study of the typical forms (*Gattungen*) in which oral traditions were preserved. Often these forms would be closely similar to forms found in the literature of other cultures of the Near East; occasionally both form and content owed much to foreign sources. Thus the findings and methods of the new *religionsgeschichtliche Schule*, which was opening the world of the ancient Orient to Western scholars, could be drawn upon by the Pentateuchal critic.[6]

In his Genesis commentary, Gunkel looked behind the present written stage of the narratives to discern the earlier stages of tradition. First there had been the creation of individual sagas or legends (*Sagen*), which were the basic units of tradition. Then there had been the drawing together of the *Sagen* into collections (*Sammlungen*) which usually centered on one character or pair of characters in the stories. All of this, Gunkel stressed, took place before the creation of J or E, which drew together many such collections into unified epic narratives.[7]

In his analysis of the rise of J and E, Gunkel placed much more emphasis on the earlier collections of *Sagen* than on the creative work of the "authors" of sources. The "authors" themselves were viewed primarily as "collectors" who took over the already existing groups of traditions — traditions which showed their varied origins by their variety of styles and contents.

This variety shows that the legends of E, and still more decidedly those of J, do not bear the stamp of a single definite time and still less of a single personality, but that they were adopted by their collectors essentially as they were found.[8] In the sources of J and E, materials from very early periods stand side by side with later material. Thus, by implication, the efforts of literary critics to locate and date the origin of the sources must be based on the general background reflected in the various traditions, and on the theological emphases apparent in *Traditionssammlungen*, rather than on isolated geographical or political-historical references.

His analysis of the form and content of individual narratives demonstrated for Gunkel the independence of J and E. Sometimes he found the older form of a story in E, as in E's Joseph narrative, where Reuben is the protagonist of the eleven brothers, while J modernizes and replaces the no longer existing Reuben tribe with Judah. More often, Gunkel believed, J had the older form of a story, as in the Jacob-Laban cycle where J's narrative is much less wordy and stated more naively than E's. Similarly, in the J narrative the magical effects of the mandrakes are spoken of without embarrassment, whereas E makes the story illustrate the gracious power of God (Gen 30:14ff.). The important point is that such examples demonstrate the independent evolution of J and E from a related common body of early traditions.[9]

Gunkel retained the traditional eighth-century date for E, but this date had much less significance in his view, for the final writing down of this body of traditions was simply the culmination of a long period of collection and sifting of oral and written traditions.[10] The long editorial process was more important for understanding the history of the traditions than the date which could be fixed as the *terminus ad quem* of the process.

What Gunkel had done in his Genesis commentary was carried on by his student, Hugo Gressmann, in a study of the Moses traditions, *Mose und seine Zeit*.[11] Like Gunkel, Gressmann came to view J and E as collections of traditions rather than unitary documents. "One will achieve a satisfactory explanation of the evidence only if one conceives of JE as redactors or collectors."[12] Gressmann was led to this conclusion, as was Gunkel, by the lack of complete unity of style and conception within J and E. Instead of theorizing a multitude of different written documents (J_1, J_2, E_1, E_2, etc.), Gressmann followed Gunkel in picturing the "authors" of the sources as editors of already formed complexes of tradition. Still adhering to the theory of E's independence from J, Gressmann also set *ca.* 750 B.C. as the probable date for the final form of E.[13]

What are the results of the Gunkel-Gressmann approach to the Pentateuchal traditions? First of all, these scholars replaced the too purely *literary* approach of previous critics with one that assumed continuous growth and change in sacred traditions which were both oral and written. J and E were no longer viewed as "documents," but as collections of traditions which reflected, at every point in their evolution, the on-going life of the people of Israel. Secondly, and as a corollary, questions of absolute date and individual authorship receded as the collections of traditions came to be seen in relation to a long process of history, reflecting the work of many minds and memories. At the most we can speak, Gunkel said, of "schools of tradition." Finally, Gunkel's approach meant that the stylistic peculiarities of individual authors could not be expected in the Pentateuchal sources. Instead, we find only the sorts of characteristic words and phrases which will reflect the usage of a school or circle of tradition, or perhaps of a particular region in ancient Israel.[14]

It was perhaps inevitable that when authors and documents were disposed of, as by Gunkel and Gressmann, the sources symbolized by "J" and "E" could not long survive. The disappearance of J and E as independent written sources is precisely what we encounter in the Scandinavian successors of Gunkel, Johannes Pedersen and Ivan Engnell.

(B) The Disappearance of Separate Sources

In his *Israel: Its Life and Culture, I-II*, published in English in 1926, Johannes Pedersen first suggested that it was frequently not possible to separate J from E in the Pentateuch.[15] This was only a mild prelude to his published rejection, in 1931, of the whole literary-critical structure by means of which most modern scholars had understood the Old Testament.[16] Included in this abandoned structure was, of course, the Documentary Hypothesis of Pentateuchal origins.

Pedersen's main point was the close association of the Wellhausenist theory with nineteenth-century Hegelian evolutionism — an association which makes the entire structure untenable, once the Hegelianism that supported it is rejected. This Hegelian view of the evolution of religion as a neat, unilinear process must be rejected, Pedersen maintained, as a rationalistic, idealized schematization which has no relation to the actual development of religion in Israel or among any other people.

The careful source-analysis which was the glory of German scholarship in the nineteenth century must be viewed realistically as part of this rationalistic construction, Pedersen continued, and its severe limitations accepted.

> The view of the Israelite literary sources which has been current since the middle of the nineteenth century has been adopted by modern historical scholarship. This view presupposes that each document can be placed precisely in time and that its value as a source can be defined precisely. This source-critical method is undoubtedly of significant value for the study of antiquity, when one is concerned with establishing events and external data. But it must be used with stringent limitations when it is a question of describing the literature of a people. When we have this much clear, then we will also see that the minute separation of the different levels of the Pentateuchal sources and their distribution to definitely specified periods in time, viewed in an historical perspective, is of questionable significance.[17]

Three years later Pedersen applied his views more specifically to a particular set of Pentateuchal traditions, namely the Exodus-Passover complex in Exod 1-15.[18] He viewed these traditions as the cult-legend of Passover, which had evolved out of the cultic celebration of Israel's historical experience of deliverance. The literary-critical method of source-analysis missed the essential meaning of these traditions, which arose and were elaborated over the course of centuries of life and worship in Israel. "The festival legend which is rendered here with the utmost brevity cannot be any purely literary production of late origin."[19]

Pedersen did not attempt to ignore the contradictions and variants among the traditions of the Exodus, but insisted that these simply point to a series of originally oral additions which grew up around the initial nucleus. For example, with reference to the different depictions of the departure from Egypt in Exod 13:17-19; 14:2-4, 5-7, 19, 21, Pedersen maintained that ". . . they do not point to different parallel and continuous narratives."[20] Pedersen especially objected to the attempts of literary critics to rate the different notices concerning the event at the Sea in terms of their historicity — the J source's east wind being valued as the most "natural"and therefore the most "historical" and therefore the earliest.

> If, as indicated above, the basis of source-analysis is less than secure, it is an even worse error to set aside, in the ancient narratives, whatever does not agree with our understanding of nature, and by this means to create a "natural" account, which is then expounded as "historical." A more accurate examination will show that the supposedly natural account is not as natural as is commonly thought.[21]

In criticism of Pedersen it should be noted: (1) Exod 1-15, because of the intimate connection of Passover and Exodus, is the only portion of the Pentateuch which shows such clear signs of use as a "cult legend." The same analysis could hardly be applied to Gen 12-50. (2) The results of source-critical analysis can be called into question much more easily in Exod 1-15 than in other parts of the Pentateuch, especially Genesis.

In favor of Pedersen, we comment: (1) The association between the Documentary Hypothesis and Hegelianism needed to be pointed out, and Hegelian-influenced ideas of religious evolution questioned in the light of new knowledge; (2) Source-analysis must be limited to its proper sphere — the study of the literature once it has become literature — and not used as a vehicle for presenting a tendentious view of the cultural and ideological history of Israel.[22]

Like Pedersen, the Swedish scholar Ivan Engnell begins by mounting a thorough-going attack on the philosophical presuppositions that governed the work of Wellhausenist critics. "The whole literary-critical system," writes Engnell, "is based upon a complete misunderstanding of the actual situation. It reflects a modern anachronistic *book view*, and attempts to interpret ancient biblical literature in modern categories, an *interpretatio europeica moderna*."[23] Any appraisal of the Old Testament literature which hopes for authentic understanding must discard such academic fantasies as "documents," "editors," and scissors-and-paste composition. Instead we must appreciate fully the profound and central importance of oral transmission in the development of the Biblical traditions.

Applied to the Pentateuch, this means that we cannot reckon with continuous narrative sources such as J and E. These must be replaced by cycles or complexes of tradition, such as the Passover cult-legend of Exod 1-15 and the Patriarchal narratives of Gen 12-50, which stand as a preface to the Passover complex.[24] Within these complexes there are, to be sure, doublets and other signs of overlapping traditions, but these do not establish the existence of continuous strands.

How does Engnell deal with the literary-critical claim that the presence of continuous parallel sources is proved by linguistic characteristics which accompany the parallels? Gen 12:10-20, for example, is paralleled by a very similar story in Gen 20:1-17. In the former, *Yahweh* is used; in the latter only *Elohim* appears. Engnell's reply seems to be that the variations of the use of the different divine names are not sufficiently constant to make literary analysis possible on that basis alone. No source limits itself entirely to one divine name. To some extent, he argues, the variations represent the theological and stylistic preferences of a single traditionist (as also claimed by Volz and Rudolph; see below, pp. 12-15); to some extent they appear to be merely arbitrary. In any case, comparison with the LXX text and with variant Hebrew texts demonstrates that the present usage in the MT must be to a large extent the result of later editing. The other linguistic arguments of literary critics can find even less support, says Engnell, once the nature of oral transmission and the development of traditions is evaluated accurately.[25]

As to the alleged theological characteristics of the sources, Engnell refuses to see anything in these arguments but the presuppositions of modern scholars. "In reality these criteria are based upon nothing but an a priori, evolutionistic concept, which is inseparable from the documentary hypothesis and dictates to it."[26]

How are we to assess the success of Engnell's attack on the imposing structure of literary criticism? It is certainly legitimate to question, as Pedersen had previously done, the evolutionistic presuppositions of the founders of literary criticism, and also to raise questions about their overly academic description of ancient Israelite literary activity. This last point had already been well established by Gunkel, although he did not go so far as to break completely with the literary-critical method.

Nevertheless, as we will attempt to show in the following chapter, there is more to be said for the literary-critical position than Engnell would have us believe. There are in fact, especially in Genesis, narratives which are given in double accounts, and in which each account displays distinctive vocabulary elements and distinctive theological or religious emphases. These linguistic and theological constants (such as *Elohim* vs. *Yahweh*) are found throughout the Pentateuch in conjunction with contradictions and repetitions in the narratives. "The existing doublets," comments Aage Bentzen, "are linked together through ever-recurring constant elements of formal and material nature, even if we are not in all cases able to reconstruct strictly coherent narratives."[27] At the very least, these constants lead us to say, in regard to E, that there is good evidence for the incorporation into the Pentateuch of a body of traditions which used the name *Elohim*, and which shared, as a central and inescapable feature, a definite interest in and close acquaintance with an early form of prophecy. While this is a good deal less than was said by older literary critics about E, it is a minimal statement in the light of the evidence.

Engnell's handling of the variation in divine names must also be criticized. First of all, let it be said that Engnell does not develop any new arguments with regard to the text-critical problems. He merely reiterates, citing Dahse, Wiener, Cassuto, Volz, and others, that the presence of textual variants in the LXX and other texts, where the MT reads *Yahweh* or *Elohim*, undercuts the possibility of using these names to establish separate sources.[28] Now some of the scholars cited by Engnell had presented their arguments in the context of highly idiosyncratic theories which are themselves shaky. This is especially the case with Dahse's work, where it is argued that the divine names in both the LXX and the MT were distributed in accordance with lectionary selections, thus replacing the original random distribution with a "pericope distribution."[29] None of these scholars, moreover, had the advantage of the new access of knowledge and problems presented by the Dead Sea Scrolls and related manuscript finds; the whole problem, like so much in textual criticism, will have to be worked through again in the light of this new knowledge.[30]

In any event, we can reply to Engnell that the use of different divine names, while it was the first criterion to be used historically, is by no means the only criterion, but is used in conjunction with other evidence.[31] That the whole literary-critical edifice does not rest on this foundation alone is demonstrated by the fact that Hupfeld first distinguished the Elohist traditions from the Priestly traditions by the use of other criteria altogether, since both E and P use the name *Elohim*.[32]

Finally, and most importantly for our purposes in the present study, the textual variants in the divine names by no means undermine our analysis of the content of the E tradition, as presented below in Chapter II. While more detailed comments will be made in the proper context in that chapter, let us simply remark in a summary fashion here that there are no important textual variants to the Masoretic *Elohim* in the Genesis passages which we assign to E with any degree of certainty, and only a few significant variants in Exodus, where the divine name criterion admittedly has less force anyhow.[33]

Engnell's attempt to explain the variation in divine names as resulting from stylistic and theological preferences of a single author can, perhaps, be improved upon if the separate sources of Yahwistic and Elohistic traditions are taken seriously as distinct tradition circles. An important study by Robert G. Boling on the use of *Yahweh* and *Elohim* in the Psalter can provide at least an analogical argument. Boling showed that Hebrew authors or circles of tradition, like their Canaanite counterparts, could regularly employ one name as the preferential "A word" in the first line of a couplet and another name as the "B word" in the second line.[34] This explains the Yahwistic Psalter and the Elohistic Psalter as collections coming, respectively, from circles in which *Yahweh* or *Elohim* is the "A word," with the other name being used in the less preferred position.

While Boling's analysis does not directly explain the use of *Yahweh* by the Yahwist tradition and *Elohim* by the Elohistic tradition, it does suggest that the two could be products of tradition circles in which these names were current as preferred designations of the Deity, at the same time explaining how the other name could be used by either school as the less preferred designation. This argument gains in force if we consider the prose of J and E as stemming from originally poetic accounts, which is highly probable.[35]

Engnell claims that *Elohim* suggests a "more theological" and "abstract-cosmic" understanding of God, while *Yahweh* suggests a more "historical-factual" meaning. This interpretation of the connotations of *Yahweh* and *Elohim* is also offered by Cassuto, and was first suggested by ancient rabbinical exegetes. In relation to some passages it is a valid observation, but certainly cannot be applied in every passage: e.g., when Jacob wrestles with the Deity and then asserts, "I have seen *Elohim* face to face," this is not a very "abstract-cosmic" idea of God! (Gen 32:31).[36]

As to the use of *Elohim*, with which we are primarily concerned, we suggest two related considerations. First, we have evidence that the use of this type of plural of the word "god," in speaking of one deity, is very ancient in Semitic literature. The Canaanite city-lords, whose correspondence with the fifteenth- and fourteenth-century Pharaohs is preserved in the Amarna tablets, flattered the Egyptian ruler with the address *ilānīya*, "my gods," or "my pantheon." This usage, as Albright suggests, may have been drawn from the cultic sphere, where a high-god was similarly addressed as "the totality of gods, the equivalent of the entire pantheon."[37] It is conceivable that *Elohim*, as a plural of *el* analogous to the type of plural evidenced by *ʾāmāhôt* ("maid"), was taken over from Canaanite cultic language by the early Israelites as they identified their patriarchal deity or deities with the Canaanite high-god El.[38]

The second and related consideration is that the E tradition, which prefers the very ancient designation *Elohim*, was preserved in northern Israel, where Yahweh was strongly identified with El, as witnessed by Jeroboam's use of the bull, an El symbol, in his temple to Yahweh at Bethel.[39] In other words, insofar as *Elohim* can be construed as a plural of *El*, the preference for *Elohim* might be a regional peculiarity resulting from a strong cult of El in pre-Israelite North Canaan.

To return to our review of the impact of form-criticism, we conclude that the observations of Gunkel, Gressmann, Pedersen, and Engnell have made some very significant alterations in the literary-critical analysis of the Pentateuch and of E. Among the most positive contributions is the reminder that we must look to the life of the people and to their oral traditions for the living source of the Pentateuchal narratives, and must reckon with the continuing influence of oral traditions even after the crystallizing of traditions into writing had begun. Secondly, we must reckon with schools or circles of tradition rather than with individual authors, with editing and collection rather than creative writing. But we must still insist on the possibility of literary analysis of this now written literature, and maintain as well the importance of the undeniable constants, theological and stylistic, which distinguish the main collections of tradition.

(C) The Rejection of E as an Independent Source

During the last years of Gunkel's life, and coincident with the work of Pedersen and Engnell, another line of criticism was being carried forward which also led to the rejection of E as an independent narrative source. Using literary rather than form criticism, Sigmund Mowinckel, Paul Volz, and Wilhelm Rudolph reached some of the same results that Engnell had reached through his emphasis on oral tradition: the rejection of the variations in the divine names and other linguistic "constants" as critical criteria, and the development of a theory of Pentateuchal composition through a long process of somewhat random additions to an ancient nucleus.

(1) Mowinckel

In an article entitled "Der Ursprung der Bil'amsage," published in 1930,[40] the Norwegian scholar Sigmund Mowinckel announced his break with the Wellhausenist analysis of E. Regarding "E" as simply a convenient symbol for a process, rather than a unitary document, Mowinckel asserted: (1) that there never was an independent "E document," with its own traditions about Israel's origins; (2) instead, "E" signifies a long process of explanatory and corrective additions to the J epic, with a *terminus ad quem* in the Exilic period. In this process (here Mowinckel thoroughly agrees with his Scandinavian colleagues, Pedersen and Engnell), the development of oral rather than written traditions is primary; yet there is a curiously academic-sounding process of editing hypothesized for the end of the development.

> Therefore, the individual narratives will have retained the final form in which the Elohist, in quite a different period, appropriated them. We may generally assume that the tradition which he recorded had earlier formed a fixed oral composition, dependent on J, somewhat like the Icelandic sagas before their fixation in writing. Within this complex, one narrator would tell a narrative in one fashion, another in another fashion, always modifying in accordance with the views and conditions of the changing times. The "Elohist" is the person who, after the downfall of the nation, recorded the whole corpus of already coherent material in his own peculiar language; indeed, he also made alterations here and there, polished the style, and eliminated material, all in accordance with his own ideas. Perhaps he is also the one who independently formulated the story of the latest, immediately preceding, period. — This whole process is what we include in and symbolize by the ideogram "E".[41]

In fact, E here disappears altogether as a separate source, as Mowinckel himself makes clear in later statements of his thesis in which he examines the whole corpus of Pentateuchal traditions.[42]

It remained for the German scholars Paul Volz and Wilhelm Rudolph, working both together and separately, to carry out a thorough-going analysis of the E traditions, attacking the solutions of the earlier literary critics point by point. This they did in a series of publications which appeared in the 1930's.

(2) Volz and Rudolph

In a monograph entitled, *Der Elohist als Erzähler ein Irrweg der Pentateuchkritik?*,[43] of which Volz and Rudolph each wrote one part, the two scholars answered their own question with a resounding "Yes!" The documentary hypothesis developed in the Wellhausen school is a dogma, Volz said, which has concealed the literature from sensitive and realistic investigation. To support this claim, Volz makes the following points:

(1) The literary-critical method is "unnatural." The existence of two separate literary sources with almost the same contents (J and E) is improbable, and the type of editorial work attributed to the redactor of JE is incredible in ancient Israel, being rather the creation of nineteenth-century *Privatdozenten*. The ridiculous analysis that breaks up the Pentateuch into half-sentences and isolated words points up the unnaturalness of this method of approaching ancient literature.

(2) Literary criticism of the Pentateuch has made use of incorrect methods.

For example, the supposed differences in the use of the names *Yahweh* and *Elohim*, and the use of "Horeb" in one context and "Sinai" in another, is simply the result of the *one* main author's varied literary style, or of his faithful use of older traditions.

(3) There are better ways of solving the problem of literary relationships. The methods of criticism which have been applied to the prophetic books should be used on the Pentateuch as well: we should assume an original text by one author, with later additions and explanations being added over the course of centuries.[44]

(4) "The method of dividing into sources frequently and to a serious degree destroys the original unity and artistic beauty of the stories and of the entire narrative work."[45]

On the positive side, Volz presents this theory: There is one basic connected narrative in the Pentateuch, the J tradition. The J narrator himself is not so much an author as a collector of traditions. To his original work the rest of the Pentateuch was added over the course of centuries in the form of glosses, explanations, and commentary. Accordingly, the "E document" is simply a group of additions to the basic narrative, having no continuous narrative stream of its own. The same is true of P.[46]

Rudolph's section of the work offers an explanation of the variation in the divine names in the Joseph stories. He claims that the stories are contributed by one author who uses *Yahweh* when he himself is telling the story, but has his characters use *El-Shaddai* when they are speaking in Palestine and *Elohim* when in Egypt.[47]

Rudolph goes on to glance briefly at some other passages in Genesis which are commonly attributed to E: Gen 20; 21:8-21, 22-32; 31:2, 4-16; 35:1-4, 7. He finds that there is indeed a certain unity of thought and intention in these narratives, in that they are all obviously aimed at defending the morally-dubious actions of a central character. Rudolph attributes these passages to "an interpolator who improved the J-tradition at certain points." He concludes,

> If one wishes to go further and designate as "the Elohist" this interpolator who improved on the J-tradition at certain points, one can do this. But when one considers the small number of passages that can be thus designated, it should become clear that there is no question of speaking of a source in the sense of the previously accepted E, or of an author analogous to the J narrator.[48]

The careful work of Volz and Rudolph, later extended by the latter to cover the entire Hexateuch, offers an opportunity for scholars to review the whole literary-critical method which lies behind the commonly-accepted Wellhausenist solution of Pentateuchal origins. For this opportunity, and for the careful work which was carried out by Volz and Rudolph, scholars have reason to be grateful. Nevertheless, the writer believes that these authors have not dealt fairly with all of the evidence.

(1) We repeat, first of all, that the variation between *Yahweh* and *Elohim*

cannot be viewed simply as an example of the rich and varied style of a single author, since the names are accompanied by certain other constants, both theological and linguistic.

(2) It is true that there are actually only a few extensive Elohistic narratives which parallel Yahwistic narratives, and that these are all in Genesis. But if even a small number of important constants can be established on the basis of these parallel narratives, then we have a basis for detecting Elohistic passages which lack J parallels.[49]

(3) It is true, as Volz and Rudolph claim and as we have already said, that there was considerable academic myopia involved in the development of the neat Wellhausenist scheme. But if narratives can be detected throughout the Pentateuch which generally use *Elohim* and which display a consistent theological emphasis, what is to prevent us from postulating an E epic tradition, imperfectly preserved, which parallels the J epic? A realization of the weaknesses and fallacies built into the literary-critical solution should not blind us to the data which the theory attempted to explain. (More detailed criticisms of Volz and Rudolph will be made from time to time in the following chapter, when we will discuss actual passages attributed to E.)

To sum up our findings thus far, we do not believe that either Pedersen and Engnell or Mowinckel, Volz, and Rudolph, working from their disparate points of view, have succeeded in doing away completely with E, although they have forced considerable qualifications into the older view and have prevented any simple acceptance of the literary-critical solutions of nineteenth-century scholars. A school or circle of E-traditionists at work in the early years of the northern kingdom, and having their own separate version of the pre-monarchical epic tradition, remains a possible explanation for the evidence. The full statement of this view, however, must await a presentation of the work of Gerhard von Rad and Martin Noth.

(D) *The Structure and Origin of the Hexateuch*

The publication in 1938 of Gerhard von Rad's *Das formgeschichtliche Problem des Hexateuch* signalled a new departure in Pentateuchal studies.[50] While accepting in large measure the Wellhausenist scheme concerning the sources and their dates, von Rad concerned himself with a more fundamental problem: how did the epic which lies behind the present Pentateuch come to be formulated, and what was its original structure?

Von Rad found this answer in the outline of certain passages which appear to be liturgical summations of the faith of early Israel, capsule statements of the *Heilsgeschichte*: Deut 26:5*b*-9; 6:20-24; Josh 24:2-13. Von Rad calls the last passage "the Hexateuch in miniature."[51] These passages or similar "credos" must have been recited in the tribal-league cultus as confessions of faith, and were later used as the framework for the Hexateuchal narrative of Israel's origins. Thus the Hexateuch represents a baroque elaboration, on a gigantic scale, of Israel's primitive confession of faith.[52]

Comparison of these credal outlines with the Hexateuch itself, however, shows that the credos omit something of tremendous significance for Israel. They speak of the Promise to the Patriarchs, the Exodus from Egypt, and the Conquest of the land promised to the fathers, but say nothing of the Sinai covenant. The explanation for this, says von Rad, is that the Sinai tradition was maintained quite separately from the Patriarchs-Exodus-Conquest tradition, and brought into literary connection with this three-fold historical tradition after the breakdown of the amphictyony. In short, the Hexateuch owes its present form to the Yahwist, who himself enfleshed the bare bones of the credo with scores of ancient traditions, and brought together the two great tradition-complexes of early Israel into an epic whole.[53]

Von Rad's contribution through this study has been felt in all quarters. His analysis of the significance of the "cultic credos" has thrown new light on these passages and on the whole Hexateuch, and his concern with the origins of the Hexateuchal tradition as a whole has given new life to studies in this area. The main weaknesses of his theory are in two areas:

(1) An analysis which severs the Exodus-Conquest tradition from the Sinai tradition, only to bring them together in a purely literary manner at the finish, separates through analytical scholarship something which for early Israel was inseparable. The recital of Yahweh's saving intervention for his people, his past graciousness to his "vassal" Israel, was precisely what must have formed the prelude to the covenant ceremony itself.[54] This is demonstrated with inescapable force by the studies of Mendenhall and Baltzer on ancient covenant forms.[55] The covenant ceremony must have been the occasion for the recital of the *Heilsgeschichte*; the covenant itself is naturally omitted in the recital of past history, for it is recalled and renewed following the recital in the actual ceremony, as in Josh 24.

(2) The second point is closely related to the first, and it involves the question of the contribution of the Yahwist. Von Rad, like many before him, has reconstructed the development of the Hexateuch along lines which are too purely literary. It is incredible that a single author, writing in Solomon's time, should have drawn together the allegedly separate traditions of Exodus-Conquest and Sinai Covenant, severing them and many other narratives from their original cultic contexts, in addition to creating the Primeval History (Gen 1-11) out of similarly scattered and heterogeneous fragments of past traditions, forming the whole into an epic history stretching from Creation to the conquest of Canaan.[56] To theorize such a literary composition is to ignore the function of oral literature in the whole life of an ancient people. At the same time, von Rad fails to see the natural way in which the epic narrative could have been rooted in the historical recital which had its cultic *Sitz im Leben* in the covenant ceremonies.

When we turn to the work of Martin Noth in this area, the second objection is overcome. In Noth's view the relation of J and E can be explained only if both are seen as the heirs of an older common tradition, which Noth designates "G" (*Grundlage*). This ancient pre-monarchical epic tradition already contained narratives grouped around five "themes": the deliverance from Egypt, the leading into the Promised Land, the promise to the Patriarchs, the leading in the Wilderness, and the revelation on Sinai. Like von Rad, Noth holds that these traditions or themes were originally separate, reflecting memories of historical events which occurred in the life of separate groups. They were drawn together, put into a chronological sequence, and given an all-Israel orientation during the tribal-league period. This basic tradition thus lay ready to be used independently by both Yahwist and Elohist, writing in a later period.[57]

As suggested above, we believe that Noth is moving in the right direction when he theorizes the dependence of J and E upon a previous "G," thus minimizing the purely literary activity of both later schools, and emphasizing instead the origin of the epic traditions in the life and worship of the people in the pre-monarchical period. But when we attempt to describe the development of this vast body of tradition more precisely, we run into considerable difficulty, for there is much that we do not know. Certainly Noth's theory of separate traditions at separate sanctuaries is no help in understanding how the traditions came to be drawn together. We now have good reason for believing that the sacred history was recited as a prologue to the covenant ceremony, yet there is much in the Pentateuch which would have no obvious place in such a recital, such as the picaresque Jacob-Laban cycle, which incorporates sanctuary legends without being dominated by them.

Perhaps the best explanation is that there existed in the early tribal-league period a poetic epic, incorporating ancient popular traditions as well as more specifically religious traditions such as sanctuary legends. Salient points from this common body of traditions were drawn into the covenant ceremonies and summed up in the prologue to the covenant, thus being given a specifically all-Israel and sacred-historical cast. These prologues were in turn summarized into the very short credos mentioned by von Rad. The prologue and credal summaries, which would be periodically recited to all Israel in cultic contexts, would then be in a position to exert formative influence back upon the folk-epic tradition, which gradually would come to assume a more or less fixed sacred-historical framework and theological orientation. J and E would then be later prose recensions of this common epic tradition.[58]

Recent studies have questioned Noth's reconstruction of early Israel as an amphictyonic league, and have also challenged von Rad's arguments for the existence of early summaries or "credal" recitals of the sacred history.[59] I do not consider that these questions about Israel's precise degree of organization (or disorganization!) in the tribal league period, or questions about the precise date, authorship, and genre of passages like Deut 26:5*b*-9 fundamentally undercut the reconstruction offered here. Israel, after all, did exist prior to the monarchy, and did have a cultus. I am proposing that this cultus had its roots in the character of Israel as a covenant community, and that the covenant structure itself contained some form of historical recital, as evidenced above all by Josh 24; cf. also Josh 8:30-34; Deut 27:15-26.[60]

In addition to the historical prologues of the covenant formularies, which may be reflected in the passages just cited, the early epic tradition must have been recapitulated in songs and hymns. As P. D. Miller points out, one of these hymns — Exod 15 — has "credentials as a genuinely ancient recital of the saving events which are far sounder than those of the 'credos'."[61]

To return to Noth's sketch of the origins and early growth of JE, it is significant that Noth, like von Rad, retains so much of the Wellhausenist scheme in his identification of the J and E sources, using literary-critical methods to accomplish minute separations in the text.[62] In regard to the dating of the sources, however, Noth follows his own course:

> The question whether J or E is the earlier is disputed; E is usually taken to be the less ancient, but this cannot be proved for certain. In any case E in fact stands much nearer to the pre-literary stage of the Pentateuchal tradition than J, at whatever date the work may have been set down in writing.[63]

Whichever source is earlier, Noth holds, there is no doubt that J has been taken as the basis of the Tetrateuch (Genesis through Numbers), with E worked in secondarily to supplement the J narrative. Thus he would agree with the contention of Volz and Rudolph that E as it now stands has no independence from J, although he maintains, as we do, that E once formed a separate and independent tradition.[64]

(E) Conclusions

We have moved quickly over this review of modern critical work, omitting discussion of some interesting side-developments in order to proceed more rapidly into an analysis of the content, scope, and characteristics of E. After that we can state our own theory concerning the date and provenance of this tradition.

The past half-century of criticism has called into question the presuppositions and findings of earlier literary critics with regard to the Pentateuch and its sources. The Wellhausenist solution has withstood the attack, at least to the extent that we must still reckon with various identifiable collections of tradition which went into the final fabric of the Pentateuch.

Many of the linguistic criteria cited by earlier authors are not sufficient basis for carrying out minute source division — to this extent Engnell, Volz, Rudolph, and others, are correct — but there still remain some constant features, theological and linguistic, which enable us to designate some passages "J" and others "E."

The theory of individual authorship must give way, as Gunkel saw, to the more reasonable theory of a group or tradition-circle. As Noth emphasizes, no single author created the outline of either J or E; both have their roots in an amphictyonic epic tradition.

Finally, as Noth convincingly shows, the Tetrateuch must be separated from the Deuteronomistic History, and treated separately from the latter complex. This means that we cannot speak of the continuation of J and E into the Conquest narratives of Joshua, but must deal with the history of the Deuteronomic historian's traditions without recourse to our explanation of Pentateuchal traditions.[65]

---

[1]So often and so well has the story of Pentateuchal criticism in the past century been told that it would be pretentious to add yet another summary. For the original identification and description of E, see Hermann Hupfeld, *Die Quellen der Genesis und die Art ihrer Zusammensetzung* (Berlin: Wiegand & Grieben, 1853). This description was elaborated in Abraham Kuenen's *An Historico-Critical Inquiry into the Origin and Composition of the Hexateuch* (London: MacMillan & Co., 1886), and particularly in the highly influential publications of Julius Wellhausen, *Die Composition des Hexateuchs und der historischen Bücher des AT* (Berlin: Georg Reimer, 1889), and *Prolegomena to the History of Ancient Israel* (New York: Meridian Books, 1957; German original, Berlin, 1883). See also J. Estlin Carpenter and G. Harford-Battersby, *The Hexateuch* (2 vols.; London: Longmans, Green & Co., 1900); S. R. Driver, *An Introduction to the Literature of the OT* (New York: Meridian Books, 1956; 1st pub. London, 1897); Hans-Joachim Kraus, *Geschichte der historisch-kritischen Erforschung des AT von der Reformation bis zur Gegenwart* (2d ed.; Neukirchen: Neukirchener Verlag, 1969): For the period since 1900, some of the most helpful reviews are: Joseph Coppens, *The OT and the Critics* (Paterson, N.J.: St. Anthony Guild Press, 1942); C. R. North, "Pentateuchal Criticism," *The OT and Modern Study* (ed. H. H. Rowley; Oxford: Clarendon Press, 1956) 48-83; John Bright, "Modern Study of OT Literature," *The Bible and the Ancient Near East* (ed. G. E. Wright; Garden City, N.Y.: Doubleday, 1961) 18-31; R. J. Coggins, "A Century of Pentateuchal Criticism," pub. in two parts, *CQR* 166 (1965) 149-161; 413-425. A number of articles by G. E. Wright should also be mentioned as particularly useful: "Recent European Study in the Pentateuch," *JBR* 18 (1950) 216-225; "OT Scholarship in Prospect," *JBR* 22 (1960) 182-193; "Cult and History: A Study of a Current Problem in OT Interpretation," *Int* 16 (1962) 3-20; "Modern Issues in Biblical Studies: History and the Patriarchs," *ExpT* 71 (1960) 3-7.

[2]"Die Composition des Hexateuchs, III," *Jahrbücher für Deutsche Theologie* 22 (1877) 478.

[3]Cf. Carpenter and Harford-Battersby, *Hexateuch* 1. 171-179.

[4]*Genesis übersetzt und erklärt* (HKAT; 2d ed.; Göttingen: Vandenhoeck & Ruprecht, 1902).

[5]H. Gunkel, *The Legends of Genesis*, an English translation of the Introduction to the Genesis commentary cited above (New York: Schocken, 1964) 88-122.

[6]Cf. Kraus, *Erforschung* 295-367.

[7]Gunkel, *Legends* 123-144.

[8]*Ibid.*, 125. For a very helpful recent account of Gunkel's work and method see M. Buss, "The Study of Forms," *OT Form Criticism* (ed. J. Hayes; San Antonio: Trinity University, 1974) 1-56, and J. Wilcoxen's "Narrative," in the same volume, pp. 57-78.

[9]Gunkel, *Legends* 126-127.

[10]*Ibid.*, 142.

[11](Göttingen: Vandenhoeck & Ruprecht, 1913).

[12]Gressmann, *Mose und seine Zeit* 372. (Here and throughout this work, where no published

English translation exists I have made my own translation).
13 *Ibid.*, 373.
14 Gunkel, *Legends* 133-135.
15 (London: Oxford, 1926) 27.
16 "Die Auffassung vom AT," *ZAW* 49 (1931) 161-181.
17 Pedersen, "Auffassung" 174-175.
18 "Passahfest und Passahlegende," *ZAW* 52 (1934) 161-175.
19 *Ibid.*, 168.
20 *Ibid.*, 171.
21 *Ibid.*, 172.
22 Cf. Aage Bentzen, *Introduction to the OT* (2 vols.; Copenhagen: G. E. C. Gad, 1948) 2. 63.
23 *A Rigid Scrutiny: Critical Essays on the OT* by Ivan Engnell (trans. and ed. by John T. Willis; Nashville: Vanderbilt University Press, 1969) 53; originally pub. as an article, "Moseböckerna," in *Svenskt bibliskt Uppslagsverk* (2d ed., 1963). See also C. R. North, "Pentateuchal Criticism," *OT and Modern Study* 65.
24 As summarized in Bentzen, *Introduction* 2. 20-21.
25 Engnell, *Rigid Scrutiny* 54-56; cf. North, "Pentateuchal Criticism," *OT and Modern Study* 66-67.
26 Engnell, *Rigid Scrutiny* 56.
27 Bentzen, *Introduction* 2. 45.
28 Ivan Engnell, *Gamla Testamentet: En traditionshistorisk Inledning* (Stockholm: Svenska Kirchens Diakonistyrelses Bokforlag, 1945) 195-196, esp. 195, n. 2.
29 Johannes Dahse, *Textkritische Materialien zur Hexateuchfrage* (Giessen: A. Töpelmann, 1912). Cf. the reply of John Skinner, *The Divine Names in Genesis* (London: Hodder & Stoughton, 1914).
30 See F. M. Cross, Jr., *The Ancient Library of Qumran and Modern Biblical Studies* (rev. ed.; New York: Doubleday, 1961) 163-194. See also Cross's "The History of the Biblical Text in the Light of Discoveries in the Judaean Desert," *HTR* 57 (1964) 281-299; and Dominique Barthélemy, O.P., *Les devanciers d'Aquila: Première publication intégrale du texte des fragments du dodécapropheton* VTSup 10 (Leiden: Brill, 1963), with the bibliographies cited in these works.
31 Cf. Skinner, *Divine Names* 1-11.
32 *Ibid.*, 8-9.
33 See below, p. 24; pp. 73-74, notes 92, 100.
34 Robert G. Boling, "Synonymous Parallelism in the Psalms," *JSS* 5 (1960) 221-255.
35 See D. N. Freedman, "Pentateuch," *IDB* 3. 711-727. Freedman describes the underlying source of J and E, which he (like Noth) designates "G," as a "poetic composition, orally transmitted, relating the official story of Israel and its forebears. It is to be dated in the twelfth-eleventh centuries B.C, and finds its cultic locus in the amphictyonic festivals" (714).
36 See Engnell, *Gamla Testamentet* 198, n. 4; *Rigid Scrutiny* 56; cf. U. Cassuto, *The Documentary Hypothesis and the Composition of the Pentateuch* (Jerusalem: Magnes, 1961) 125-145. H. Ringgren deals briefly with the subject in his article, "אלהים," *Theol. Wörterbuch AT* (ed. G. J. Botterweck and H. Ringgren; Stuttgart: Kohlhammer, 1973) 1. 285-305, esp. 304-305.
37 W. F. Albright, *From the Stone Age to Christianity* (2d ed.; Garden City, N.Y.: Doubleday, 1957) 213.
38 Cf. also the plural forms of "goddess" found in Ugaritic and Aramaic: $^{\circ}lht;$ $^{\circ e}l\bar{a}h\hat{\imath}n$. On the linguistic problems associated with the plural form $^{\circ}el\bar{o}h\hat{\imath}m$ in Hebrew, see recently H. Ringgren, "אלהים," *Theol. Wörterbuch zum AT*. 292. On the identification of the patriarchal deity with El, see F. M. Cross, Jr., "Yahweh and the God of the Patriarchs," *HTR* 55 (1962) 225-259; and, more recently, Cross, "אל," *Theol. Wörterbuch zum AT* 1. 259-279; and Cross, *Canaanite Myth and Hebrew Epic: Essays in the History of the Religion of Israel* (Cambridge: Harvard University Press, 1973) 1-75.
39 Cf. Cross, "Yahweh and the God of the Patriarchs," 257-258; Cross, *Canaanite Myth and Hebrew Epic* 72-75.

⁴⁰*ZAW* 48 (1930) 233-271.
⁴¹Mowinckel, "Bilʾamsage," 271.
⁴²In addition to the article cited above, n. 40, see Mowinckel's *Two Sources of the Predeuteronomic Primeval History* (Oslo: Jacob Dybwad, 1937); and, more recently, *Tetrateuch-Pentateuch-Hexateuch* BZAW 90 (Berlin, 1964); see also Mowinckel, *Erwägungen zur Pentateuchquellenfrage* (Norway: Universitetsforlag, 1964) 1-138.
⁴³BZAW 63 (Giessen, 1933).
⁴⁴ Volz-Rudolph, *Erzähler* 14-21.
⁴⁵*Ibid.*, 179.
⁴⁶*Ibid.*, 21-25.
⁴⁷*Ibid.*, 148-151.
⁴⁸*Ibid.*, 179.
⁴⁹Cf. the important article by H. W. Wolff, "The Elohistic fragments in the Pentateuch," *Int* 26 (1972) 158-173. Wolff identifies the "fear of God" as the most prominent theme of the Elohistic passages, and points out that E links together successive narratives in which this "fear" is tested.
⁵⁰BWANT 4. Folge, 26 (Stuttgart, 1938). Printed also in Gerhard von Rad, *Gesammelte Studien zum AT* (Munich, 1961) 9-86 and, in English trans. in *The Problem of the Hexateuch and other Essays* (New York: McGraw-Hill, 1966) 1-78.
⁵¹Von Rad, *Gesammelte Studien* 16.
⁵²*Ibid.*, 58-81. Cf. also von Rad's *Genesis: A Commentary* (rev. ed.; Philadelphia: Westminster, 1972) 13-43.
⁵³Von Rad, *Gesammelte Studien* 20-33; 60-62.
⁵⁴Cf. G. E. Wright, "Cult and History: A Current Problem in OT Interpretation," *Int* 16 (1962) 3-20; and, recently, a thoughtful critique by E. W. Nicholson, *Exodus and Sinai in History and Tradition* (Richmond: John Knox, 1973) 1-32.
⁵⁵G. E. Mendenhall, "Law and Covenant in Israel and the Ancient Near East," *BA* 17:2 (May, 1954) 26-46; and 17:3 (Sept., 1954) 49-76; reprinted in *The Biblical Archaeologist Reader 3* (ed. Edward F. Campbell, Jr. and David Noel Freedman; Garden City, N.Y.: Doubleday, 1970) 3-75. See also, Klaus Baltzer, *The Covenant Formulary* (Philadelphia: Fortress, 1971). Cf. also W. Beyerlin, *Origins and History of the Oldest Sinaitic Traditions* (Oxford: Basil Blackwell, 1965), who comes to the same conclusions. See, however, D. McCarthy, *Treaty and Covenant* (Rome: Pontifical Biblical Institute, 1963) for a view which calls into question some parallels with Hittite suzerainty treaties adduced by Mendenhall, Baltzer, and Beyerlin; cf. Nicholson, *Exodus and Sinai* 33-52.
⁵⁶Cf. Martin Noth's criticism of von Rad in *A History of Pentateuchal Traditions* (Englewood Cliffs, N.J: Prentice-Hall, 1972) 38-41.
⁵⁷*Ibid.*, 38-41.
⁵⁸"The epic cycle of the Israelite league was taken up into the prose Epic (JE) sources in the course of the early monarchy. The Pentateuch itself may be described as the baroque elaboration of these Epic sources"; F. M. Cross, *Canaanite Myth and Hebrew Epic* (Cambridge: Harvard University Press, 1973) ix.
⁵⁹See G. W. Anderson, "Israel: Amphictyony; ʿAm; Kāhāl; ʿĒdâh," and J. Philip Hyatt, "Were there an Ancient Historical Credo in Israel and an Independent Sinai Tradition?" in *Translating and Understanding the OT* (ed. H. T. Frank and W. L. Reed; Nashville: Abingdon, 1970) 135-51, 152-170.
⁶⁰In addition to the works of Mendenhall, Baltzer, and Beyerlin cited above (n. 55), see Delbert R. Hillers, *Covenant: The History of a Biblical Idea* (Baltimore: Johns Hopkins Press, 1969) and F. M. Cross, "The Cultus of the Israelite League," *Canaanite Myth and Hebrew Epic* 77-121.
⁶¹Patrick D. Miller, Jr., *The Divine Warrior in Early Israel* (Cambridge: Harvard University Press, 1973) 166-175.
⁶²Noth, *Traditions* 5-41.
⁶³Noth, *Exodus* (Philadelphia: Westminster, 1962) 15.
⁶⁴Noth, *Traditions* 20-41.
⁶⁵See below, pp. 60-63.

CHAPTER II

The Content and Scope of E

In our discussion of past and current scholarly evaluations of the Elohist tradition, we distinguished three broad stages in the development of criticism: (1) the identification of the E tradition by the methods of literary criticism; (2) the rejection of this identification in the light of form- and tradition-criticism; (3) its defense on the basis of different literary-critical methodology. We saw that the attackers of the older critical methods and findings were justified at least to the extent that they pointed up fallacies in the presuppositions and methodology of the earlier literary critics.

In the following pages we shall attempt to show that there is significant evidence for the existence of E as a unified and extensive tradition, parallel to the J tradition. In our analysis we shall not identify a given passage as E except where the evidence seems quite clear. Many discussions have been vitiated by the assumption that wherever there are two non-Priestly traditions, one must be J and the other E. We shall not make this assumption, for there are many passages which must be designated as having undeterminable origin. In accordance with the conclusion of the preceding chapter, we shall not assume that the E traditions are the product of a single author, thus displaying an unvaried style and vocabulary. We shall assume instead that these traditions are the product of a school or circle, possibly extending over a considerable period of time.

Because the evidence in the patriarchal narratives of Genesis is clearest, we begin with an analysis of these traditions. Then we shall discuss the traditions of the Mosaic period. Lastly, we shall consider the question whether E can be clearly detected in the preceding and following sections of the Hexateuch; i.e., in the Primeval History (Gen 1 — 11), and in the account of the Conquest (Josh 1 — 11).

(A) The Patriarchal Narratives, Gen 12 — 50

Since the work of Astruc in 1753, the variation in the use of the divine names has been the first criterion for the separation of sources in Genesis. Similarly, our analysis will begin with an examination of passages in which *Elohim* is used as the divine name. A list of these passages in Genesis follows:[1]

chapter	verses
17	3, 9, 15, 18, 19, 22, 23
19	29
20	3, 6, 11, 13, 17
21	2, 4, 6, 12, 17, 19, 20, 22, 23
22	1, 3, 8, 9, 12
25	11
27	28
28	4, 12, 17, 20
30	2, 6, 8, 17, 18, 20, 22, 23
31	7, 9, 11, 16, 24, 42, 50
32	1, 2, 3, 29, 31
33	5, 10, 11
35	1, 5, 7, 9, 10, 11, 13, 15
39	9
40	8
41	16, 25, 28, 32, 38, 39, 51, 52
42	18, 28
43	29
44	16
45	5, 7, 8, 9
46	2
48	9, 11, 15, 20, 21
50	19, 20, 24, 25

The use of *Elohim* is not in itself sufficient basis for postulating a continuous Elohist source; this usage must be accompanied by the presence of other "constants" which characterize the style and interests of the Elohist narratives.[2] Such constant features, however, can be clearly determined only comparatively; i.e., in passages where we are able to compare an Elohist narrative with a Yahwist account. Furthermore, such narratives must be of sufficient length to assure us that we are dealing with a separate and unified tradition.

An examination of the above-listed passages, after the elimination of texts which are unanimously assigned to P,[3] results in only *three* extensive Elohist narratives which have clear parallels in Yahwist accounts: Abraham and

Sarah at the court of Abimelech, Gen 20:1-17 (parallel to 12:10-20; cf. 26:6-11); the expulsion of Hagar and Ishmael, 21:8-20 (parallel to 16:1-14); Abraham and Abimelech at Beersheba, 21:22-34 (parallel to 26:17-33). The rest of the non-Priestly occurrences of *Elohim* are in passages which do not have clear Yahwist parallels, or in passages where Yahwist and Elohist elements are intertwined.

In our discussion of these three passages we shall attempt to establish significant characteristics of the Elohist narratives which distinguish them from their Yahwist parallels. Once we have determined a few constant features of the Elohist traditions, we shall be in a better position to discuss the Elohist passages which lack J parallels, and passages where the two are mingled.

(1) Texts Having Yahwist Parallels

(a) Abraham and Sarah at the court of Abimelech, Gen 20:1-17. — The outstanding peculiarities of the Elohist version of this tradition, when compared with the J (Gen 12:10-20), are (1) The theme of divine revelation or communication, taking place in a dream (חלום, vss. 3, 6); (2) The statement that Abraham was a prophet (נביא, vs. 7); (3) Abraham's intercession (יתפלל, vss. 7, 17); (4) The emphasis on questions of moral integrity (תם לבב, vss. 5, 6), innocence, (נקין כפי, vs. 5) righteousness (cf. צדיק, vs. 4), sin (חטא, vss. 6, 9), and fear of God (יראת אלהים, vs. 11).

Every one of these features importantly distinguishes the Elohist tradition from its J parallel. In the Elohist narrative the narrator speaks in the moral and religious categories of sin, guilt, justice, innocence, and the fear of God; in Gen 12:10-20, on the other hand, the story-teller emphasizes the beauty of Sarah, and the danger of Abraham's undermining the divine promise.[4] Here in Gen 20, significantly, the patriarch is expressly designated a prophet; his prophetic office is that of intercession, and it is only by his intercession that the pagan king can be freed from his guilt.[5]

These elements in the Elohist narrative, all of which are quite lacking in the J parallel, do indeed introduce "a completely new theological concern" into the Patriarchal narratives.[6] Moreover, these concerns richly delineate the circle in which the tradition received such a peculiar stamp. They point to an environment in which a specifically religious presentation of history is being worked out, a group which idealizes the prophet and is concerned with questions of revelation.

That this chapter is the *locus classicus* of the E tradition has generally been assumed.[7] Even Paul Volz acknowledged it as the work of a hand other than the Yahwist's, though of course he did not consider the tradition to be independent of J or even part of a continuous source.[8] At this stage in our presentation we can only note its peculiarities in theological emphasis, and watch for their reappearance in other passages. Similarly, we cannot yet say whether various stylistic features (in addition to the use of *Elohim*) point to a characteristic vocabulary, distinct from J. Scholars have especially noted the use of ʾāmāh (maid, female servant), in contrast to J's use of the synonymous word šipḥāh.[9] This, however, remains dubious, since šipḥāh appears in vs. 14.[10]

(b) *The expulsion of Hagar and Ishmael, Gen 21:8-21.* — The second of our three Elohist narratives, the story of the expulsion of Hagar and her child, finds its J parallel in Gen 16:4-14. Significantly, the theme of divine revelation through a night dream (cf. 21:4 and 20:8), which was an important distinguishing mark of the Elohist narrative of Gen 20, is again prominent here. In the J account, Abraham simply acts in accordance with Sarah's wishes and allows her to expel the slave woman (16:6). In the Elohist account, however, Abraham is disturbed at Sarah's demand until a revelation from God instructs him to expel the slave and promises progeny through both Ishmael and Isaac (21:11-14). A second revelation occurs when Hagar hears the voice of the "angel of God" calling "from heaven" (vs. 17; cf. J's story of a direct encounter with the angel, 16:11). The use of this motif, like that of the divine speech in a night dream, suggests that the Elohist narratives were shaped in a group which was concerned to emphasize a particular type of revelation — one which in Israel was frequently associated with prophecy.[11] This group is also concerned with theological and ethical problems associated with right and wrong, guilt and innocence, in a way that is simply not characteristic of J.

Past commentators, who unanimously assign this passage to E,[12] have pointed to the use of *Elohim* (vss. 12, 17 thrice, 19, 20); and the use of ʾāmāh, where J has šipḥāh (16:1, 5,8).[13] As before, we must remain cautious, but the existence of two Elohist passages with several important theological concerns in common — the theme of divine revelation and the questions of guilt, innocence, and the fear of God — strengthens the hypothesis that we are dealing here with a significant and independent body of traditions.

(c) *Controversy and Agreement with Abimelech, Gen 21:22-34.*—The third Elohist narrative which has a J parallel (Gen 26:26-33), the story of the controversy and covenant with Abimelech in Gen 21, is actually made up of at least two originally separate traditions: vss. 22-24 and vss. 25-34. Neither of these strands displays the theological concerns of E as clearly as the two narratives discussed above. However, we do find a clear relationship between the first of these traditions (21:22-24) and the previous E tradition about Abraham and Sarah at the court of Abimelech.

Abimelech, as a result of the near-disaster brought about by his attempt to take Sarah as his wife, now recognizes Abraham as a man of God — a man "under the protection and blessing," as von Rad remarks, of a "very powerful God."[14] This prompts Abimelech to seek some assurance that he will not again be exposed to danger because of Abraham's presence, and because of Abraham's apparent propensity for deception (21:22-23).

At the same time, it is apparent that Abimelech is indeed one who fears God, as was stressed in 20:6, 11. He is a just man, sensitive to God's presence, even though Abraham had mistakenly thought that there was "no fear of God at all" in Abimelech's court. Abimelech is now depicted as one who has "dealt loyally" with Abraham (21:23) and who recognizes the patriarch as a true man of God (21:22).

The second tradition contained in 21:22-34 concerns a separate question — that of water rights at a well. This latter story leads into a pair of explanations of the name "Beersheba," one associating the root $šb^c$ with "seven" and the other with the word "oath" (vss. 29-30 and 31, respectively; cf. the J parallel in 26:32). The narrative containing this double etymology is not to be divided between J and E.[15] It is connected with other Elohistic traditions by the Abimelech figure and by the use of *Elohim* (vss. 22-23). Other linguistic peculiarities, such as those cited by Gunkel, are of dubious value in assigning the narrative to E.[16]

The J parallel to this Elohist tradition is found in the Isaac stories, Gen 26:12-25. There the emphasis is placed on the riches of Isaac, which demonstrate that he is the recipient and bearer of blessing. "The nations represented by the Philistine king necessarily move into relation to Isaac as one blessed by Yahweh."[17] As Wolff suggests, one has only to compare the E and the J accounts to see how heavily the J narrator has underscored the theme of "blessing."[18] In comparison, the E account appears almost skeletal; it is probably much closer to the original patriarchal traditions.

(d) Conclusions. — Of these three narratives, at least the first two appear to be of value in establishing the characteristics of the passages which use *Elohim*. The third passage (21:22-34) is clearly linked with the first story of Abraham's dealings with Abimelech. Its existence and style suggest a varied collection of E narratives concerning the patriarchs, not all of which have been visibly worked over in accordance with E's characteristic theology. Thus, there appear to be various strata in the E traditions, probably stemming from different oral tradition cycles and different locales as well.

Kilian points out the close connection of Abraham with Beersheba in all of the Elohistic Abraham narratives. The purpose of 21:22-34, in Kilian's opinion, is to document Abraham's relation to Beersheba by attributing both the name of the town and the origin of the El-Olam cult there to Abraham.[19] This might also constitute a clue that the original place of transmission of these E Abraham traditions was Beersheba. At any rate, the evidence suggests the inclusion in E of some very ancient traditions, dating before the split into northern and southern kingdoms and, indeed, probably premonarchic in their earliest oral form.

The theological interests of E, in any case, are clear. There is much concern with problems of revelation and questions of sin, guilt, innocence, and the fear of God. In conjunction with these interests, which would seem most natural in an early prophetic group, we found the actual designation of Abraham as a prophet — a term not used elsewhere in Genesis. This, too, suggests that the traditions have been shaped by a group which is itself prophetic, and which tends to project prophetic leadership into the past.

We should note, incidentally, that no text-critical problems arise here: all of the occurrences of *Elohim* which we have mentioned are matched by *ho theos* in the LXX.

Now we shall turn to exensive narratives which employ the name *Elohim*, displaying some of the E characteristics already noted, but which do not have Yahwist parallels.

(2) Texts Lacking Yahwist Parallels

(a) The command to sacrifice Isaac, Gen 22:1-19. — The theological and stylistic similarities between this striking narrative and the traditions we have already discussed indicate an intimate connection between them. Again in this narrative Abraham receives a revelation through God's speaking to him and again, it is implied, this revelation takes place at night (vs. 3). As in 21:17 the angel calls from heaven (vss. 11, 15). As in 21:11 the "fear of God" is a vital concern.

The major critical difficulties in this story are: (a) the use of *Yahweh* in vss. 11, 14, 15, while *Elohim* is otherwise used throughout (vss. 1, 3, 8, 9, 12); and (b) the question whether vss. 15-19, or part of that text, are to be regarded as a later addition to the original narrative. Certainly these verses represent an abrupt change from the lapidary style of the preceding story, with its suspense and restrained pathos, and the transition ("And the angel of Yahweh called to Abraham a second time from heaven") is suspiciously awkward.

The most probable solution is that the E narrative is contained in vss. 1-14, 19, while vss. 15-18 represent a later addition in the style of the J promises to the patriarchs (cf. Gen 12:2; 15:5; 16:10; 32:13; 24:60). The passage betrays its late and secondary character not only by its patchwork appearance, resulting from the use of motifs from several of the promise formulas, but also by the phrase *ne'um Yahweh* ("oracle of Yahweh") in the mouth of an angel.[20]

The use of *Yahweh* instead of *Elohim* in vs. 11 can be explained as a late harmonization of the original narrative with the secondary material in vss. 15-18, while the use of *Yahweh* in vs. 14 is made necessary in the etymology of the name *Moriah*.[21]

The substance of the story (22:1-14), however, may with good reason be attributed to the same circle which produced the narratives of Gen 20 and 21:8-21. The major themes of this story — revelation, testing, obedience, and the fear of God — are fully consonant with the characteristic theology of the Elohist narratives we have been discussing. *Elohim* is used consistently in this narrative, with the exceptions explained above.

Past critics, who attribute this tradition to E almost unanimously,[22] point to certain vocabulary and stylistic peculiarities in addition to the use of Elohim. The most important of these are: (a) the formula used to introduce the story, "And after these things it happened that . . ." (ויהי אחר הדברים האלה, vs. 1); (b) the formula by which the divine communication opens, "He said to him,

'Abraham!' And he said, 'Here I am.'" (ויאמר הנני), ויאמר אליו אברהם ויאמר הנני, vss. 1, 11);
(c) the use of נסה, "to test," with the Deity as subject (vs. 1).

Of these usages, the most important is perhaps the revelatory formula in vss. 1, 11, since this is closely connected with what we have seen to be a major theological concern in the other E traditions discussed. None of the above features, however, may be regarded as valid marks of an "E style" unless they are to be found consistently in conjunction with other weighty criteria. An examination of the passages in which these phrases occur, as listed in the tables of Carpenter and Harford-Battersby,[23] shows that these expressions rarely occur in such undoubted E contexts.

(a) "And after these things it happened that. . ." (ויהי אחר הדברים האלה) occurs verbatim in Gen 39:7 and 40:1; it appears without the ויהי in Gen 15:1 and with the plural אחרי in Gen 48:1. Disregarding these minor variations, the expression occurs in only two passages which can for other strong reasons be labeled "E": the present passage (22:1) and Gen 40:1. Of the remaining two, one (Gen 39:7) appears in a passage otherwise generally attributed to J;[24] and the other (Gen 15:1) in a notoriously complex passage where E is closely fused with J, if there is an E tradition present at all.[25] The expression also occurs three times in the Deuteronomistic History (1 Kgs 13:33; 17:12; 21:1).

(b) The formula, "And God said to him, 'Abraham!' And he said, 'Here I am.'" (ויאמר אליו אברהם ויאמר הנני), or some variation of it, occurs in the context of divine revelation elsewhere in Gen 31:11; 46:2; Exod 3:4*b*.[26] Other uses of the phrase as a response occur in Gen 27:1, 18; 37:11 (conversations between father and son); 1 Sam 3:4, 5, 6, 8, 16 (Samuel's answers both to Eli and to Yahweh); 1 Sam 22:12; 2 Sam 1:7 (response to Saul), and Isa 6:8 (the prophet's response to Yahweh). It thus appears that *hinnēni*, "here I am," was a regularly used reply in ordinary speech, especially between persons related by intimacy or respect (father-son, king-subject). In the E traditions, this form of reply is stylized as the appropriate response to the Deity in a revelation scene.

(c) The verb נסה ("to test"), with God as the subject, occurs also in Exod 15:25; 16:4; 20:20; Deut 33:8, all designated "E" by Carpenter and Harford-Battersby. Only one of these (Exod 20:20) occurs in a passage which can on other grounds be assigned to E.[27]

As pointed out in recent studies by Wolff and Kilian, the "testing" of faith and obedience ("the fear of God") is an important theological theme in E narratives. For Kilian, E's main goal in Gen 22 is to present the testing of Abraham in story form, and to assert that he passes the test by his faith and obedience. A secondary, but still important aim, is to present Abraham as a model of trust and obedience for others to follow.[28] Wolff comments that "Genesis 22 . . . confirms our assumption that the Elohist was especially concerned to teach the true fear of God," through presenting, here and in many other passages, a test of obedience.[29]

Our conclusion must be that the linguistic peculiarities of E which are cited in connection with Gen 22 are of rather small value in themselves. Far more important is the deeper understanding of the characteristic theological emphases of E which can be gained from this narrative. The patriarch Abraham, formerly described as a prophet and intercessor (Gen 20:7, 17), whose actions are placed above blame (20:12), is now tested, that God may know whether he is indeed one who "fears God" (22:1, 12). This powerful narrative deepens the meaning of the "fear of God" first mentioned by E in 20:11 in a way which is positively dreadful.[30] Fear of God here is not merely religion or even awe. It is absolute obedience to the word of God — "obedience which does not hold back even what is most precious, when God demands it, and commits to God even that future which he himself has promised."[31]

The motif of obedience, together with the theme of divine revelation, again suggests a real basis for the attribution of E to a prophetic circle. The famous pronouncement of Samuel is to the point:

> Has Yahweh as great delight in burnt offerings and sacrifices,
> As in obeying Yahweh's voice?
> Behold, to obey is better than sacrifice,
> And to hearken than the fat of rams! (1 Sam 15:22)

In concluding our discussion of Gen 22, let us note the great importance of the identification of this passage as E. If this entirely independent tradition can be assigned to the same body of traditions which is visible in Gen 20:1-17 and 21:8-34, then E can be thought of as a continuing narrative strand not dependent upon J. In short, the identification of Gen 22:1-14 as E undercuts the whole argument of Volz and Rudolph that E never existed as a body of traditions independent of J. Volz recognized this when he wrote,

> Our study now stands before an extremely important question, for if this chapter were derived from E and were transmitted only (or even principally) by E, then it would be proved *that E was an independent narrator, possessing his own peculiar material.*[32]

It is clear that several features of the narrative of 22:1-14, 19, tie this tradition very closely with the Elohist traditions of Gen 20 — 21, most notably the use of *Elohim*, the theme of the fear of God, and the pattern of nocturnal revelation. These are among the classical marks of E. The designation of all of these passages as E can scarcely be avoided.

In addition to the linguistic and theological criteria just mentioned, these E traditions of Gen 20 — 22 are unified by their very marked idealization of Abraham as a man of God, a prophet, and a model of faith, and by their localizing of Abraham in and around Beersheba. The narrator of Gen 22 even takes pains to record Abraham's return to Beersheba after the offering of Isaac (22:19), thus tying this narrative to the one which precedes it (cf. 21:33). These facts suggest that we are not dealing with *ad hoc* corrections and expansions of a basic J narration, as Volz and Rudolph thought, but with the fragments of a carefully unified and systematic presentation of Israel's patriarchal traditions.[33]

(3) The Joseph Narratives, Gen 37; 39—50

Among the patriarchal narratives the Joseph stories are remarkable both for their length and for their literary unity. This unity makes them resistant to the customary applications of source criticism. Furthermore, the clues elsewhere supplied by the divine names are almost entirely lacking: *Yahweh* is used only in Gen 39. These considerations suggest that the Joseph stories had their own peculiar history of transmission.

Nevertheless, from Wellhausen on source criticism has been applied to these stories, and considerable agreement has been reached as to the portions to be assigned to J, E, and P. Such diverse authors as Carpenter and Harford-Battersby,[34] von Rad,[35] Pfeiffer,[36] and Noth[37] present analyses which are similar, differing only in details.

Although he followed methods of source-criticism in his Genesis commentary, Gunkel described the total composition of the Joseph tales as a *Novelle*, and pointed to the impossibility of separating individual portions from the narrative as a whole, which has a profound organic unity.[38] In a later writing, Gunkel dispensed with source criticism and assumed that both the J and E versions of the Joseph story had essentially the same content and style of presentation. Aware of the danger of breaking up the inner unity of the *Novelle* through a mechanically applied source analysis, Gunkel commented:

> By tradition, we should undertake our task on the basis of source-critical results. Just now this has been judged unreliable by Smend, but this presents no insuperable stumbling-block to us. For it is precisely in the Joseph narrative (as also in the Jacob story) that the sources or the alleged sources agree in the essentials of the composition. On the other hand, any future division into sources will not be able to pass over this study of the over-all composition, if it is to avoid the danger of tearing apart that which intrinsically belongs together.[39]

Wilhelm Rudolph, in his study of the Joseph story, enthusiastically applauds Gunkel's suggestions about the limitations of source criticism, and proceeds to an analysis which is intended to demonstrate the almost perfect unity of the narrative. He either discards the material and linguistic variations which first suggested that the stories were composite, or else attempts to explain these inconsistencies on artistic or esthetic grounds. The variation between the divine names *Yahweh, Elohim,* and *El-Shaddai* is represented by Rudolph as the deliberate stylistic variation of one author: *Yahweh* is used when the narrator himself speaks; *Elohim* is used in the speeches of the characters in the story when they are in Egypt; *El-Shaddai* occurs only in the speeches of the characters when they are in Palestine.[40] The alternate application of the names "Jacob" and "Israel" to the patriarch does not point to J and E usages; the single author may simply interchange these names promiscuously.[41] Material contradictions, doublets, and repetitions in the narrative are either disproved or otherwise explained.[42]

As will appear in the following discussion, Rudolph's treatment is highly artificial and ignores the conjunction of material contradictions and linguistic peculiarities which point to the combining of very similar J and E versions of the story, with P editing. This does not mean that the extremely detailed analysis of Carpenter and Harford-Battersby or of Martin Noth can be upheld; but it does mean that we cannot altogether dispense with source criticism in our analysis of these narratives. Even recent scholars whose whole emphasis is on the fine literary unity of these narratives — for example, Gerhard von Rad and Lothar Ruppert — have been unable to suggest an analysis much different from the classical literary-critical explanation that the Joseph story comes to us in intertwined J and E strands, with a P framework.[43] Donald Redford, who argues for the unity of the narrative even more strongly, has been forced to acknowledge a "Reuben strand" and a "Judah strand," which pretty much coincide with the old E and J divisions.[44] Redford refuses, because of his theory concerning the date of the Joseph story, to call these strands E and J. This is not persuasive, especially because there are definite characteristics of E in the so-called Reuben strand.[45]

(a) *Joseph's dream and early days in Egypt, Gen 37; 39.* — In the first chapter of the Joseph narratives we encounter a parade example of the combination of two originally contradictory narrative strands. In 37:21-23, first Reuben and then Judah appear as spokesmen for the eleven brothers. A little further on we meet confusion over the fate of Joseph: was he stolen from the pit by the Midianites, or sold by his brothers to the Ishmaelites? (37:28*a*, 29-30, 36; as compared with 37:25*b*; 39:1).

It is assumed by most critics that two narratives are reflected here. In one, Reuben pleads for the life of Joseph and has him placed in a pit or dry cistern (vss. 21-24), whence he is stolen by the Midianite traders who happen by on their journey towards Egypt (vss. 28*a*, 29, 36). In the other narrative, Judah is the leader of the brothers and Joseph is sold by them to Ishmaelite traders at Judah's suggestion (vss. 25-27, 28*b*, 39:1).[46] This explanation of the peculiarities of the story is far more convincing than the strained reconstruction offered by Rudolph, who must assume that the Midianites take Joseph from the pit while the brothers are negotiating with the Ishmaelites, and that Reuben does not know of the sale when he returns to the pit for Joseph.[47]

> The narrative is, in the relation of Volz and Rudolph, exceedingly clumsy — which contrasts very peculiarly against their constant emphasis on the idea of the artistic cleverness of the Yahwist. It is — in spite of all antagonists of the documentary hypothesis — more "natural" to assume two interwoven tales, of which one (v. 28) does not know the proposal of Judah in vv. 26f., but presupposes the strategem of Reuben from v. 20, countered by the theft of vv. 28-29. That the "recensions" cannot be separated completely throughout the entire chapter, is — as everywhere — no argument against these traces of two narratives which must have been — in other parts — so highly alike to one another that combination cannot be verified in other parts. To all this must be added that Rudolph only by means of much sophism can evade the fact that the two "motives," the sale and the theft, are mentioned separated from one another later in the narrative, cf. 45:4f. and 40:15.[48]

The Content and Scope of E

Since the divine names are not used anywhere in ch. 38, we have no clue in that chapter alone as to the sources of the two narrative strands. But the continuation of the Judah-Ishmaelite strand in ch. 39, together with the frequent use of *Yahweh* in that chapter, indicate that we should associate this strand with the Yahwist narrative. If, therefore, 37:25-27, 28 *b*; 39:1-23 are J, we may tentatively identify 37:21-24, 28*a*, 29-30, 36, with E.[49]

(b) Joseph in prison and the Pharaoh's dreams, Gen 40 — 41. — The above identification is supported by signs of the Elohist tradition in Gen 40 — 41. *Elohim* appears throughout these chapters (ten times: 40:8; 41:16, 25, 28, 32, 38, 39, 51, 52); *Yahweh* is not used. An explicit reference to Joseph's being *stolen* from the pit (41:15) connects this section with the Reuben-Midianites strand in ch. 37.[50] Moreover, there is no difficulty in connecting the religious outlook of these chapters with what we have seen of E's theological emphases. Much interest is shown in the revelation of God's purpose through dreams; technical terms of dream interpretation are used in an easy and natural way, and the whole episode falls into the classic pattern of ancient dream reports.[51] Yet dream interpretation is taken out of the sphere of divination and put into the hands of Joseph, a man "in whom is the spirit of God" (41:38; cf. 40:8). Thus in this narrative, as in Gen 20, we may be encountering the work of early prophetic circles in Israel in which ancient divinatory practices were brought into the realm of Yahweh's sovereignty — circles in which precisely this question was being asked, and answered affirmatively: "Do not interpretations belong to God?" (40:8)

We conclude that chs. 40 — 41 are largely E, while ch. 39 is J. With the E traditions of chs. 40 — 41 we identify the traditions reflected in 37:21-24, 28*a*, 29-30, 36 (the Reuben-Midianite strand). Further certainty is impossible, in spite of the various traces of a double tradition concerning Joseph's beginnings in Egypt.[52]

(c) Joseph's first meeting with his brothers and their return to Canaan, Gen 42. — There are contradictions and irregularities in this chapter which apparently point to the presence of both J and E strands. For example, in vss. 14-16 Joseph proposes sending one brother back to Canaan to fetch Benjamin while the rest remain hostages in Egypt. Later, he takes Simeon as a hostage and sends the rest back. Furthermore, the brothers discover the money replaced in their sacks when they camp for the night (vss. 26-28); later (vs. 35), they make the same discovery in Jacob's presence after arriving in Canaan.

The best solution to these discrepancies is to assign two major sections of the chapter (vss. 13-26 and 28*b* to 38) to E. These sections are highly important because they are unified; their content is decisive for understanding the chapter as it now stands.[53]

Vss. 1*a*, 2-3, 6-7 and 11*b* can then be taken as fragments of the E narrative which led up to these major sections. The remainder of the chapter is assigned to J, where it serves as an introduction to the J narrative which comprises practically all of the following two chapters (Gen 43 — 44).[54]

The reasons for ascribing the substance of this chapter (vss. 13-26, 28*b*-38) to E are: (a) the use of *Elohim* (vss. 19, 38*b*); (b) the depiction of Joseph, like Abraham before him, as one who "fears God" (vs. 19); (c) the position of Reuben as spokesman for the brothers (vss. 22, 37-38), together with references in his speeches to the Reuben strand of ch. 37 (42:37-38).

(d) The brothers return and meet again with Joseph, Gen 43. — In ch 43 the role of Judah as spokesman (vss. 3, 8-10) suggests J. The use of *Elohim* by the Egyptianized Joseph might be stylistic (43:29), since a foreigner would not be expected to use *Yahweh*. Simeon's incarceration in Egypt, reported in the E narrative of 42:13-26, 28*b*-38, does not serve as the motive of the brothers' return, and the report of the brothers' first encounter with Joseph is given differently than in the E tradition of ch. 42 (cf. 42:29-37; 43:3-7).[55] "Israel" is used consistently in ch. 43, while in the E sections of ch. 42 the patriarch was called "Jacob." Thus, ch. 43 can be quite clearly distinguished from 42:13-26, 28*b*-38, and may be linked to J by the use of "Israel," and especially by the position of Judah.[56]

(e) Joseph's cup and the intervention of Judah. — In ch. 44 Judah again acts as the spokesman (cf. 44:13, 16, 18-34, with 42:37), and again the captivity of Simeon is forgotten in the recital of Joseph's past dealings with his brothers (44:18-34). The chapter is thus a continuation of the J tradition of ch. 43; nothing positively points to the inclusion of any E materials.[57]

(f) Joseph reveals his identity, Gen 45. — Ch. 45 presents a less homogeneous appearance than the preceding chapters; most critics have found traces of both major sources here. The most serious difficulty is in the contrasting accounts of the invitation to Jacob. In 9-15, Joseph invites Jacob and his family to immigrate to Goshen immediately; in vss. 16-20 the Pharaoh himself issues a gracious invitation for Jacob to come and settle anywhere in Egypt. The former tradition is continued in 46:13 — 47:5, which assumes that the Pharaoh must later be informed of Jacob's arrival and grant him permission to stay. Verses 9-15 are closely connected with vss. 5-8, while vss. 16-20 are continued in vss. 21-28.

The simplest solution is to regard vss. 5-15 as basically E, because of the use of *Elohim* (vss. 5, 7, 8, 9), and vss. 16-28 as basically J because of the use of "Israel." In addition, we might distinguish two traditions about Joseph's self-revelation to his brothers, vss. 2-3 and vss. 1, 4.[58] This division remains conjectural. We must agree with Skinner that "the sources . . . are here so intimately blended that a complete analysis is impossible."[59]

(g) Jacob and his sons in Egypt, Gen 46 — 50. — Critics agree that the substance of 46:6-27 is P or secondary.[60] But 46:1-4 represents a theophany tradition that is certainly Elohistic. In 46:1-4, God speaks to Jacob "in visions of the night" (במראת הלילה) at Beersheba (vv. 1-2). The form of address (Jacob!) and the reply (Here I am!) follow closely the pattern pointed out in the E narratives of Gen 20 and 22.[61] Theologically, this passage is significant in stressing that momentous events in the history of the people of God are

accompanied by divine revelations. Jacob's decision to go to Egypt is thus lifted out of the realm of the ordinary; it is no longer prompted merely by his desire to see a long absent son.[62]

In the very interesting section 47:13-28, relating the assumption of direct control of property by the Egyptian crown, no clear indication of source is present, except in vss. 27-31 where P editorial work is visible.[63]

The very complex composition of ch. 48 is suggested by the presence of P wording in 48:3, 4, 7,[64] and by the intrusion of the blessing in vss. 15-16. E material is suggested by the use of *Elohim* in vss. 9, 11, 15, 20, 21, but the blessings themselves are probably independent traditional material and are not likely to show anything specific about E's theology. Noth treats the chapter as basically E (vss. 1, 2, 7-14, 17-22), with secondary redaction indicated by the insertion of the blessing (vss. 15-16). He admits, however, that this does not solve the problems: "The pre-priestly literary part of Gen 48 is very broken and no longer in its original form."[65]

Passing over Ch. 49,[66] we encounter in Gen 50 a passage which is undoubtedly from E, and which is of great significance for what it reveals of the theology of the E Joseph story and of the E source as a whole. In 50:15-26 the dream which led to the hostility of Joseph's brothers has its last fulfillment: the brothers surround him and prostrate themselves as Joseph's slaves out of fear for their lives, now that Jacob is dead. In this scene and in Joseph's speech in response we see strong evidence of E vocabulary and theological concern in the recurrent use of *Elohim* (vss. 19, 20) and in the discussion of the brothers' sin and guilt, which God has turned into good (vss. 15-21). The concluding verses of Genesis (50:22-26) likewise use *Elohim*, and are certainly integrally related to the scene in which Joseph forgives his brothers. We should view these verses, with their depiction of the old age and death of Joseph, as the conclusion of E's patriarchal narratives.

The E Joseph stories can deepen considerably our understanding of the theological characteristics of this source. As Wolff has shown, the theology of E is revealed most often in the dialogue ascribed to central characters in the stories.[67] In the case of the Joseph stories, there are three dialogue passages which are highly significant: the scene which we have just discussed, in which Joseph forgives his brothers (50:15-21); a similar scene in 45:3-8 in which Joseph first reveals his identity to the brothers and responds to their guilty dismay; and 46:1-4, God's address to Jacob in a vision.

In these dialogues we note first of all the very striking portrayal of Joseph as a model of leadership because of his wisdom. Joseph is wise in the full Hebraic understanding of that trait, as von Rad has so strikingly emphasized: he is humble in his recognition that both he and his brothers are simply instruments in God's gracious plan (cf. 41:16 in the *JB* translation: "I do not count. It is God who will give Pharaoh a favorable answer."). Joseph is the epitome of the wise man and perhaps of the prophet too in his knowledge of God's purpose, whether revealed by dreams (Gen 40 — 41) or simply known in some mysterious way through reflection on the past, present and future: "The evil you planned to do me has by God's design been turned to good, that he might bring about, as indeed he has, the deliverance of a numerous people" (50:20; *JB*). Joseph's wisdom, like that celebrated in Israel's wisdom writings, has its beginning in his fear of God (42:19). Here the characteristic Elohistic theme of the fear of God, previously understood as trust and obedience under the direst stress of God's testing, is deepened to include the prophetic understanding of human history as a reflex of God's plan of saving the life of his people from destruction (45:5, 7; 50:20).[68]

Lothar Ruppert has recently emphasized the parallels between this E depiction of Joseph and the figure of Moses in the E traditions of Exodus.[69] While it would be easy to push the comparison too far, it is instructive to note how E shapes the old traditions around certain models of charismatic leadership, beginning with Abraham. Each of these figures (Abraham, Jacob, Joseph, and finally Moses) receives divine revelations and serves the furtherance of God's plan in a significant way. In the process, these leaders are idealized in a way that is foreign to the Yahwist traditions, which always emphasize the worldly success and prominence of Israel's great ones.[70] As we will again comment at the end of the next chapter, E's presentation here is surely influenced by the prophetic movement and probably directly shaped by followers of early prophetic leaders in Israel.

Consistent with E's peculiar idealization of the Israelite forefathers is the strong emphasis on a divine plan which is known in advance and understood by men because God reveals himself, in the later words of Amos, "to his servants the prophets" (Amos 3:7). As shown by the revelation to Jacob in 46:1-4, the other half of Amos' statement might apply to E as well: "Surely the Lord God does nothing without revealing his secret to his servants the prophets" (RSV). On the eve of his departure for Egypt Jacob hears God speak to him in a vision, revealing that the projected journey is indeed part of the divine plan which stretches from the past ("I am God, the God of your father") into the future ("I myself will go down to Egypt with you. I myself will bring you back again; Joseph's hand shall close your eyes.")[71] The same conception of sacred history as an overarching plan is evident in Joseph's answers to his brothers in 45:3-8 and 50:12-26. What is manifested here is a strong didactic tendency — one which contrasts sharply with the Yahwist tendency to give precedence "to naked event as against all reflections."[72] That is to say, the Elohist does not hesitate to communicate in the most explicit way, through the speeches of his characters, a theological understanding which is quite forthright and definite.[73] In this respect, E is much more like the priestly tradition than J.

It is in this light that we should understand another extremely important observation of H. W. Wolff, an observation that applies especially strongly to E's Joseph narrative: E, in strong contrast to J, knits his narratives together by means of strategically placed references, primarily in dialogue sections, to preceding and following events. Thus in 45:5-15 Joseph refers back to his brothers' having sold him into Egypt, as first related in Gen 37, then to the beginning of famine in Egypt (chs. 41-42), to his own appointment as chancellor of Egypt (ch. 41). He then looks forward in time to the coming of Jacob and his whole family to dwell in Egypt. Similarly, God's speech to Jacob in 46:1-5 places the patriarch in Beersheba, the central locus of E's Abraham and Isaac narratives, and identifies *Elohim* as "the God of your father," the God who will go with Jacob into Egypt, and who has already ordained that Joseph should close the eyes of Jacob when he dies.

Here we have only touched the surface of the reminiscences and anticipations found in E's Joseph narratives which constitute, as Wolff says, "a veritable network of such connections."[74] The important point, for our purposes, is to see this as expressing the whole theological understanding of the E school. History can be narrated this way only because God lays out his plans and purposes, communicates them to "his servants the prophets," and mysteriously guides historical happenings toward their ordained conclusion. This theology of history allows for the uniquely coherent style of story-telling which is notable throughout the Elohist traditions. It also strongly suggests that E was once a coherent and comprehensive presentation of Israel's sacred history — and not, as Volz, Rudolph, and Engnell asserted, merely a string of editorial additions to a Yahwist base.

(4) Texts in which J and E are Mingled

To this point we have been discussing two types of E material in Genesis: (a) those few extensive passages which have clear parallels in J (cf. chs. 20 — 21); and (b) those which are fairly extensive, but have no J parallels (22:1-14; 40 — 41; 46:1-4; 50:15-26). In addition, we have indicated the very great probability that other passages in the Joseph stories are from E (42:13-26, 28*b*-38; 45:2-3, 5-15; 48:1, 2, 7-14, 17-22), but were prevented from making definite identification by the fine literary unity of the whole Joseph narrative. Throughout our treatment the evidence of the first chapters discussed remained primary in importance, for it was only there that E traditions could be viewed in strict parallel with J.

We turn now to another group of passages — texts in which J and E narrative strands appear to have been closely intertwined, but which do not display the coherence and homogeneity of the Joseph novelette. Here again we will move in the realm of probability rather than certainty, owing to the complexity of the redactional process which has brought the traditions into their present appearance of unity.

(a) *The call of Abraham, Gen 15.* — More than one scholar has commented upon the literary complexity of this important chapter, and many have seen in one of the strands the beginning of the Elohist epic.[75] Two major strands were first identified, vs. 1-6 and vss. 7-21;[76] later scholars offered more complex analyses, of which Noth's is typical:[77]

J = vss. 1*abβ*, 2*a*, 3*b*, 4, 6-12, 17, 18 (19-21)
E = vss. 1*bα*, 3*a*, 5, 13*a* (13*b*), 14*abα* (14*bβ*), 15, 16

Noth, like Gunkel before him, assigns the base narrative to J, with the contrasting E tradition worked in secondarily.[78]

In strong contrast to this analysis Volz, as we might expect, assigns the entire chapter to J, asserting that "here as well the juxtaposition of two so entirely different narratives is very characteristic of the great originality and boldness of this superb narrator."[79]

While on the one hand we cannot offer such a complex and minute analysis as that of Gunkel or Noth, we cannot, on the other, agree with Volz. There is good reason to believe that here, as so frequently in the Pentateuch, different narrative traditions reflect different tradition circles. The chief question is whether one of these strands can be assigned with any certainty to E. Our opinion is that we cannot make this identification with certainty, even though possible indications of E are visible, especially in vss. 1-6.

The introductory phrase "after these things" (אחר הדברים האלה) in 15:1, for example, appears at the beginning of two E narratives elsewhere in Genesis (22:1; 41:1). The revelation through a vision (מחזה) and the implication that Abraham is regarded as a prophet ("the word of Yahweh came to Abram," היה דבר יהוה אל אברם . . . לאמר) in 15:1*a* point even more strongly to E. With this verse has been connected the revelation narrative of vss. 12-16, which likewise implies a night vision or dream and also uses the expression, "Amorites" which is often regarded as a sign of E style.[80]

At the same time, these allegedly E verses contain the name *Yahweh* (vss. 1, 2, 4, 6, 13), but never use *Elohim*; they make use of the phrase mentioned above, "the word of Yahweh came to . . ." (. . . היה דבר יהוה אל and הנה דבר יהוה אליו; vss. 1, 4), which is used elsewhere only in later literature, particularly in the Deuteronomistic history.[81]

In one recent study by Kilian, vss. 4 (in part), 5-6, 13-14 (in part) and 16 are taken as definitely E, on the grounds that they display the same emphasis on faith as seen in Gen 22, and the same revelation of the divine plan of history that we saw in the Joseph stories. These themes, together with the revelation in a night dream or vision, certainly do suggest at least an E substratum.[82]

The most that we can say is that Gen 15:1-6 and possibly vss. 13-16 contain the remnant of an E tradition of the call of Abraham, but that these verses have been worked over by later writers, under Deuteronomic and prophetic influence. A certain and detailed statement about the original E substratum cannot be ventured.[83]

The Jacob Narratives, Gen 25 — 35

This large narrative complex may be viewed, following Gunkel, as a composite assembled from several smaller collections: (1) the Jacob-Esau stories; (2) the Jacob-Laban cycle; (3) legends about cult sites founded by Jacob; (4) stories about the birth and later fortunes of the children of Jacob.[84]

Although some of the older commentators believed that E material could be found throughout these traditions,[85] there is no clear evidence of E before Gen 28.[86] Accordingly we shall begin with the narrative of Jacob's theophany at Bethel, Gen 28:10-22.

(b) Jacob's dream at Bethel, Gen 28:10-22. — The narrative appears to be skilfully woven from two original stories, and it is possible to designate them J and E because of clear criteria. 28:10 connects with the preceding J narrative of ch. 27, so we assign it to J. In the theophany itself, two strands are visible: (a) vss. 11-12, 17-18, 20-22; (b) vss. 13-16, 19. The former tells of a dream in which Jacob sees the "angels of God" ascending and descending on a "ladder" whose base is the spot where he is sleeping and whose top reaches the sky. Upon awakening Jacob exclaims, "How awe-inspiring this place is! This is nothing less than a house of God; this is the gate of heaven!" (*JB*) He sets up his stone pillow as a sacred pillar and pours oil on it. Then he vows to return and worship here, if he is preserved on his journey. The use of *Elohim* in this strand, together with the motif of revelation by dream, point clearly to the E source.[87] In fact, the E tradition provides the bulk of this narrative; into it has been inserted the parallel J narrative of the founding of Bethel.

The J story, by contrast, uses the Tetragrammaton (vss. 13, 16) and has Yahweh speak directly to Jacob (vs. 13) with a repetition of the characteristic Yahwist form of the promise to the patriarchs (vss. 13-14; cf. Gen 12:2-3, 7).

This narrative again illustrates the Elohistic emphasis on revelation through a dream or night vision. Here, however, the dream is solely visual: its meaning is conveyed by the symbol of the heavenly ladder rather than through the divine word. As we shall see, the sanctuary of Bethel has a particular importance for the E tradition, as already suggested by this extensive narrative of the founding of the sanctuary there by Jacob, with the explicit attempt to legitimize the tithe to be paid.[88]

We should note also the characteristic Elohist method of marking important turning points in Israel's sacred history by a revelation vouchsafed to the patriarch or leader; we saw the same pattern on the eve of Jacob's departure for Egypt. Here, as Jacob flees from Beersheba, he is given such a revelation and prays that God will go with him and some day return him to his father's home. Thus the Elohist has used an old story of the founding of a sanctuary to express again his understanding of Israel's fathers as prophets or quasi-prophets — the revelation elevates even the worldly Jacob to a new role — and to communicate his faith in a God who holds man's past, present, and future together in his purpose.

(c) Jacob arrives and serves Laban fourteen years, Gen 29:1-30. — In spite of attempts to divide this section between J and E,[89] no sufficient evidence exists for such analysis. There is no good reason to deny that the whole narrative is J.[90]

(d) The sons of Jacob, Gen 29:31 — 30:24. — In these traditions about the birth and naming of Jacob's sons there is considerable evidence of a composite narrative. For example, *Elohim* appears in 30:2, 6, 8, 17, 18, 20, 22, 23; *Yahweh* in 29:31, 32, 33, 35; 30:24. Further, there are two explanations of the names Issachar (30:16, 18), Zebulun (30:30) and Joseph (30:23). Indeed, in the last-mentioned passage *Elohim* is used with the explanation of "Joseph" as אסף and *Yahweh* is used with the explanation as יסף. It appears, then, that both J and E contained etymologies of the tribal names, and that here they are mixed together. It would be impossible to separate them with any certainty, however,[91] and the results would be of dubious value in any case.

(e) Jacob's wealth and his departure from Laban, Gen 30:25 — 32:2. — Signs which point to considerable E narrative material in this section include (a) the use of *Elohim* in 31:7, 9, 11 (אל in 13), 16, 24, 42, 50; 32:2, 3;[92] (b) the revelation in a dream (חלום) in 31:10-11, 24; (c) reference to the E portion of the Bethel narrative, 31:13 (cf. 28:17-18).

The two accounts of Jacob's activity as a sheepbreeder are skilfully joined by the editor so that the first (J) account tells of the events themselves, while the second (E) account (31:4-16) is presented as Jacob's own recital and justification of his actions. But the two differ not only in detail (cf. 31:7-8 with 31:32-33), but also in general theological import. Whereas J portrays Jacob simply as a clever and fortunate adversary to Laban, E justifies Jacob's actions as obedience to divine revelation. Both the divine revelation and the idealization of patriarchal behavior are recurrent hallmarks of the E traditions. In the account of Jacob's flight (31:17-24), the familiar element of revelation by dream also occurs (31:24). In the dialogue of Jacob's dream, which is introduced with E's regular formula ("Jacob!"..."Here I am!" 31:11) explicit reference is made to the E account of the dream at Bethel, with a command that Jacob now must prepare for the return to Canaan (31:11, 13). E thus again carefully connects major episodes in his ongoing narrative, and at the same time stresses the divine impetus which moves history along towards the fulfillment of God's plan.

The substance of the dream dialogue does present some difficulties, for in addition to God's address to Jacob and the command to return to Canaan (vss. 11, 13), vs. 12 instructs Jacob to watch the mating of the sheep and goats. This direction does not belong immediately before Jacob's departure. Furthermore, it breaks the expected sequence of the divine call ("Jacob! Jacob!"), Jacob's response ("Here I am") and the beginning of the divine speech ("I am the God of Bethel"). Von Rad is undoubtedly correct in labeling vs. 12 "an inept insertion" which reflects the desire of an editor to attribute Jacob's trickery in sheep-breeding to a direct divine command.[93]

This minor addition, which probably comes from the E school as an addition to the original E narrative here, shows how the figure of Jacob is idealized by E. E's Jacob is "almost without moral offense ... God has frustrated Jacob's knavery (vs. 7b), God was with Jacob (vs. 5b), God has given Jacob Laban's flocks, and finally God has called him to leave Laban and go home.''[94] Precisely as in the case of Abraham, whose lie was not really a lie (Gen 20:12), E manages to excuse Jacob's rather dubious ethical behavior. God then protects Jacob from Laban's possible retaliation by speaking to Laban in a dream ("Take heed that you say not a word to Jacob, either good or bad," RSV, 31:14), just as he warned Abimelech in a dream not to sin against Abraham (20:3-7).

We conclude that the substance of 31:1-24 derives from E, with vss. 4-16 as a unified narrative section containing several important E characteristics.[95]

In the following passage, depicting Laban's pursuit of Jacob and their treaty (31:25 — 32:3) there are several signs of affinity with the E strand. Not only is *Elohim* used absolutely (31:42, 50; 32:1, 2), but the phrase אלהי אברהם without the identification of the Deity as Yahweh, appears several times (31:29, 42, 53).

The only passage in this section which cannot be linked to E with any certainty is the complex covenant account of vss. 43-54. Here there are many signs of a double recension, including the explanation of the two place-names (vss. 48b, 49a); the erection of two sacred monuments (vss. 46, 48, 51, 52; and vss. 45, 51, 52); two covenant meals (46b, 54); and two reports of the contents of the treaty (vss. 50, 52). The narrative reflected in vss. 45, 49, 50, 53b, 54, has been most commonly attributed to E,[96] but the basis for this identification (mainly the use of *maṣṣēbāh* which J supposedly avoids[97]) is not sufficient to bear the weight of such a complex analysis.

In the especially strong and vivid narrative of 31:25-42, which is largely E,[98] the strong ridicule of Laban's household gods is very significant as the first open condemnation of pagan religion in the Pentateuch. Laban's gods are so lacking in power and holiness that a woman sat upon them in her menstrual uncleanness! (cf. Lev 15:20). No comparable disparaging of pagan gods is found anywhere in J. We must conclude that the E tradition is particularly concerned to oppose pagan religious practices and to ridicule their adherents. This is not at all strange if E is to be linked with early prophetic circles in Israel (cf. 1 Kgs 18:25-29).

(f) Jacob prepares to meet with Esau and wrestles with God, Gen 32:3— 33:20. — None of the criteria of E so far recognized are found in this section before 33:5.[99] In 33:4-11, recounting the meeting of Jacob with Esau, *Elohim* is used three times (33:5, 10, 11). There are no other recognizable signs of E in this section, however, and no dislocation or unevenness in the narrative. We must conclude that the whole section is JE, with J as the basis, and E only visible in 33:5-11.[100]

(g) The Rape of Dinah and Jacob's alliance with the Shechemites, Gen 34. — Modern critics view this narrative as a literary complex, but are not in agreement on the exact analysis.[101] Several signs of at least two original narratives are found. For example, in. vss. 4, 6, 8-10, Hamor represents his sons' interests in trying to win Dinah, while in 11-12 and 19 Shechem himself

deals with the sons of Jacob. In vss. 25-26, 30-31, Simeon and Levi alone avenge Dinah, while in 27-29 all the sons of Jacob take part in attacking "Shechem." Further, in the main body of the story Jacob does not appear at all (vss. 13-29). This suggests that the narrative was originally concerned with the Simeon and Levi tribes' attempt to gain a foothold around Shechem in very early times, and that the connection with the cycle of Jacob narratives is secondary.[102]

At any rate, nothing in the entire narrative points clearly to E material, although it is possible that a combination of J and E stories led to the present complex account.

(h) Jacob at Bethel, 35:1-8. — There is considerable reason to relate this passage to E. The name *Elohim* is used three times (vss. 1, 5, 7) and *El* is used twice (vss. 1, 3). The close connection with the Bethel theophany of 28:11-22 (E) and with the reference to that event in 31:13 (also E), can be seen by comparing the texts of 28:20; 35:3; 31:13; and 35:1 (RSV):

28:20   Then Jacob made a vow, saying, 'If God will be with me and will keep me in this way that I go, and will give me bread to eat and clothing to wear . . ."

35:3   "Then let us arise and go up to Bethel, that I may make there an altar to the God who answered me in the day of my distress and has been with me wherever I have gone."

31:13   "I am the God of Bethel, where you anointed a pillar and made a vow to me. Now arise, go forth from this land, and return to the land of your birth."

35:1   God said to Jacob, "Arise, go up to Bethel, and dwell there; and make there an altar to the God who appeared to you when you fled from your brother Esau."

Vss. 16-20 continue the story of the journey of Jacob and his household and so would appear to be from E, although positive indications are lacking.

That the entire narrative has a definite relation to the establishment of royal worship at Bethel in the time of Jeroboam I is suggested by Albrecht Alt.[103] It is significant, as Alt points out, that E places so much stress on the Bethel sanctuary, making it the point of departure and return for the patriarch Jacob; this is one of the strongest suggestions thus far of the north Israelite provenance of E.[104] Northern provenance is also indicated by the phrase, הסירו את אלהי הנכר אשר בתככם (vs. 2) which appears almost verbatim in the northern traditions of Josh 24:23; and I Sam 7:3, although it does not indicate any *literary* connections between E and these traditions.[105]

(5) Summary

We are now in a position to sum up our findings thus far. In the patriarchal narratives of Gen 12 — 50 we have isolated E passages in every major section. Dominating these texts is the interest in and acquaintance with prophecy and problems of revelation. Subsidiary motifs are the use of dreams and visions as revelatory media, the idealization of patriarchal behavior, an emphasis on a divine plan of events and divine guidance toward fulfillment of that plan, the themes of obedience and testing, and a disparaging of foreign gods.

We have also pointed to a few purely stylistic features which recur in these traditions. Especially notable is the set form in which revelation accounts are cast, as in Gen 22:1, 11; 46:2. Equally significant are the heavy use of dialogue in depicting events, and the tendency to tie the narration together by reminiscences and predictions. E also tends to use places, especially sanctuary sites, as focal points for whole series of episodes. Beersheba is such a focal point for the Abraham, Isaac, and even the Joseph narratives, while the site from which the Jacob stories radiate and to which they return is Bethel.

It is important, methodologically speaking, that the reliable stylistic constants of E are few compared with the vocabulary tables in the work of Carpenter and Harford-Battersby. We believe that we must be cautious about depending upon stylistic features which do not represent any characteristic theological emphasis, for it seems that we are dealing primarily with a school of thought, a cluster of particular theological emphases, rather than with a single writer.

If this means that we are much less certain about attributing isolated verses to specific sources, it also means that we can be quite certain about the identification of the passages which are the most important theologically. Among these are certainly the following: Gen 20:1-17; 21:8-21; 22:1-14; 28:11-12, 17-22; 31:4-16; 35:1-5, 7-8, 16-20; 40; 41; 42 (in large part); 46:1-4; 50:15-26. The hypothesis that E was an important, independent, and continuous tradition receives emphatic support from this array of passages.

(B) The Exodus and Sinai Covenant Traditions: Exodus 1 — 34

The separation of the strands of tradition in the Book of Exodus is notoriously difficult. The criterion of the divine names becomes less available after Exod 3:13-15, though the E tradition still appears to use *Elohim* by preference in most passages. Clear signs of composition exist throughout the book, but it is often impossible to go further than the distinction between "JE" and "P." Thus in Exodus, even more than in Genesis, our designation of passages as "E" can only reflect varying degrees of probability.[106]

Even where we are able to distinguish E traditions with considerable certainty, it will become evident that the total amount of E material in Exodus is not nearly so great as the amount of J and P. The explanation for this must be that the editor has taken J as the base narrative, adding variant E traditions only as supplements. The only exception to this is in the Sinai pericope, where the situation is reversed and E is the dominant narrative tradition, the J version of the covenant being displaced to ch. 34.[107]

(1) The Mosaic Birth and Call Narratives, Exodus 1 — 3

The narratives of the birth, early life and call of Moses include some passages which can quite probably be assigned to E. The first clue to the presence of E in ch. 1 is the contradiction between vss. 15-21 on the one hand, and vs. 22 on the other. Two different stratagems for getting rid of the Hebrew children are described in these passages.[108] This material contradiction is accompanied by differences in language: vss. 15-21 speak of "the king of Egypt," while vs. 22 uses the term "Pharaoh." On this basis alone, vs. 22 would appear to stem from the same tradition as vss. 8-12. As for vss. 15-21, we can assign them to E because of the use of *Elohim* and the theme of the fear of God (vss. 17, 20, 21; cf. Gen 21:11; 22:12; 42:18).[109] Thus, we may see a rough division in the chapter between J's tradition (vss. 8-12, 22) and E's narrative (vss. 15-21), assigning vss. 1-7, 13-14 to P.[110]

It is striking that God is mentioned in the first chapter of Exodus only in these E verses — and in the characteristic E context of "the fear of God." The midwives' disobedience of the Egyptian pharaoh is extensively developed in this E passage, in sharp contrast to J's laconic statements in vss. 12, 22. The Elohistic understanding of the fear of God is presented here in a new way to mean not only trust and obedience toward God, but obedience to God even if it means direct disobedience to earthly legal powers: "The midwives feared God, and did not do as the king of Egypt commanded them . . ." (vs. 17). For their courage in adhering to his commands and promises, God visibly rewards the midwives: "So God dealt well with the midwives; and the people multiplied and grew very strong. And because the midwives feared God he gave them families" (vss. 20-21).[111] In Noth's words,

> The midwives' fear of God proves to be a real factor in history, and God afterwards gives express and visible confirmation to the midwives that this fear of God was the right course, and that he stands with those who fear him against all earthly power, by 'dealing well' with them (v. 20*a*).[112]

We shall comment more fully in the next chapter on the implications of this theme of conflict with earthly power, in relation to the date and provenance of E. This theme seems clearly to point to an anti-monarchic circle, probably a prophetic circle, as the chief tradent of the E traditions.

The story of the call of Moses and the revelation of the divine name *Yahweh* in Exod 3 is clearly composite. For example, the Deity twice declares that he has seen the oppression of his people (vss. 7, 9), and twice announces their deliverance (vss. 8, 10). Close examination reveals — perhaps more clearly here than in any other place in the Pentateuch — even more doublets, suggesting that both J and E (as would be expected) find the call of Moses and the first announcement of the coming exodus from Egypt to be absolutely crucial events in Israel's sacred history.[113]

Definite signs of E style are noticeable in vss. 1*b* ("Horeb, the mountain of God"),[114] 4 ("Moses, Moses! And he said, Here I am."),[115] 6*b* ("for he was afraid to look at God"),[116] 11a ("But Moses said to *Elohim*"), and 12 ("you shall serve *Elohim* upon this mountain"). In addition, we note the use of *Elohim* in vss. 13, 14, 15.

Vss. 13-15 are crucial, for here the Elohist stresses the introduction of the name *Yahweh* at the time of Moses, accounting thereby for the use of *Elohim* in the narratives to this point.[117] There is, however, some unevenness in the text, especially in the connection of vss. 14 and 15. The "moreover" (ʿôd) which introduces vs. 15 appears suspiciously editorial. It would appear that since the direct answer to the question of vs. 13 is found in vs. 15, vs. 14 must be an addition to the original narrative, with the purpose of explaining the name *Yahweh* etymologically. The ʿôd of vs. 15a would then be redactional, added after the insertion of vs. 14.[118]

We identify the E portion of Exod 3, then, as vss. 1, 4b, 6, 9-13, 15.[119] Here Moses' call is depicted as leading to a role which is that of a prophet — and more than a prophet. He is to play an actual role in the event of deliverance by bringing Israel out of Egypt (vs. 10). This contrasts with J's presentation of Moses as simply conveying news of the coming deliverance of Israel (vss. 7, 8, 17). Noth is probably correct in suggesting that E shows more reflection and refining of the tradition here, while J follows closely the preliterary tradition that it was Yahweh who brought Israel out of Egypt.[120]

A refining and elevation of Moses' role is also visible in E's strong emphasis on the communication to him of the divine name *Yahweh* as the validation of his mission. Moses is thereby made to share in a significant way in the divine saving activity and in the inner intentions and plans of God.[121] This revelation of the name is, in fact, the climactic element in J's story, which is the appearance of God in the burning bush. At the same time, of course, a major turning point in E's total narration of the sacred history is reached: from now on, Israel will know Yahweh by his proper name.

A number of scholars have pointed to the very evident parallels between the call of Moses and the later prophetic call narratives.[122] It is important to recognize, however, as Richter does,[123] that both J and E depict Moses as a prophet, and both apparently depend upon a pre-prophetic call genre or *Gattung* which is found also in the narratives concerning Gideon and Saul, who were called to be holy-war leaders or "judges."[124] In other words, we are here encountering a reflex of a very ancient type of call narrative which provided the basis for later stories of the call of the classical prophets.[125] In terms of the history of traditions, the northern kingdom is doubtless the source of this genre.[126] The E tradition of Moses' call in Exod 3 stands very close to the original frame of reference of such narratives, with its emphasis on the political and military leadership which Moses will combine with his role of messenger.[127]

(2) The Plague Narratives, Exodus 4 — 12

The narrative of the empowering of Moses to work signs in 4:1-23 contains only a few verses which appear to belong to E, vss. 17, 18, and 20b. These verses are marked by the delivering to Moses of a rod, described in vs. 20b as מטה האלהים whereby he shall do signs. In the contrasting J tradition, vss. 1-12, the rod is used in the first sign. This E tradition further contrasts with J in that Moses returns to Egypt alone, taking with him the rod (vss. 18, 20b; cf. Exod 18:2-4), while in J he takes his wife and children with him (vss. 19, 20a).[128]

The older commentators found, in the passages just discussed (Exod 1 — 6), means whereby E passages in the plague narratives (Exod 7 — 12) might be distinguished. First, the rod given to Moses as a means of working signs (4:17) appears later as a miracle-working instrument in the hand of Moses (7:20b; 9:23; 10:13; cf. 10:22). On the basis of Moses' use of the rod, it is suggested, these verses ought to be assigned to E.

A second peculiarity which has been thought to point to E in the plague narratives is the way the Hebrews are depicted as living in close proximity to their Egyptian neighbors in passages such as Exod 3:21; 10:21-23; 11:2. This intermingling of Hebrews with Egyptians, found also in P (Gen 47:11), is contrasted with J's picture of them settled in the land of Goshen (Gen 45:10), where they are removed by distance from the effects of the plague (Exod 8:18 [EV 8:22]; 9:26).

Using these two alleged criteria, scholars assigned fragments of the plague narratives of Exod 7-12 to E; viz., 7:15, 17b, 20b, 23; 9:8-12, 19-23a, 24a, 25a, 31, 35; 10:12-13a, 14a, 15b, 21-23; 11:1-3.[129]

It is questionable whether such analysis is profitable when the data are so meager and so precarious. J appears to furnish the framework of the plague stories with an account of seven plagues, while the P tradition supplements these and rounds off the number of plagues to ten.[130] Even if there are also a few fragments which can be distinguished from the basic J-P narrative and assigned to E, they are not of sufficient clarity to justify minute analysis.[131]

(3) The Deliverance from Egypt, Exodus 13 — 17

Scholars have assigned only fragments of Exod 13-17 to the E tradition. Driver, for example, designated as E only 13:17-19; 14:10b, 16a, 19, 20a, 15:20-25, 27; 17:1b-2b, 4-6, 8-16.[132] In a very similar analysis, Holzinger attributed these fragments to E:[133] 13:17-19; 14:15aβ, 16a, 19a, 21b?, (22?), 23, 25a, (26?), 27a?, 31aβb; 15:20-21; 17:8-16; 14:16a, 23 are attributed to E only "in part." Noth designates as E only 13:17-19; 14:5a, 7, 11, 12, 19a, 25a; 17:3.[134]

In regard to these passages there is general agreement on only one, 13:17-19. The ascription to E of these verses is probably correct, since *Elohim* is used four times and since the passage alludes to the E tradition of Gen 50:25-26 by the mention of Joseph's bones being brought out of Egypt by the departing Hebrews.[135] The tradition is remarkable in its depiction of the Hebrews as armed for battle (חמשים, vs. 18).[136]

In Exod 14 we cannot be at all certain that E narrative material forms part of the complex of traditions. The surprising statement that the Hebrews *fled*

The Content and Scope of E

from Egypt (vs. 5a) can be connected with E only on the basis of the expression "king of Egypt" instead of Pharaoh, as in vs. 5b (cf. 1:15, E). Verse 19a appears to be an E fragment, because of the mention of the "angel of *Elohim*" protecting the Hebrews (cf. J's "pillar of cloud" and "pillar of fire" in 13:20-21; 14:19b). Again, the fragments are so small, and their identification so tenuous, that no important discussion can spring from them.[137]

There is no question about the antiquity and importance of the great Hymn at the Sea, Exod 15:1b-18. But it stands independent of all the narrative strands in its presentation of the event of deliverance and is probably earlier in formulation than either J or E.[138] If the song comes to us as part of the J tradition,[139] then vss. 20-21 might represent the parallel title or *incipit* of the hymn in the E tradition.[140]

Nothing in the remaining verses of ch. 15 points clearly to E. Verse 25b fits poorly in its context, and is presumably a fragment of a once longer account of law-giving and testing. It has often been assigned to E on the basis of the occurrence of נסה as in Gen 22:1.[141] But the verb may be just a play on the name מסה (17:7).[142] Originally, the reference was probably to a place of legal transactions, as suggested by the use of חק , משפט, and the dispensing of law — a place like the עין משפט of Gen 14:17.[143] Finally, 15:26 has many contacts with Deuteronomic theology and style, but none directly with E.[144]

Traces of E do not appear again until ch. 17.[145] There it is quite clear that two accounts are interwoven, recounting a rebellion against Moses (vss. 1b-7), and a battle with the Amalekites (vss. 8-16).

Doublets in the account of the ריב or complaint against Moses include vss. 1b-2. as opposed to vs. 3. Both passages tell of the lack of water and the people's complaint (vs. 2, ריב; vs. 3, לון). Verse 3 presumes a geographical setting which has been excised (שם); vs. 2 lacks any mention of place. The account in vs. 3 appears to be continued in vss. 4-7.[146] The use of the miracle-working rod of Moses points to E as the source of this passage.[147] The narrative of vss. 4-7, then, is part of an E version of the common and widespread tradition that the Hebrews constantly rebelled against Moses and Yahweh in the wilderness (cf. Num 20:1-3; Deut 6:16; 8:16; 9:22).[148]

The narrative concerning the battle of the Hebrews with Amalek in vss. 8-16 is usually attributed to E because of the rod which Moses wields (vs. 9; cf. vss. 11-12).[149] The story is an old tradition of holy war set in the desert period. It would fit better in the Wandering narratives of Numbers, where Joshua is the designated successor of Moses; his appearance here without introduction is rather sudden. The stress upon the early leadership of Joshua, however, characterizes the E strand in Exodus; it is reflected also in E's version of the Sinai covenant tradition (see below).

We can note also that E again shows a definite tendency to exalt the position of Moses; his elevation of the rod is necessary for victory. This motif was seen in the story of Moses' call, where he is given the rod and empowered to lead the Hebrews out of bondage (Exod 3:12-13; 4:17, 20).

(4) Jethro's Visit to the Israelites, Exodus 18

The evidence indicates that in Exod 18 we are dealing with a primarily E tradition which has been supplemented and expanded by a redactor.[150] That the narrative developed in this manner, rather than through a combining of sources, is shown by the impossibility of constructing two or more parallel accounts from the chapter. Moses' father-in-law arrives with Moses' children, meets with Moses, hears the news concerning God's deliverance of the Hebrews, offers sacrifice, and shares a sacred meal with Aaron and Moses (vss. 1-12). Afterwards Jethro observes Moses' administration of community legal affairs and suggests a reform, which is then carried out (vss. 13-28). Nowhere is there any sign of the juxtaposition of two parallel accounts.

In fact, the original narrative tradition has been supplemented in two ways; first of all, by the addition of the name "Jethro" and possibly the further description, "father-in-law of Moses," where the original tradition probably simply had "priest of Midian." Secondly, there are expansions in vss. 1*b* and 8-11, both of which have the same pious motive: to amplify the actions of Yahweh in saving his people from Egypt.[151] In these portions of the text, significantly, the name *Yahweh* is used six times (vss. 1*b*, 8, 9, 10, 11). Elsewhere, *Elohim* is used consistently (vss. 1*a*, 5, 12, 15, 16, 19, 21, 23) for a total of eleven times. This use of *Elohim*, together with two other characteristic E motifs ("fear of God" and "mountain of God" in vss. 5, 21) appear to make the identification as E secure. Other supplements may occur in vss. 2*b*, 3*b*-4, as Noth thinks, although such an explanation of the meaning of names can be early as well as late in Hebrew literature.[152]

As Noth comments, it is remarkable to find, in the middle of the Pentateuch, such a passage as this — one which clearly has no parallel or counterpart in either J or P sources.[153] This very fact, however, suggests again that E is not merely an expansion or commentary upon a J base (so Volz, Rudolph, and Engnell). If that were true, we should be unable to explain the existence of an extensive, independent narrative such as this one.

Furthermore, Exod 18 contains allusions to independent E traditions about Moses' family. The E traditions suggest, for example, that Moses had left his family in Midian before returning to Egypt (Exod 4:18, 20*b*),[154] and that he had two sons instead of one, as in J (2:22).

The Elohist here again emphasizes the importance of the fear of God. Those who are appointed judges within the Israelite community must be men who fear God (יראי אלהים, 18:21). As in Gen 20, this certainly means integrity of character and concern for doing what is right. But another dimension of this "fear of God" in a judge would certainly be reliability and rejection of dishonest gain.[155]

It is impossible to be certain whether E intends to depict the meeting with Jethro as taking place at Sinai — which E customarily designates "Horeb" or "the mountain of God" — or at some other sacred mountain in the wilderness. The description of the meeting place (in "the wilderness, where his camp was, at the mountain of God," vs. 6) appears to be overloaded; one or more of the three descriptive phrases has been added by a later editor — but which one? "In the wilderness" suggests an attempt to tie this narrative to the wilderness stories, while "at the mountain of God" clearly ties it to the Sinai account.[156]

In any case, there is present here a theme which ties the Exod 18 tradition closely to E's Sinai account. This is the theme of Aaron and the elders of Israel sharing a sacred meal in the presence of God, depicted in 18:12 and in 24:9-11. As suggested by J. M. Schmidt, this might represent a fragment of a very old tradition — one that is actually more ancient than the developed Sinai narrative of either J or E — in which E depicts Moses' father-in-law in his priestly role, meeting with Moses and the elders at the holy mountain of God, offering sacrifice, and then giving instructions for the sacral approach to Yahweh, as in 24:1, where Jethro rather than Yahweh might be the speaker.[157]

E. W. Nicholson has also recently discussed Exod 18:12 and 24:1, 9-11 in the context of his argument that neither fragment originally depicted a *covenant* meal.[158] We would be inclined to think, to the contrary, that both passages represent a covenant meal — in Exod 18 a covenant with the Midianites, represented by the priest Jethro, and in Exod 24 a covenant with Yahweh.[159]

For our purposes at this point it is sufficient to point out the probable connection between these two E fragments, and to remark on the independence and obvious antiquity of these Sinai-related traditions preserved by the Elohist.

(5) The Sinai Pericope, Exod 19— 34

The section of the Hebrew Bible relating the covenant at Sinai has probably undergone the most complex and tangled literary development of any portion of the Scriptures. This is certainly not surprising, in view of the extreme importance which the covenant assumed, historically and theologically, in Israel. The complexity and confusion of traditions, however, renders absolute certainty impossible when we undertake to separate the various strands which have gone into the final web of law and narrative.

Here we are only concerned with isolating, with whatever degree of probability we can attain, the materials to be identified as E. Our task is made somewhat more manageable by the possibility of disposing of certain passages — in addition to acknowledged P material[160] — which do not require consideration as part of the E narrative.

(a) *Decalogue and Covenant Code.* — First of all there is the question of the literary status of the Decalogue, Exod 20:1-17. Older commentators almost unanimously assigned the Ten Commandments to the E stratum. This identification was based on the use of *Elohim* in the introductory sentence (20:1), and even more on the assumption that the "E document" was the product of the "ethical monotheism" of the eighth-century prophetic movement in Israel. Since the Decalogue supposedly represented the sort of advanced ethical thought attributed to the E source generally, and since it was felt that the whole Sinai account must be divided among J, E, and P with no remainder, the ascription of the Decalogue to E seemed obvious.[161]

This view must be corrected in the light of modern research into the history of Israel's religion. Mendenhall has shown that the Old Testament covenant narratives and related passages bear a striking formal resemblance to Hittite state vassal-treaties of the late second millennium B.C.[162] Some form of the Ten Commandments could go back to the Mosaic era.[163] The attribution of the Decalogue and of the Covenant itself to the epoch of the classical prophets is thus shown to be wrong.[164] And, as we are arguing, the attribution of the E tradition to this late period is also wrong.

This does not mean that the Ten Commandments are after all E, for the conclusion of the literary critics was probably incorrect on purely literary grounds as well. Apart from the introductory phrase in 20:1 there is no use of *Elohim* in the Decalogue; on the contrary, *Yahweh* appears throughout. Furthermore, there is no necessary literary connection between the Decalogue and any narrative strand in the Sinai account. Its absence would not be felt at all if it were removed from its present context. Indeed, the connection between 19:25 and 20:18 would be improved by such an omission.[165]

Some of the same observations can be made about the literary status of the "Covenant Code," Exod 20:22 — 23:33. The introductory passage, 20:22, uses the name *Yahweh*. Thus there is no connection with the preceding verses (18-21), which use *Elohim*. The motif of Yahweh's speaking to the people from heaven, also in vs. 22, has no parallel in either the J or the E Sinai narratives; in J Yahweh comes down (ירד) to the mountain, while in E he is enthroned upon it and Moses goes up to meet him.[166]

It has been assumed that the "book of the covenant" of 24:7 is to be identified with the Covenant Code. But the covenant-ceremony narrative of which 24:7 is a part is not demonstrably related to either J or E. That it is not E is suggested by the repeated use of Yahweh (24:3, 4, 5, 7, 8). The narrative of 24:3-8, if it does refer to the Covenant Code, may have been introduced into the Sinai complex along with the Covenant Code as a secondary expansion.[167]

The internal evidence adduced for assigning the Covenant Code to E is similarly unconvincing. For example, Carpenter and Harford-Battersby state that the "judgments" (משפטים) of 24:3 are derived from the Elohistic source because of:

> their use of Elohim, 21:6, 13; 22:8, 11 (LXX); 22:28; . . . and other linguistic marks such as the designation of אמה for 'bondwoman' . . . and the repeated use of the word בעל and of דבר in the sense of 'matter' or 'cause.'[168]

The mentioned use of *Elohim*, even if we accept without cavil the LXX reading in 22:11, reflects no more than the precisely cognate and analogous uses of *ilu* in the Mesopotamian law codes. The meaning of "god" is very stereotyped and unspecific in both cases; in the Covenant Code it is simply a mark of the close relation of the code to ancient Near Eastern case law.[169]

The other linguistic criteria alleged by Carpenter and Harford-Battersby do not actually show characteristic E vocabulary in the Covenant Code, since many of the words and expressions cited occur primarily or solely in the Covenant Code. Examination of the same authors' vocabulary tables shows that seven of the sixteen listed occurrences of אמה fall in the Covenant Code; all five of the appearances of מות יומת are found there. Eleven of the eighteen cited occurrences of בעל are found in the Covenant Code, while six of the nine uses of the expression איש אל רעהו appear there. Ten of the twenty appearances of the root גנב appear in the Decalogue and Covenant Code; eight of the remaining uses occur in Gen 30 — 31; surely the reason for this concentration is subject matter rather than "characteristic E vocabulary." Not only do these vocabulary items not prove that the Decalogue and Covenant Code are E; they cast further doubt on the whole method behind the compilation and use of these frequently cited tables.

For lack, therefore, of both external and internal evidence, we exclude both the Decalogue and the Covenant Code from our consideration, and pass to the actual covenant narratives.[170]

(b) *The Sinai Theophany, Exodus 19— 20.* — Even scholars who do not see two continuous narratives in these chapters point to the composite nature of the account.[171] Particularly in ch. 19 is composition evident: three times Moses goes up on the mountain and returns; what he does on these journeys is not reported (vss. 3, 8, 29). Yahweh commands Moses to set bounds to keep the people from touching the mountain (vs. 12), but later must be reminded of his command (vs. 23). Whether Moses alone, Moses and Aaron, or Moses and all of the people receive the words of Yahweh is not clear (vss. 9, 17, 24).[172]

The older scholars explained these inconsistencies by a literary analysis which divided ch. 19 into sections derived from J and E, with an introduction by the P redactor. Carpenter and Harford-Battersby offer the following analysis:[173]

J	E	P	R^d
11b-13	2b	1-2a	3-8
18	7-11a		
20-25	14-17		
	19		

S. R. Driver's analysis, while similar, does not make use of the theory of a Deuteronomic redactor:[174]

J	E	P
3b-9	2b-3a	1-2a
11b-13	10-11a	
18	14-17	
20-25	19	

It can be seen that the main disagreement concerns vss. 3-8.

Rudolph's treatment begins, of course, by dispensing with E. Then vss. 3*b*-8 and 20-24 are excised as later additions. Rudolph claims that the remaining verses stand as a unified J narrative, if only we place vs. 20 before vs. 19. The differences in the divine names are explained as expressing desired dramatic effects: the *Elohim* of vss. 17, 19, expresses more strikingly the confrontation with the *mysterium tremendum* than would *Yahweh*.[175]

We have indicated elsewhere that this treatment of the variation in divine names is not satisfactory. Rudolph's treatment of vss. 20-24 as "a type of midrash on vss. 12-13" merits, however, serious consideration, offering the most accurate explanation of the passage.[176] These verses are intended to answer the question of later priests as to whether the warnings of vss. 12-15 apply even to the priestly class.[177]

More difficult problems arise in connection with vss. 3*b*-8.[178] The elevated style of this passage, with its *parallelismus membrorum*, makes it stand out from the surrounding prose narrative.[179] The heart of the passage (vss. 4-6) is clearly a reflective summary of the covenant theology; the rhythmic style suggests a liturgical background, perhaps in the covenant-renewal ceremonies.[180] These observations, and the parallels with Deuteronomic language,[181] have led some scholars to agree with Rudolph in thinking that the passage represents a secondary expansion under Deuteronomic influence.[182]

Two considerations make an identification as E more plausible: (a) The Deuteronomic parallels appear to derive from and expand upon this passage, rather than the reverse;[183] (b) It is quite unlikely that there are any Deuteronomic passages in the Tetrateuch.[184] The many similarities between E and D indicate that they are closely related northern schools of tradition, and it is probable that many "Deuteronomic" passages in the Tetrateuch belong to some stratum of the E tradition, rather than to D.[185]

If the passage is ascribed to E, the theological motifs are consistent with Elohistic themes so far discussed. The emphasis on the goal of Israel's history as specifically religious, the stress on obedience, and the centrality of the covenant are entirely understandable in the prophetic or prophetic-Levitical circles which we shall propose as bearers of the E tradition.[186]

In the remainder of chs. 19 — 20 (accepting the common ascription of 19:1-2*a* to P), the variation in the divine names can be taken as a starting point in separating the narrative strands. *Elohim* appears in 19:3*a*, 17, 19; 20:19, 20, 21. Are there any constant motifs which accompany the use of *Elohim* in these verses?

(a) In vs. 3*a* Moses "goes up to God," to be addressed by Israel's covenant Lord (vv. 4-6); in vs. 17 he brings the people to the mountain to meet God, where, terrified by the theophany, they ask Moses to act as their spokesman (20:19); Moses then draws nearer to speak with God (20:21). The significance of these approaches to God can be seen by comparing 19:9, 11, 18, 20. In the latter verses the name Yahweh is used, and Yahweh is depicted as coming

THE CONTENT AND SCOPE OF E 49

down upon (יֵרֵד עַל) Mount Sinai. In contrast, the verses using *Elohim* picture God as dwelling upon (or enthroned upon, יֵשֵׁב) the mountain. This conception of the mountain as the dwelling place and throne of God, to which Moses and the people go up for revelation, is the first constant which unites the E fragments.

(b) A contrast can also be seen in the theophanies connected with the two divine names. In 19:16; 20:18, 21, the theophany consists of "thunder and lightning" (קוֹל וּבְרָקִים); a "thick cloud" (עָנָן כָּבֵד); "the voice of the *shophar*" (קוֹל שֹׁפָר); and "flashes" (לַפִּדִים). But in the parallel theophany of Yahweh, there is "smoke" (עָשָׁן); "fire" (אֵשׁ); and the "trembling" (חָרַד) of the mountain. Thus, the unique features of the theophany of Elohim are the call of the *shophar*, the thick cloud, and the קֹלֹת or thunderings.

(c) The verses using *Elohim* emphasize the role of the people. They are brought out of the camp to meet God, taking their stand at the foot of the mountain (19:17). Only when the people are too frightened by the stormy theophany do they appoint Moses to act for them (20:18-20). By contrast, the people are forbidden to approach the mountain at all in the account using the name Yahweh; instead, Yahweh himself appoints Moses and comes to speak to him alone, as in 19:9.[187]

There are, then, some constants which distinguish the narrative fragments which employ *Elohim* from those using the Tetragrammaton. Through these motifs we can distinguish 19:2b-3a, 4-6, 16-17, 19 as a brief but coherent E narrative. The narrative strand thus ascribed to E finds its continuation in 20:18-21. The latter verses are connected with the E tradition of Ch. 19 by the use of *Elohim*, by the description of the theophany (cf. 20:18 with 19:16, 19), and by the prominent position given to the people (cf. 19:18 with 20:18-19). As in the earlier E fragments, God is depicted as dwelling upon the mountain (cf. 20:21 with 19:3a). Two themes previously noted in Elohistic passages elsewhere appear here as well: the emphasis on religious awe or "fear" (יִרְאָתוֹ) and the motif of divine "testing" (נַסּוֹת אֶתְכֶם, 20:20).

(c) *Exod 24*. — Ch. 24, narrating the ceremonial conclusion of the covenant, contains two very different accounts, vss. 1-2, 9-11, and vss. 3-8. Verses 3-8, in spite of the frequent use of *Yahweh*, might not be J; instead, the passage may have been introduced into the Sinai pericope along with the Covenant Code.[188] At any rate, there is no legitimate reason for assigning vss. 3-8 to E, in spite of the almost unanimous agreement of past scholars that these verses contain the E covenant narrative.[189]

It is in vss. 1-2, 9-11 that we find E's account of the sealing of the covenant. The identification of the passage as E is supported by the use of *Elohim* in the climactic verse 11 (cf. *Yahweh* in vs. 10), as well as by the community's sharing, through its representative elders, in the sacred covenant meal (cf. "c," above). We might also note the use of the verb חזה (vs. 11), which suggests that a prophetic type of revelation was received by the elders on the mountain.[190] The tradition itself, enigmatic and fragmentary in its present form, is of the greatest antiquity.[191]

The remainder of ch. 24 falls into two parts, vss. 12-15a, 18b; and vss. 15b-18a. The latter is recognized as the P introduction to the account of the Tabernacle, chs. 25 — 31.[192] Verses 12-15a, 18b serve as a bridge to the narrative of chs. 32 — 34. The expression "mountain of God" (vs. 13) suggests E, as does the apparent connection between the elders of vs. 14 and the elders mentioned in 24:1-2, 9-11. But there is some confusion, too: in the Sinai account Joshua has not been mentioned previously as Moses' minister (משרתו, vs. 13). He has, however, appeared in that capacity in the E tradition of Exod 17:8-16, and will appear again in Exod 32 — 33 (both largely E, as will be argued). Perhaps in all four passages (Exod 17:8-16; 24:13-16; 32:17; 33:11) the E tradition makes use of a traditional cycle which emphasized the position of Joshua. The Nadab and Abihu of 24:1, 9 are, in this cycle, replaced by the Joshua, Aaron, and Hur of 24:13-14.[193]

(d) *The Golden Calf, Exod 32.* — The substance of Exod 32 has been almost unanimously ascribed to the E stratum since the nineteenth century, although some scholars have attributed part of the account (especially vss. 7-14) to J.[194] The entire narrative stands as a sequel to the E covenant tradition of 24:1-2, 9-11, 12-15a, 18b, making the identification as E seem most natural.

Further indication of the affinity of ch. 32 with E is found in vss. 17-18. Here Joshua again has the role of Moses' immediate assistant, as in Exod 17:8-16 and 24:13. Ascription to E is likewise supported by the use of *Elohim* (twice in vs. 16) and by the statement that it was Moses who brought Israel out of Egypt (vs. 7; cf. Exod 3:10).

The question arises, however, whether Exod 32 can be viewed as a unity, for there are many contradictions and much unevenness in the account as it stands. Moses learns in two different ways of events at the foot of the mountain (vss. 7-8; 17-19); twice he intercedes for the people before God (vss. 11-14; 31-33); three different punishments are depicted (vss. 20; 25-29, 35), but at the same time punishment is twice said to be suspended (vss. 14, 34). These and other inconsistencies have often been noted by commentators.[195] What do they indicate about the structure of the story?

The six natural divisions in the narrative are: vss. 1-6; 7-14; 15-20; 21-24; 25-29; 30-34; with vs. 35 as a probably secondary concluding note. Of these, the primary account is contained in perfectly coherent form in vss. 1-6, 15-20. Moses, as in the E tradition of Exod 24:12-15a, 18b, ascends the mountain for a stay of forty days and nights, during which the people, encamped at the foot of the mountain, grow restless. At their urging, Aaron molds a bull to serve as a pedestal for the Deity, a symbol (like the Ark) of Yahweh's presence and leadership.[196]

The making of the bull climaxes in a great feast (חג) at which sacrifices are offered on an altar built by Aaron, and the festal cry rings out, "These are your gods, Israel, who brought you up from the land of Egypt!"[197]

Moses, descending the mountain with the completed covenant tablets, hears the tumult, identified in what appears to be an ancient couplet as "the noise of singing" (vs. 18). Angry at this rebellion against his authority, Moses smashes the tablets symbolizing the breaking of the covenant. He destroys most of the image with fire and casts the remaining particles into water, which the people are forced to drink.

This nucleus is clearly related to the Deuteronomistic historian's account of Jeroboam I's institution of bull images at Bethel and his celebration there of a festival (חג) in the eighth month (1 Kgs 12).[198] Yet neither narrative is dependent upon the other.[199] They must be seen as independent polemical accounts of the cultic institution of Jeroboam which make use of an old sanctuary legend which once probably legitimized an El cultus at Bethel.

In support of this interpretation we note that vss. 1-6 are free of any condemnation of the action of Aaron and the people. The making of the bull symbol to serve as Yahweh's pedestal is ascribed to Aaron himself; the feast that follows, far from being an act of apostasy, is a חג ליהוה, the God who delivered Israel from Egypt.[200]

Just so, in 1 Kgs 12 it is only the Deuteronomistic Historian who represents the bull images as apostasy. The underlying reason for his condemnation is not that the images themselves are to be worshipped, but that Jeroboam broke the divinely-ordained unity of Israel and spurned the chosen sanctuary of Yahweh at Jerusalem in favor of his own (more ancient) cultic center. His action, which actually may have been a restoration of ancient practices (as suggested by the use at Bethel of the old El symbol, the bull),[201] is thus credited with bringing the wrath of Yahweh upon the northern kingdom.[202]

In any case, the nucleus of Exod 32 and of 1 Kgs 12 would be the cult-legend which validated the bull symbolism, tracing it back to Sinai and to Aaron. The use of such an old cult legend is suggested first of all by the position of Aaron as the one who fashions the image and recites over it — as Cross remarks — "a classic Yahwistic cult formula."[203] Secondly, there is the mention of a pilgrim feast by Aaron, and the insistence that the bull miraculously "emerged" from the fire.[204]

It is this very legend which, ironically, the Elohist uses to condemn Aaron's actions. Upon Moses' descent the image must be utterly destroyed and the feast disrupted; the breaking of the covenant tablets hammers home the lesson. In this way the Elohist tradition unmistakably registers condemnation of Jeroboam's cult and priesthood, relating it to the primal apostasy of Israel at Sinai.

Inserted into this narrative and joined to its conclusion are numerous secondary traditions: vss. 7-14, 21-24, 25-29, 30-34, 35. These supplements aim at excusing Aaron's participation in the making of the calf (vss. 21-24), defending the interests of the Levitical priests (vss. 25-29), and explaining why the apostasy of Israel/Jeroboam was not immediately and visibly punished. Vs. 35 supplies a fitting punishment which could be intended as a sequel to vs.

20.²⁰⁵ Although these passages were undoubtedly added to the original E narrative of vss. 1-6, 15-20, we cannot attribute them to the early Elohist tradition, since they lack the typical linguistic and theological motifs of E, and in part contradict the base narrative.

That E engages in a polemic against the cultus of Jeroboam I significantly aligns the E schools with the same prophetic or prophetic-Levitical groups which castigate Jeroboam's actions in the traditions preserved in 1 Kgs 12 — 13. The basis of the condemnation seems to be: (a) the flouting of the prophetic authority (in Exod 32 represented by Moses), and (b) the shattering of the divinely-created unity of the people (in Exod 32:15-20 represented by the sharp contrast between Moses and Joshua on the mountain and the people below in the camp, as well as by the breaking of the covenant tablets). E thus associates itself with early prophetic groups in Israel who held to the ancient ideal model of Israel as a covenant people, and stems, we may suggest, from the period shortly after Solomon's death in which these issues were raised most acutely in Israel.²⁰⁶

(e) *Preparations for departure; the Tent of Meeting, Exod 33.* — That this chapter falls easily into four quite separate passages has been seen by most commentators. The natural divisions are vss. 1-3*a*; 3*b*-6; 7-11; 12-23.²⁰⁷ The disagreement among scholars concerns the sources of these passages.

Of the older writers, Driver's division is typical:²⁰⁸

J = vss. 1, 3-4, 12-23   E = vss. 5*a*, 5*c*-6, 7-11
R^JE = vs. 5*b*   gloss = vs. 2

A similar analysis is offered by Beyerlin:²⁰⁹

J = vss. 1, 3*a*, 12-17 (18-23)
E = vss. 3*b*-4, 5-6, 7-11

Against these typical attempts to see in the chapter the continuation of J and E, Noth has claimed that the whole chapter is simply a collection of unrelated traditions, partly Deuteronomic (vss. 1-6) and partly pre-Deuteronomic (vss. 7-11).²¹⁰

Rudolph calls 33:1-3*a* "the initial portion of the J narrative vss. 12-17*a*," and designates 3*b*-6 and 7-11 as additions related to Exod 32.²¹¹

Rudolph's observations give a clue to the analysis of the text. Verses 3*b*-6, 7-11 are indeed related to Exod 32, and also to Exod 24:13 and 17:8-16 — all of which are Elohist passages.

The relatedness of this entire set of passages is suggested, first of all, by the presence in all of them of Joshua, who is depicted as Moses' servant and "executive officer" (17:9-10; 24:13; and 32:17 where, in continuity with 24:13, Joshua is with Moses on the mountain and not a part of the rebellious Israelite community below). In 33:11, similarly, Joshua accompanies Moses in the Tent of Meeting and does not leave it, even when Moses returns to the camp.

Secondly, this set of passages is related by the extraordinary emphasis placed on Moses' elevated status and his separation from the people. Through him comes Israel's power to wage holy war in the wilderness (17:8-16); through him the covenant is made and then, by the smashing of the tablets, its annulment is announced (32:10). In 33:7-11, Moses' status is defined more exactly and described in still more elevated terms: Moses is the one with whom Yahweh speaks "face to face, as a man speaks with his friend" (33:11). This extreme intimacy, of course, contradicts the tradition of 33:20, which states the common Israelite belief that a man cannot behold Yahweh and live, and serves to set Moses apart from all other representatives of the community as the prophet *par excellence*. This depiction of Moses' role is clearly related to Elohist passages which we shall discuss below, Num 11:17, 24-30; 12:4-8. In those passages, especially 12:4-8, as in the traditions of Exod 32 — 33, Moses is not only the supreme prophet but also the supreme priest. In this respect he stands above and apart from Aaron, as is shown most tellingly in Exod 32. Here the Elohist is doubtless engaging in an immediate polemic against the priesthood of the Bethel sanctuary, with its bull image and royal sponsorship.[212]

Another interesting point of contact with Elohist traditions is pointed out by Beyerlin. This is the theme of the discarding of ornaments by the people (33:3b-4, 5-6) which is also found in the E tradition of Gen 35:2-4. In the latter passage this putting away of ornaments is linked with the renunciation of foreign gods. The connection with Gen 35, and indirectly with Josh 24:14, 23 (where the renunciation is ordered in the same terms, but without mention of ornaments) suggests that the Elohist is here drawing on a cycle of traditions associated with the Shechem sanctuary.[213]

Thus in Exod 33:3b-6 and 7-11 the Elohist tradition joins together materials which relate to the wilderness sojourn which originally contain a number of different themes: Israel's apostasy and continued rebellion in the desert; the establishment of the Tent of Meeting as a medium of Yahweh's presence, and the role of Moses as prophet and priest. These traditions are connected, as we have shown above, with other Elohist traditions, both in Exodus and Numbers. The single unifying theme which can now be discerned in the E traditions of Exod 33, however, is, as Beyerlin suggests, "the question of God's presence among his people on their way to Canaan."[214] Here E has to deal with a paradox: God's distance from the people must be maintained, as in the Sinai theophany of 20:18-21 — especially because the people are a rebellious lot, led by a rebellious priest. Yet the same Yahweh who graciously revealed his name to Moses and caused Moses to lead them out of Egypt must be present among his people or else they will die in the wilderness. The solution is two-fold: the Tent of Meeting is established outside the camp (33:7), and Moses, with his assistant Joshua, stands between God and the people as intercessor, priest, and prophet just as he stood for them as covenant mediator on Sinai.[215] In this way, in spite of the rebellion of the people, Yahweh can continue to be present to his people through Moses' office and through the institution of the Tent of Meeting. As we will suggest in the next chapter, this may very well reflect E's solution to an analogous problem which arose in tenth-century Israel: how can Yahweh make himself known to his people in spite of the apostasy of Jeroboam in his cultic "innovations"[216] at Bethel. E's implied answer to this tenth-century issue would be that Yahweh is still present and revealing himself through prophetic-levitical groups who are the successors of Moses and Samuel.[217]

(C) The Wilderness Wandering, Num 10 — Deut 34

After the great P interpolation, Exod 35 to Num 10:28, the JE narrative is taken up again in Num 10:29. In the remainder of Numbers the P material is easily distinguished, but J and E are often impossible to separate. "The purely linguistic data are indecisive; much turns on interpretation and relation to other passages, the origin of which is also often doubtful."[218]

(1) Rebellion in the Wilderness, Numbers 11 — 12

The remark of Gray cited above refers specifically to chs. 11 — 12, in which the following passages have often been claimed for E: Rebellion at Taberah (11:1-3); Moses' spirit given to seventy elders (11:16-17, 24-30); God's answer to the rebellious talk of Miriam and Aaron (12:1-15).[219] These passages do not use *Elohim*. They can only be assigned to E on the basis of certain motifs which connect them with other Elohist passages. These characteristic motifs are:

(1) The intercession of Moses for the people in 11:1-3, and for Miriam in 12:13. This intercessory prayer is part of E's picture of the prophetic role, as we saw in connection with Gen 20:7, 17-18, where the same expression (*hitpallēl*) is used. The expression occurs in the Hexateuch only in these two passages and in Num 21:7.[220]

(2) The depiction of the Tent of Meeting outside the camp in 11:16-30; 12:4 (especially 11:26, 30, where it is explicitly said to be outside the camp). This description of the Tent and its function, together with the associated theophanic language (11:17, 25; 12:5) are clearly connected with Exod 33:7-11. We argued that the latter passage was E because of its emphasis on Moses as the recipient of revelation, and because of the role of Joshua in 33:11, and also because of the way in which characteristic E theological concerns were brought out. Identification of the present passage as E, therefore, rests partly on the correctness of our earlier argument in relation to Exod 33:7-11.

(3) The description of Joshua as Moses' minister (*mᵉšārēt mōšẹh*) in 11:28.

(4) The role of the seventy elders (11:16-17, 24-25), to which we compare Exod 18:21-26; 24:1, 9-11.

(5) The depiction of the prophetic activity of the elders and of Eldad and Medad in 11:24-30, and, in more general terms, also in 12:6. The type of ecstatic behavior described is similar to that attributed to Balaam, Saul, and

others, and suggests that the present tradition was preserved in circles allied with early prophecy (cf. also *wayeḥezû ẹt hā⁾ᵉlōhîm*, Exod 24:11).

(6) The description of Moses as possessing the prophetic spirit to a unique degree; even a portion of his spirit causes the rest to prophesy. To him God speaks "mouth to mouth," and not in dreams and enigmatic visions (12:7-8).

Thus, while detailed linguistic criteria fail us here, there is every reason to connect Num 11:1-3, 16-17, 24-30 and the substance of ch. 12 with E. Only in the E tradition have we seen such an idealization of prophecy (11:29), such heavy use of prophetic terminology, and such an exalted description of Moses as the super-prophet. As we will argue later, the associations with the Samuel, Elijah-Elisha, and Deuteronomic traditions support ascription to a northern, prophetically influenced stream of tradition.[221]

(2) The Balaam Pericope Num 22 — 24

Although many scholars have attempted to unravel the JE narratives contained in Num 13 — 21, this type of analysis would not contribute to our present task. In fact, the criteria for such division are lacking, there being but one use of *Elohim* (21:5) and no appearance of characteristic E vocabulary or theological emphases. No clear evidence of E passages can be found before the Balaam pericope, Num 22 — 24.[222]

The many inconsistencies and doublets in the narrative of Num 22 — 24[223] have led all of our major commentators to see in these chapters the conflation of two or more sources. The customary division into J and E narratives (here including the poems as well) is reflected in Carpenter and Harford-Battersby:[224]

E = 22:2-3*a*, 8-10, 12-16, 19-21, 36*b*, 38, 40-41; plus all of ch. 23 except vss. 28 (J); vss. 27, 29 (R^{JE})

J = 22:3*b*-7, 11, 17-18, 22-36*a*, 39; plus all of ch. 24.

Gray and Noth give analyses which are quite similar to the foregoing.[225] Even Rudolph, rejecting the theory of two parallel narrative sources, recognizes the following separate strands:[226]

(a) 22:3-21, 36-41; 23:1-26; 24:25 — an independent narrative from pre-monarchical times;
(b) 22:22-34 — an equally old but separate tradition, once longer than its present form;
(c) 24:3*b*-9 — a separate poem of the time of Saul;
(d) 24:15*b*-19 — a poem from the time of David;
(e) 23:27, 28; 24:1-3*a*, 10-15*a* — from the J author of the era of David or Solomon, who also put the above material together, furnishing these verses in order to connect the various strands.

Even though the inconsistencies of the narrative of Num 22 — 24 are accompanied by the use of *Yahweh* in some passages and *Elohim* in others, the usage appears to be so inconsistent that it cannot be used to distinguish sources.[227] Rudolph has tried to detect, for example, an underlying system in which, say, *Elohim* was used by the narrator himself, *Yahweh* being used only in the speeches of Balaam and Balak. But Rudolph is able to apply this scheme only by juggling the very confused textual evidence of the various versions.[228] He finally comes to the rather weak conclusion that ". . . [the Yahwist] uses *Yahweh* in the narration if no special circumstance exists, and has foreigners sometimes say *Elohim* and sometimes *Yahweh*."[229]

Eissfeldt analyses the relation of the usage of the divine names to the narrative strands which he distinguishes and concludes, "There is no recognizable system in the use of the divine names in either narrative."[230]

The reason for the breakdown of regular usage here is undoubtedly theological. Countless scribes and story-tellers must have puzzled over the tale of a foreign seer who acted as Yahweh's prophet. Would such a stranger use Yahweh's personal name? Would he not speak instead of *Elohim*? But if he were acting as a prophet of Yahweh, must he not validate his office by speaking explicitly in the name of Yahweh? These questions and the attempts to answer them have hopelessly confused the use of Yahweh and Elohim in the Masoretic text and in the versions.[231]

In spite of the confusion in the use of the divine names, a strand of narrative can be identified which is transparently E. The basis of the identification is the familiar theme of prophetic revelation in a night dream or vision.

The narrative strand in which this theme appears is found first in 22:3-21, 36-40. *Elohim* comes to Balaam in the night and instructs him. What *Elohim* tells Balaam to do he must do: "Though Balak were to give me his house full of silver and gold, I could not transgress the command of Yahweh my God, to do less or more" (22:18*b*; cf. 22:8-9, 19-20). These passages form a clear contrast to the inserted narrative about Balaam's encounter with the angel of Yahweh (22:21-35). In the latter story the obedience of Balaam to Yahweh is brought about through a highly amusing conversation between Balaam and his ass. The Elohist story in 22:3-21, 36-41 is much less earthy and more reflective, showing a radical concern for the nature of prophetic obedience and for the certainty of the divine revelation. "Have I any power at all to speak anything? The word that God puts in my mouth, that must I speak" (22:38). We are reminded of Joseph's question, "Do not interpretations belong to God?," and of the obedient response of the boy Samuel, "Speak, for your servant is listening" (I Sam 3:10).

Is the Elohist narrative here discussed a unity? Most commentators have treated the whole of ch. 22 as a conflation of J and E, finding J not only in the inserted pericope of vss. 22-35, but in other verses throughout the chapter.[232] It appears to the present writer that this analysis has been mistaken. We must instead regard the chapter as composed of two main blocks of material, vss. 2-

21, 36-40 on the one hand, and vss. 22-35 on the other. The inconsistencies of the E narrative of vss. 2-21, 36-40 should not be ascribed to the insertion of fragments from a parallel J narrative, but to the growth of the tradition in the course of transmission in E circles. For example, Carpenter and Harford-Battersby and even Noth regard vs. 3 as a conflation of two sources. Might it not rather be the remnant of an underlying verse narrative, with *parallelismus membrorum*? If we omit *kî rab hû*ʾ in the middle of vs. 3 as an explanatory gloss, the remaining words scan 4+4, with exactly eleven syllables on each side of the bicolon: ויגר מואב מפני העם מאד :: ויקץ מואב מפני בני ישראל The other inconsistencies, such as the varied designations of Balaam's visitors (vss. 5, 7, 8, 14, 15, 18, 21), should perhaps be described as the variants which have grown up within one E narrative tradition.[233]

Similarly, 22:41 — 23:26 can be treated as a unified narrative, probably E, which parallels 23:27 — 24:25, generally assumed to be J. 23:27 forms the transitional verse which makes the parallel narratives appear to be consecutive. The unity of 22:41 — 23:26, and its connection with the Elohist material of ch. 22, is shown by the almost verbatim recurrence of the formula which introduces prophetic speech:

22:38 "the word which God puts in my mouth"
(הדבר אשר ישים אלהים בפי)
23:5 "and Yahweh put a word in Balaam's mouth"
(וישם יהוה דבר בפי בלעם)
23:12 "that which Yahweh puts in my mouth"
(את אשר ישים יהוה בפי)
23:16 "and he put a word in his mouth"
(וישם דבר בפיו)

This formula, or any equivalent formula, is lacking in ch. 24. Ch. 23 is also tied together and related to the Elohist narrative in ch. 22 by the recurrence of "the princes of Moab" (שרי מואב) in the successive scenes (vss. 6, 17; cf. 22:13, 15, 21).

To summarize, the E tradition appears to be preserved in 22:2-21, 36-40; 22:41 — 23:26. In these passages, as we have seen, two closely related themes are found — themes which we have found again and again in Elohist passages: the word of God "which encompasses all events and which is adequate for all challenges,"[234] and the necessity for human obedience to that word.

In God's addresses to Balaam the customary E formula for the "call" is lacking: we do not find God calling "Balaam, Balaam!" or hear Balaam replying "Here I am" (הנני). Since this formula is also lacking in the case of the pagan Abimelech in Gen 20, we may conclude that such a call formula is not considered appropriate for Balaam, the pagan diviner and soothsayer. Nevertheless, the power of God's word as the Elohist understands it is celebrated by the very fact that God can reveal and effect his purpose even through a pagan prophet who serves involuntarily.

(3) The Baal-Peor Incident (Num 25) and Israel's Settlement of Transjordan (Num 32)

The precise sources of the remaining chapters in Numbers and of the narrative material in Deut 31 and 34 are, with the exception of Priestly passages, impossible to determine with absolute certainty. Both the P editing process and the addition of the Deuteronomistic history have brought about such displacements and omissions that we can no longer be certain where or how the JE narratives reached their conclusion. This, at any rate, is my conclusion.[235] Nevertheless, since it has been very commonly held that the epic-derived sources continue to appear in Num 25; 32; Deut 31 — 34, we must examine the evidence in some detail.

The Baal Peor narrative in Num 25:1-5 has usually been attributed to JE and, on the basis of apparent doublets in these few verses, scholars have gone on to distinguish traces of separate J and E accounts. Thus, Carpenter and Harford-Battersby separate vss. 1*a*, 3*a*, 5, from vss. 2, 3*b*, 4, and conclude, "The close correspondence of vs. 2 with Exod 34:15 makes it certain that this account is derived from J; the reference to the judges (vs. 5) confirms the belief that the other elements must be drawn from E" (cf. Exod 18:21).[236]

Now it may be true that the tradition of 25:1-5 distinguishes itself sharply from the remainder of the chapter. In vss. 6-18 the people with whom Israel falls into apostasy are not Moabites, as in vs. 1, but Midianites; and Yahweh's sentence is executed not by judges, as in vs. 5, but by a priest. Thus, the P tradition, responsible for the rest of the chapter, is clearly set off from vss. 1-5. It is furthermore quite probable that vss. 1-5 are the remains of an ancient tradition of Israel's early apostasy, and may very well come from J.[237]

At the same time, there is little basis for the division of 25:1-5 into two parallel accounts, and certainly none for the ascription of a few scraps of this narrative to E. There is no necessary contradiction, for example, between Israel's "yoking himself to the Baal of Peor" (vs. 3) and Israel's "worshipping their gods" (vs. 2). Surely the Moabites could worship both Chemosh, their national deity, and also various manifestations of the Canaanite Baal.[238] Verses 4-5 could, moreover, be read in sequence, so that (a) Moses immediately executes chiefs of the people to avert the divine fury; and (b) gives orders to his officials (שפטי ישראל) to dispatch any individuals who had directly participated in the pagan sacrifices. In any case, the narrative as we have it is a mere torso; this prevents us from drawing definite conclusions about its history.[239]

In Num 32 there is even less readiness to assign particular verses to J and E, even among scholars who ordinarily display little restraint in such matters. Carpenter and Harford-Battersby refuse to assign any part of the chapter to E, though they propose that vss. 39-42 might be J, assigning the rest of the chapter to P.[240] According to Gray, "A strict analysis of the chapter as between JE and P cannot be satisfactorily carried through."[241] Procksch assigns a few fragments to E (vs. 1*a*, except the words מאד עצום; vs. 3, vss. 16-

17, 20*b*, 34-38, 40) on the slender basis of a hypothetical reconstruction of the Elohist account of the Conquest.[242] But there is simply no evidence for such a reconstruction, and all stylistic and theological characteristics of E are lacking. We must conclude with Noth,[243] "The description of the occupation given by E within the old Pentateuchal tradition has also been omitted in consideration of P. Even in Num 32 E elements are no longer demonstrable."

(4) The Last Days of Moses, Deuteronomy 31 — 34.

First of all we exclude from consideration the two poems which, with their prose introductions, comprise Deut 32 — 33. It has been common to regard one or both of these poems as coming from the E tradition, but in fact there is no basis for this in either language or theology.[244] The poems, as has now been well demonstrated, are both extremely ancient and have their own independent history of transmission.[245] Most probably they were drawn into the final edition of Deuteronomy as part of the series of appendices which comprise chapters 31 — 34.[246]

In Deut 31 a series of dislocations in the text suggests that a writer put together narrative parts written on separate scraps, without much regard to their order.[247] Verses 14-15, 23 stand out especially as being not only out of place, but contradictory to the rest of the chapter. Apart from these verses the chapter has four sections: (a) an address of Moses giving a final charge to Israel, vss. 1-6; (b) Moses' final charge to Joshua, vss. 7-8; (c) Moses writes the law and gives instructions for its public reading in the future, vss. 9-13; (d) an introduction to the Song of Moses (Deut 32) in two parts (vss. 16-22 and vss. 24-30), which predict the apostasy and punishment of Israel alluded to in the Song.[248]

In the midst of the above material, which clearly comes from the hands of Deuteronomic editors, vss. 14-15, 23 tell of Moses and Joshua at the Tent of Meeting, where Joshua receives the divine commission as Moses' successor. These verses have been attributed to E, as Carpenter and Harford-Battersby argue, on the following grounds: (a) the prominence ascribed to Joshua (cf. Exod 17:8-16; 24:13; 32:17; 33:11); (b) the reference to the Tent of Meeting (cf. Exod 33:7-11; Num 12:4-10); (c) the theophany of Yahweh in the pillar of cloud at the Tent (cf. Exod 33:9; Num 13:5); and (d) the promise of Yahweh to be with Joshua as he was with Moses (cf. Exod 3:12).[249]

Clearly, conclusions must rest on the analysis of the earlier passages cited as parallels, especially Exod 33:7-11 and Num 12:4-10, since the verses in question must come from the same stream of tradition.[250] We argued previously that Exod 33:7-11 and Num 12 were E, primarily on the basis of the position of Moses as the recipient of revelation and, in the case of Num 12, because of the obvious prophetic interests of the narrator. In addition, the figure of Joshua as Moses' minister ($m^e\check{s}\bar{a}r\bar{e}t$) connects the Tent of Meeting passages (including the present one) with a series of other passages ascribed to the E tradition in which Joshua has this role.

Consequently we believe that the arguments for attributing Deut 31:14-15, 23 to the E tradition are strong, but we recognize that the argument depends on the identification of a number of other texts.

Deut 34 appears to depend, as scholars have long noted, on the final P edition of the older historical sources, and also shows Deuteronomic or deuteronomistic editing.[251] Vss. 1-4 or 1-6 are commonly attributed to J, vss. 7-9 to P (cf. Num 27:18-23), and vss. 10-12 to E, or to a deuteronomistic editing of an E fragment.[252] It is true that vss. 10-12 reflect the same stream of tradition which is visible in Exod 33:7-11; Num 12; Deut 31:14-15, which we have just argued is to be identified with the E tradition. We note in 34:10-12, as typical of the E strand, the express designation of Moses as a prophet receiving the direct revelation of the Deity. Accordingly, we are inclined to attribute 34:10-12 to E.

Admittedly, however, a Deuteronomic editor — perhaps the writer of the Deuteronomistic history — has worked over these verses, drawing the fragments of tradition into his framework and style. Since the Deuteronomic school is rather closely related to the E school, we cannot in the end be certain whether he drew the tradition directly from the E prose epic, or whether he drew independently upon a common stock of Northern E-D traditions.

(D) The Conquest, Josh 1— 24

The now widely accepted thesis of Martin Noth that the books Deuteronomy through 2 Kings comprise a single historical work has forced a radical change in scholars' understanding of the Book of Joshua.[253] Whereas it was once almost universally agreed that Joshua represented a continuation of the Pentateuchal sources — hence the widespread use of the term "Hexateuch" — it has now become questionable whether we can speak of these sources at all in the Deuteronomistic account of the Conquest. Instead, it appears that the JE account of the Conquest of Palestine has been replaced, save perhaps for a fragmentary account of the Transjordanian stage of the process (Num 25; 32), by the account of the Deuteronomistic historian. And in fact, despite the opinions of outstanding scholars to the contrary, we cannot be at all sure that the old epic traditions ever contained an account of the Conquest.[254]

Noth's theory, in broad terms, is that the historian responsible for the collection and editing of Deuteronomy — 2 Kings, living during the Exile, used the seventh-century Deuteronomic Code as the theological foundation of his work. He set this older corpus at the beginning as a sort of programmatic preface, providing it and the work as a whole with an introduction (Deut 1:1—4:43)[255] Fragments of older narratives, probably coming from JE, were added at the end to complete the story of Moses' life (Deut 31; 34), and two ancient poems (Deut 32—33) were inserted as fitting conclusions to Moses' farewell address.[256]

The Book of Joshua was built up, Noth believes, out of a mass of ancient narrative and annalistic materials, including a series of etiological tales which form the bulk of chs. 2 — 11 and had already existed as a distinct collection by the ninth century.[257] These tales were made into a history of the Conquest by the historian, and provided with an introduction in ch. 1 and a conclusion in 11:21 — 12:24. The boundary and city lists of chs. 13 — 22, and the covenant ceremony tradition of ch. 24, formed no part of the original Deuteronomistic work which, in Noth's view, ended with the farewell address of Joshua in ch. 23.[258]

Three scholars may be mentioned who, with varying emphases, maintain that the sources of chs. 1 — 12 are the same as the sources of the Pentateuch: Otto Eissfeldt, Artur Weiser, and John Bright. Eissfeldt continues to insist that the Pentateuchal sources, including his "L-source," are to be traced through Joshua and even through Judges and 1-2 Samuel.[259] For Weiser, the narrative base of Josh 1 — 12 and 24 is the E strand, though this has been edited and supplemented by a Deuteronomic reviser, whose work is clearly evident, for example, in 1:10-18. J, on the other hand, appears only in short passages which do not determine the character of the work as a whole, which is thus basically E.[260] Bright, though he is otherwise heavily indebted to Noth in his analysis of Joshua, maintains that the JE prose epic is the source from which the Deuteronomistic historian drew the account of the Conquest in chs. 2 — 11, and that ch. 1 contains traces of this ancient source (vss. 1-2, 10-11).[261] Bright states clearly the arguments which are typical of those scholars who trace the Pentateuchal narratives into Joshua:

> (i) The major emphasis of J since Gen 12, and of E since Gen 15, has been that Israel would one day inherit the Promised Land (cf. Gen 12:1-3, 7; 13:14-17; 15:7, 13-16 and *passim* throughout Genesis, Exodus and Numbers). Without an account of the way in which this actually came to pass the narratives of J and E would be a torso. Either chs. 1 — 11 give that story or it has been lost — an unlikely supposition in view of the fact that the rest of JE is preserved.
> (ii) Num 32:1-17, 20-27, 34-42 (JE) tell how the Trans-Jordan tribes received their heritage. Is it not likely that JE would also inform us how the other tribes fared? (iii) Finally, in Num 25:1-5 we find Israel encamped at Shittim, where the JE document of the Pentateuch leaves them. It is precisely at Shittim that 2:1 takes up the story. For these reasons we must regard the older narratives of chs. 1 — 11 as JE.[262]

With regard to the first point made by Bright, we quote the remark of another recent scholar: "The argument from the promise of the land cannot stand apart from the demonstration of literary contacts. The only literary contact on which everyone agrees is with Deuteronomy and the rest of the Deuteronomic history . . ."[263] We cannot maintain that the source of chs. 1 — 12 (or 2 — 11) is JE unless we can show definite points of stylistic and theological contact with J and E in individual narratives.

Secondly, in answer to points (ii) and (iii) above, we may say that certain aspects of the Joshua account complement and continue, geographically and temporally, the JE traditions in Numbers (though we have seen how uncertain is the analysis of the Num 25 and 32 passages upon which Bright depends). But this does not demonstrate that the Joshua narratives are from the same traditions which we have traced from Genesis, for they might come from an independent account of the Conquest which circulated separately from the common epic tradition.

Hence we must examine the concrete evidence for the relation of the Joshua narratives in chs. 1 — 11 and 24, to JE, and specifically — since that is our interest here — to E. Doublets and inconsistencies in the narratives will not serve as proof unless they are accompanied by some of the constants which have previously been seen to characterize the E traditions.[264]

The main features which are appealed to in Carpenter and Harford-Battersby's work as signs of E in Joshua are "Joshua the son of Nun, Moses' minister" (1:1) and "Joshua the son of Nun" (2:1; 6:6; 24:29); "according to the number of the tribes of the children of Israel" in 4:5, reminiscent of the covenant ceremony in Exod 24:4; Joshua's elevation of a spear during the conquest of Ai in 8:18, 26, which is compared with Moses' use of the rod in Exod 17:8-16; "Amorites" in 10:5-6; 24:8; "*Elohim*" in 24:1; "the hornet" in 24:12 (cf. Exod 23:28); "forgive" (נשא) in 24:19 (cf. Gen 50:17; Exod 23:21; 34:7 [J]); "set them a statute and an ordinance" in 24:27 (cf. Gen 21:30); the burial of Joseph's bones (24:32; cf. Gen 50:25).[265]

This list of parallels with the language and content of the E tradition in the Pentateuch is not only scanty, it is riddled with uncertainties. "Joshua the son of Nun" appears elsewhere in the Deuteronomistic history in Deut 1:38 and Judg 2:8, apart from the previously discussed occurrences in Deut 31 and 34, and is reflected in 1 Chr 7:27. Hence it is a feature of E language, we might theorize, which has been picked up by the Deuteronomistic school. Joshua's elevation of the spear during the battle for Ai may be a deliberate attempt to show him in the place of Moses, but this does not prove that the E circle contributed the passage. It shows only that the Deuteronomistic historian wishes to cast Joshua in the role of Moses' divinely-sanctioned successor, as is clear in Deut 3:28. The use of the word "Amorites" for the original inhabitants of Canaan can only doubtfully be ascribed to E in the Pentateuch (so Noth), and is otherwise a known feature of Deuteronomic style. *Elohim* in 24:1 occurs in a set phrase, "before God" (לפני האלהים) which refers to a cultic setting and does not show that the tradition involved here customarily uses *Elohim*; on the contrary, *Yahweh* is used in the rest of the chapter. The remainder of the E features cited depend on passages which we cannot ascribe to E with any certainty. The argument from language and content thus breaks down.

The argument from the presence of Elohistic theological motifs in Joshua is best stated by Artur Weiser:

> The E strand plays the main role dominating the picture of the conquest of the land. Yahweh's miracles at the crossing of the Jordan in 3:5ff. and at the capture of Jericho in 6, the claim in 24:23 for Yahweh alone to be worshipped, which is the practical deduction from the story of the conquest which God has directed, all reveal the Elohist's tendency to lead up to exhortation, which can be observed elsewhere in E.[266]

The Content and Scope of E

Admittedly, the tendency toward a didactic presentation of history is present in the E tradition in the Pentateuch. But it is no argument for the assigning of passages in Joshua to E because (a) these passages must still be shown, through language and manner of presentation, to be closely similar to E; and (b) the hortatory shaping of the historical traditions is precisely what we find also in the Deuteronomic school. Thus it is *a priori* unlikely that we should be able to separate the similar hortatory emphases of the Elohist and Deuteronomic traditions, especially in a book which is admittedly very heavily edited by the Deuteronomic school. Weiser himself, speaking of Deuteronomy, remarks, "The Elohist tradition with its fight against strange gods and heathen customs and with its hortatory view of history is carried on [in Deuteronomy]. . . ."[267] In discussing the Deuteronomic version of Joshua, Weiser writes, "The Deuteronomic revision, the form in which we now have the Elohist tradition of Joshua, agrees with the picture given by E of the conquest of the land as a whole. . . . The tradition derived from E of the conquest of the land as a whole and the extermination of its inhabitants means for the theological outlook on history of the Deuteronomist the abolition of the danger of syncretism."[268]

We conclude that if the Deuteronomistic picture of the conquest is in agreement with that of "the E tradition," and if it is not certain how the two traditions are to be distinguished in their hortatory emphases, and if in addition there are no really recognizable marks of E language and style, then we are in no position to claim E as a basis for the work of the Deuteronomistic historian in Joshua. The most that the above scholars have been able to demonstrate is the very close relationship between the E school and the school of Deuteronomy (see below, Ch. IV).

(E) The Primeval History, Gen 1—11

As the concluding part of our treatment of the content and scope of E, we must consider the possibility that there are remnants of E traditions in Gen 1—11. Here we will be directly addressing issues raised by Sigmund Mowinckel in his monograph, *The Two Sources of the Predeuteronomic Primeval History (JE) in Gen 1—11*.[269] Mowinckel is the most prominent scholar in recent times to affirm the presence of parallel J and E narratives in the Primeval history; it has otherwise been almost universally held that E began with the Abraham narratives. More recently, an argument similar to Mowinckel's has been put forward by Werner Fuss, who finds both J and E strands reflected in the doublets and apparent contradictions found, for example, within Gen 3—4.[270]

Mowinckel's argument moves in four stages, each of which must be discussed separately: (1) He first separates, through intricate literary analysis, two separate but parallel strands in the non-Priestly matter of Gen 1—11.[271] (2) He then attempts a relative dating of the two strands, finding his strand "A" to be the older, and strand "B" not only later, but dependent upon the first one.²⁷² (3) The next step is to identify the earlier strand A with the J epic, strand B with E.²⁷³ (4) Finally, Mowinckel supports both his relative and his absolute dating of the two strands by a consideration of the "Babylonian matter" in the Primeval History, which he finds limited to the later E source. He deduces that this Babylonian material came into Israel in the last period of the monarchy, hence after the composition of J, but before and during the period of E's composition.²⁷⁴

An analysis of Mowinckel's arguments seems to show up some serious flaws. With regard to the first point, to be sure, he is on fairly solid ground, even though his literary analysis is not convincing in detail. That is, Mowinckel is perfectly correct in asserting that the non-Priestly materials of the Primeval History do not form a unity, but a collection of traditions which do not agree in their presentation. The many inconsistencies, doublets, and shifts in terminology long ago led Wellhausen to postulate a long oral and written development of the Primeval History, through a series of additions and supplements to an original kernel, which he identified as chs. 2; 3; 4:16-24; 11:1-9. He concluded:

> Even though agreement cannot be reached in specific instances, the principal fact is established: what occurred was not merely a combining of large connected narratives, but rather the insertion of a number of smaller dependent fragments into these connected narratives — whether before, during, or after the uniting of large traditions. Some of the fragments were of a more learned or theoretical character, while some were of popular origin. For the oral tradition did not suddenly cease developing once it was set in writing. Instead, it continued to evolve, now interacting with the written version, and also taking up entirely new material from outside, which then itself became a part of what was fixed in writing.²⁷⁵

Wellhausen's observations (which express the older literary-critical theory with more subtlety than is usually credited to the Wellhausenists) were followed by Karl Budde and Hermann Gunkel, with one important new development: Budde and Gunkel found two parallel collections of ancient traditions lying behind the "J" primeval history. Gunkel defined their contents in detail in his Genesis commentary, and called them "J^e" and "J^j" in the belief that the awkward *Yahweh-Elohim* of Gen 2:4b — 3:24 pointed to a combination of sources which used, respectively, these two divine names.²⁷⁶ Eissfeldt's "L-source" and Pfeiffer's "S-source" represent other attempts to deal with the Primeval History by this type of literary analysis.

There can be no question, then, that Mowinckel was correct in calling our attention to the composite nature of the J primeval history, and in this he is in the company of other leading scholars. But two parallel narratives can only be derived from the account by a scissors-and-paste type of literary criticism which we must repudiate. Many of the "doublets" and "contradictions" which Mowinckel points to in Gen 2:4b — 3:24, for example, are in contexts of poetic parallelism and cannot be used to prove two different sources. Thus, he lists "3:18a parallel in substance to 3:19b; the first speaks of ʾ*adamah* and the second of ʿ*aphar*; cf. the same parallel in 2:7."²⁷⁷ But surely this passage simply reflects a common kind of poetic parallelism in Hebrew literature, not an "ʾ*adamah* source" and an "ᶜ*aphar* source!"

Furthermore, Mowinckel extends his method past the point of credibility by creating parallels where there are none in the material as it stands. For example, to cite an instance of the creation of parallels in two directions, we quote a passage from the discussion of the Cain and Abel story, Gen 4:

> Precisely on account of the kinship in spirit and motif which according to all the evidence must have existed between the older Ḳain-Abel narrative and the Romulus-Remus legend, it would be very natural, not to say necessary, to combine the narrative of 4:2-16 with the notice regarding the building of the city in 4:17*b*, and to infer that it was about this work — perhaps when offering sacrifices at the laying of the foundation stone — that Ḳain quarreled with his brother and killed him. Afterwards Ḳain completed the building of the town alone, and called it after his son Ḥanok.
>
> *The A-strand must actually have contained, at one time, some such story as this.*
>
> It has long been felt that there is a lacuna between 4:1 and 4:17, which is not properly filled up with 4:2-16. ... Evidence that the strand is broken off at 4:1 is afforded also by the incomplete text in 4:1*b*. The Ḳain-Abel narrative of the A-strand originally followed 4:1. The notice in 4:17*b* is a displaced fragment of this narrative.[278]

In discussing the sequence of events in the "B" (E) narrative strand, Mowinckel states:

> The immediate continuation of the paradise narrative in E, as in J, was the statement that the man came together with his wife, so that she conceived and gave birth to Seth, the first man born on the earth (*4:25). And then followed, in the form of a genealogy with anecdotal notices and stories inserted in it, the list of the first patriarchs on the earth, father and son for ten generations from "the Man" Adam to Noah. Of this list only the fragments 4:25*, 26; 5:28*b**, 29 have come down to us. But no doubt it was identical with P's Sethite list Ch. 5, both as regards the names and arrangement generally.[279]

Thus, parallels are inferred from "A" to "B" and from "B" to "A," and also from P to "A" and "B." But in fact we do not have two parallel narrative strands, but a *collection of traditions* about primeval times which the Yahwist uses for his own theological and literary purposes. In speaking of the work of the Yahwist, Noth comments:

> ... for the fundamental story of the Creation and the Fall (Gen. 2 and 3), which is formed as a coherent unity, he apparently followed none of the numerous creation traditions of the ancient Orient. Rather, to express what he wanted to say he drew upon various individual narrative elements, such as the garden planted by God in the form of an oasis in the wilderness or, on the other hand, in the form of a paradise on the world-mountain in the north . . . etc. These he worked together into a great composition whose essential content, however, lies not in these elements that were worked together, but rather in the central, distinctive contribution of J.[280]

With regard to Mowinckel's third point, that his "B-strand" is to be identified with the Elohist tradition, we must again demur. In answer we simply quote Mowinckel's own words:

> The arguments from linguistic statistics are too few to afford any reliable answer here, especially as the clue furnished by the divine names Yahwe and Elohim is here to some extent absent. Nor, in material of this nature, dealing with the Creation and Primeval

History, where one would expect the traditions to have attained a high degree of fixity on account of the sacredness of the subject-matter, is it probable that the compiler's religious and theological ideas have reshaped the matter to such an extent that they can serve as literary-critical arguments.[281]

In short, there are none of the linguistic criteria or theological motifs which we have been relying on for our identification of E passages. With these absent, discussion about the presence of E becomes so subjective and lacking in any effective controls as to be meaningless.

The fourth step in Mowinckel's argument, that the chief difference between the J and E primeval histories is in the presence of "Babylonian matter" in E, has been heavily criticized by W. F. Albright in a review and subsequently in an article. Albright states quite correctly that the J author must have drawn on very ancient and widespread stories and myths which were current in the Fertile Crescent by the early second millennium B.C. The cultural source of these early traditions was north Mesopotamia, rather than either Canaan or exilic Babylonia:

> . . . It is in the region between the Euphrates and the Khabur that we should look for the direct antecedents of the Hebrew people and of most of the early stories of Genesis. Babylonia had, indeed, contributed greatly, but this contribution reached Israel through the Amorites and Proto-Arameans of the Upper Euphrates region. There is nothing in the data now available to forbid my view that most of the matter in the stories of creation, of paradise, and of the antediluvian patriarchs, of the Flood, and of the Tower of Babel reached Palestine with the Hebrews before the middle of the second millennium B.C.[282]

Certainly nothing has turned up since 1938 to overthrow Albright's theory, and in fact it has received further support.[283] In any case, we cannot use a theory about the date of the entrance of prevalent ancient material into Israelite literature to support literary-critical and traditio-historical reconstructions. The literary analysis of the Primeval History and the dating of the J and E traditions must stand on their own feet.[284] No clear evidence exists of any Elohist version of the Primeval History.

(F) Conclusions

In this chapter we have shown that there is a remarkably homogeneous body of traditions, scattered from Genesis through Numbers, which is distinguished from other Pentateuchal traditions by certain features, both stylistic and theological. The most dependable stylistic features are the use of *Elohim* and a form of dialogue which occurs in scenes in which God reveals himself to a patriarch or other leader who is viewed as a prophetic figure.

Clearly associated with this latter feature are the major theological emphases of this E tradition: the interest in prophecy and in prophetic questions regarding divine revelation; stress on the human response of fear and awe toward God; obedience to the divine command as revealed to prophets; reflection on moral problems of sin, guilt, and forgiveness, with a general sensitivity to moral issues; and a thoroughly religious understanding

The Content and Scope of E

of history.

One of the crucial questions which was raised about the Elohist passages by Volz, Rudolph, Engnell, and others, was whether these passages represent a continuous epic source, or simply a body of additions to J. We are convinced that the Elohist work was an independent formulation of the epic tradition, and that this is indicated by the detailed E doublets to J narratives found in the Abraham, Jacob, and Joseph stories. E's independence is shown even more by its transmission of such a unique and theologically profound narrative as that of the sacrifice of Isaac in Gen 22.

As evident in the list given below, E passages occur in every important section of the Pentateuch and in conjunction with every major theme, from the patriarchs to the wilderness wandering. This in itself strongly suggests that E is a comprehensive literary and theological work, not just a random collection of additions to an older base narrative.

We now list the passages which we ascribe to E. Following that, we shall turn to the task of establishing the probable provenance and date of the Elohist tradition and to a consideration of its relation to other streams of tradition in Israelite religion and literature.[285]

E PASSAGES IN THE PENTATEUCH

(1) Genesis

The Abraham Narratives

The Call of Abraham	15:1-6, 13-16
Abraham and Sarah at Abimelech's Court	20:1-17
The expulsion of Hagar and Ishmael	21:8-21
Controversy and covenant with Abimelech	21:22-34
The command to sacrifice Isaac	22:1-14, 19

The Jacob Narratives

Jacob's dream at Bethel	28:11-12, 17-18, 20-22
Jacob's actions as Laban's shepherd	31:4-16
Jacob's flight and the dream of Laban	31:17-24
The theft of Laban's household gods	31:25-42
Jacob's covenant with Laban	31:45, 49, 50, 53-54
Jacob meets Esau	33:5-11
Jacob returns to Bethel	35:1-8

The Joseph story

Joseph and his brothers	37:21-24, 28a, 29-30, 36
Joseph in prison and Pharaoh's dreams	40 — 41
Joseph's first meeting with his brothers	42:1a, 2-3, 6-7, 11b, 13-26, 28b-38

Joseph reveals his identity	45:2-3, 5-15
Jacob's dream at Beersheba	46:1-4
Jacob blesses Ephraim and Manasseh	48:1-2, 7-14, 17-22
Joseph forgives his brothers	50:15-26

(2) Exodus

The Exodus from Egypt

The Hebrew midwives	1:15-21
The call of Moses	3:1, 4b, 6, 9-13, 15
Moses receives the rod	4:17, 18, 20b
The plagues of Egypt	E fragments?
The departure of the Hebrews	13:17-19
Israel at the sea	14:5a, 19a
Victory at the sea	15:20-21
Rebellion in the wilderness	17:4-7
Victory over Amalek	17:8-16
Jethro's visit	18:1-27

The Sinai Covenant

The theophany at Horeb	19:2b-3a, 4-6, 16-17, 19
Moses as mediator	20:18-21
The covenant ceremony	24:1-2, 9-11
Moses on the mountain of God	24:12-15a, 18b
The golden calf episode	32:1-6, 15-20
The tent of meeting established	33:3b-6, 7-11

(3) Numbers

The Wilderness Wandering

Israel's rebellion and the affirmation of Moses' role	11:1-3, 16-17, 24-30; 12
Balak and Balaam	22:2-21, 36-40
Balaam's oracles of blessing	22:41 — 23:26

(4) Deuteronomy

Joshua commissioned to succeed Moses	31:14-15, 23
Moses as prophet	34:10-12

¹This excludes passages in which *Elohim* is used as a common noun, as it frequently is in construct, *Yahweh ᵓĕlōhê* . . . ("Yahweh, the God of . . .), followed by a noun or proper noun; e.g., Gen 24:3, 7, 12, 27, 42, 48.

²The notion of constants was put forward by Humbert in his review of Rudolph's *Der 'Elohist' von Exodus bis Josua, TLZ* 1938, 404-406. Cf. also Bentzen's use of the term to designate "phenomena of different kinds occurring again and again, grouping themselves in such a manner as to combine the different traditions to form the collections which literary criticism calls 'sources' or 'documents,' and which — if we accept the modern theories of oral traditions — serve as indicators which must group the oral traditions in a way leading to much the same results as literary criticism has led us to, even if we cannot establish an unbroken line of narratives, so as to extract whole separate 'books' from the bulk of the Pentateuch." *Introduction* 2. 26.

³Gen 17; 19:29; 21:2, 4; 35:9-13, 15; 46:2; so Carpenter and Harford-Battersby, *Hexateuch* 1. 273-275. Essentially the same contents of P are established by Noth in *Traditions* 8-19. Cf. also S. R. Driver, *Introduction* 11-21; R. Pfeiffer, *Introduction* 188-89.

⁴ Cf. von Rad, *Genesis* 167-170, 225-230. The J narrative of Gen 26:6-11, which shows the use of the same narrative motif in the Isaac cycle, may be the most ancient version of the tale; so Noth, *Traditions* 104-105. In any case it also lacks the theological depth and detail of the E narrative in Gen 20, and is even more laconic than the parallel J story in 12:10-20.

⁵The verb used for Abraham's intercession (*hitpallēl*) is also used of the intercession of Moses (Num 11:2; 21:7; Deut 9:20, 26); Hannah (1 Sam 1:10, 27; 2:1); Samuel (1 Sam 7:5; 8:6; 12:19, 23); Elisha (2 Kgs 4:33; 6:17, 18); Hezekiah (2 Kgs 19:15, 20; 20:2, *passim* in Isa 37 — 38); Jeremiah (Jer 38:3; 42:2, 4, 20); Jonah (Jonah 2:2; 4:2); Job (Job 42:8, 20); Nehemiah (Neh 1:4, 6; 2:4; 4:3); Solomon (2 Chr 6:20). The occurrences of the verb fall into two broad groups: those passages in which it means to pray for oneself, and texts in which it means to pray or intercede for another. The meaning "intercede" comes from the notion "to seek consideration"; so E. A. Speiser, "The Stem *PLL* in Hebrew," *JBL* 82 (1963) 305. The intimate connection of intercession with the role of the prophet as suggested in the present passage is found also in other passages which derive from northern traditions (Num 12:3; Deut 9:26; 1 Sam 12:19-23; 2 Kgs 4:33; 6:17, 18; Jer 37:3; 42:2, 4, 20), and might stem originally from an early stage in the prophetic movement in which the connection with the cultus was close; so von Rad, *Genesis* 228; cf. Gunkel, *Genesis*, 195, explaining *hitpallēl* as "ursprünglich term. techn. für die Fürbitte des Gottesmannes . . . ." Hertzberg's conclusion that intercession was attributed to the prophets because they were "men of God" and not because they were prophets, does not really alter the fact that E's depiction of Abraham here is unique in the Pentateuch, and reflects a shaping of ancient traditions which uses prophets and other "men of God" as models; see H. W. Hertzberg, "Sind die Propheten Fürbitter?" *Tradition und Situation: Studien zur alttestamentliche Prophetie* (Göttingen: Vandenhoeck & Ruprecht, 1963) 63-74.

⁶von Rad, *Genesis* 230. Cf. also Wolff, "Elohistic Fragments," 162: "The Elohist has made a very involved theological problem of guilt out of the unambiguous failing of the patriarch."

⁷"The narrative vs. 1-17 (18) is unanimously ascribed to the Elohist, wherever one reckons with the existence of this document at all." von Rad, *Genesis* 226. Volz asserts, "Diese beiden Stücke werden ganz allgemein E zugeschrieben; es steht dies wie bei 22:1-14 fast als ein Dogma fest." *Elohist als Erzähler* 34.

⁸*Elohist als Erzähler* 34-36.

⁹John Skinner, *A Critical and Exegetical Commentary on Genesis*, ICC (New York: Chas. Scribner's Sons, 1910) 315; Gunkel, *Genesis* 139.

¹⁰Carpenter and Harford-Battersby suggest that the occurrence of *šiphāh* here may be a copyist's error or the result of a redactor's activity (*Hexateuch* 2. 29). Might we not instead question the assumption that E can always be identified by the use of *ᵓāmāh*? Cf. the vocabulary tables of the same authors, 1. 190. See below, p. 70, n. 13.

¹¹The dream (*hᵃlôm*) is mentioned as a vehicle of revelation in a number of texts throughout

the OT. Outside the Tetrateuch, the dream appears as a revelatory experience, but with no mention of prophecy, in Judg 7:13, 15; 1 Kgs 3:5, 15; Job 33:15; Dan 1:17; 2:1, 2, 3. In most of these passages, however, the dream is not vouchsafed to a common citizen, but to a king who, by virtue of his sacred office, is himself a channel of revelation. The remaining texts which refer to dreams either list them as one mode of revelation, along with prophecy, Urim, and divination (cf. 1 Sam 28:6; Deut 13:2, 4, 6 [EV 1, 3, 5]; Jer 23:25, 27, 28, 32; 27:9; 29:8; Zech 10:2), or describe prophecy directly as the communication of dream revelations (Joel 3:1 [EV 2:28]; cf. Num 12:6). The later texts, especially Jeremiah and Deuteronomy, reflect considerable suspicion of "dreamers" as the source of false prophesying, but even so the possibility is recognized that a true word of Yahweh may come in this fashion. The dream in the OT and later literature has been studied by E. L. Ehrlich, *Der Traum im Alten Testament*, BZAW 73 (Berlin: A. Töpelmann, 1953). For ancient Near Eastern literature generally, see A. L. Oppenheim, *The Interpretation of Dreams in the Ancient Near East*, Transactions of the American Philosophical Society 46:3 (Philadelphia, 1956).

[12]See the remark of Volz, quoted in n. 7, above. Cf. Skinner, *Genesis* 320-321; Gunkel, *Genesis* 200-202; Procksch, *Elohimquelle* 11-13. Noth (*Traditions* 35) designates vss. 6, 8-20, 21b as E.

[13]Skinner (*Genesis* 320-321) and Gunkel (*Genesis* 200-202) both mention the use of ʾāmāh in 21:10, 12, 13, as opposed to J's šiphāh in 16:2, 3, 5, 8. Of the sixteen occurrences of ʾāmāh in the Pentateuch, all designated "E" by Carpenter and Harford-Battersby (*Hexateuch* 1. 190), eight are in the Covenant Code, which can scarcely be expected to display characteristic E vocabulary (see below, pp. 45-47). Of the remaining eight, five occur in Gen 20:1-17 and in the present text. Of the rest (Gen 30:3; 31:33; Exod 2:5), only one (Gen 31:33) can with any certainty be ascribed to E — and on other grounds. We must conclude that the use of ʾāmāh is not in itself sufficient grounds for assigning a passage to E, although it might be of significance in conjunction with other features.

[14]von Rad, *Genesis* 236.

[15]The division into J and E is defended in Carpenter and Harford-Battersby, *Hexateuch* 2. 30-31; similarly in Gunkel, *Genesis* 205-207 and Procksch, *Elohimquelle* 10. Some of the older commentators, however, viewed the tradition as entirely E; see J. Wellhausen, *Die Composition des Hexateuchs und der historischen Bücher des AT* (Berlin: Georg Reimer, 1889) 29; Rudolph Smend, *Die Erzählung des Hexateuchs* (Berlin: Georg Reimer, 1912) 42-43. Von Rad (*Genesis* 236-237) regards the passage as a unity and attributes it to E. Volz (*Elohist als Erzähler* 40) also regards it as a unity, but of course assigns it to J. In any case, the arguments for dividing the narrative into two documentary sources are not convincing.

[16]Gunkel (*Genesis* 205) mentions "Worte wie das selten vorkommende ונכד נין 23 u.a." This certainly does not constitute proof that the passage is E! Cf. the criticisms of Volz, *Elohist als Erzähler* 39-40.

[17]H. W. Wolff, "The Kerygma of the Yahwist," *Int* 26 (1966) 149.

[18] *Ibid.*, 149. Wolff's entire article constitutes a very illuminating treatment of the themes and characteristics of J.

[19]R. Kilian, *Die vorpriesterliche Abrahamsüberlieferungen, literarkritisch und traditionsgeschichtlich untersucht*, BBB 24 (1966) 309.

[20]von Rad, *Genesis* 242-243. The phrase nᵉʾum Yhwh, much used in later prophetic literature, is found elsewhere in the Hexateuch only in Num 14:28 (P).

[21]Cf. Noth, *Traditions* 35: "Quite correctly, 22:15-18 is usually excluded as a supplement. In vs. 14, even though it is an E text, one should not object to the occurrence of יהוה as an exceptional case involving the explanation of a name. On the basis of the occurrence יהוה may have been inserted secondarily into vs. 11 for an original אלהים." My analysis, as can be seen, is identical with Noth's and has been suggested previously by a number of scholars. Cf. Wellhausen, *Composition* 20; Gunkel, *Genesis* 210-212; Skinner, *Genesis* 331. Again in this chapter, I should note, the LXX and MT are in agreement on the divine names. The Syriac disagrees in vss. 11 and 15, reading malʾak ʾĕlōhîm instead of malʾak Yahweh. This presents no problem to my analysis, since these verses are secondary in any case.

The Content and Scope of E

²²So Procksch, *Elohimquelle* 12-13; Wellhausen, *Composition* 20-22; Eissfeldt, *Hexateuch-Synopse* (Leipzig: J. C. Hinrichs, 1922) 33-34; Noth, *Traditions* 132; cf. Volz, as quoted above, n. 7.

²³*Hexateuch* 1. 190-192.

²⁴Carpenter and Harford-Battersby (*Hexateuch* 1. 274) attribute all of Gen 39 to J except for vss. 4*b*, 6*ac*, 7*a*, which are designated "E." Noth (*Traditions* 30) assigns the entire chapter to J, as does von Rad (*Genesis* 364).

²⁵See below, pp. 33-34.

²⁶See the discussion of the individual passages below, pp. 30-33, 36-37, 40-41.

²⁷See below, pp. 48-49.

²⁸R. Kilian, *Isaaks Opferung: zur überlieferungsgeschichte von Genesis 22* (Stuttgart: Verlag Katholischer Bibelwerk, 1970) 59.

²⁹Wolff, "Elohistic Fragments" 164.

³⁰See Søren Kierkegaard's great work, perhaps still the most profound analysis of the theological implications of Gen 22, *Fear and Trembling*.

³¹Wolff, "Elohistic Fragments" 164.

³²"Unsere Untersuchung steht hier vor einer überaus wichtigen Frage, denn wenn dieses Kapital von E stammen würde und nur in ihm (oder auch nur in der Hauptsache von ihm überliefert wäre) so wäre damit erwiesen, *dass E ein selbständiger, eigenes Gut enthaltender Erzähler gewesen wäre*" (*Elohist als Erzähler* 43; the italics are in the original).

³³Wolff, "Elohist Fragments" 167-168: "The Yahwist strung his materials together rather loosely.... The Elohist proceeded more deliberately and within the separate accounts themselves expressed connections to earlier or later narratives." Cf. Kilian, *Abrahamsüberlieferungen* 311: "Die Zusammengehorigkeit der Kap. 20. 21. 22 ist fraglos; einmal spielen sie in dem einen südlichen Lebensbereich von Abraham und Isaak und zum anderen sind sie durch die eine elohistische Sprache und Eigenart auch innerlich zusammengehalten."

³⁴*Hexateuch* 1. 274.

³⁵*Genesis* 347-440.

³⁶*Introduction* 144, 169-170.

³⁷*Traditions*, 8-36.

³⁸Gunkel, *Genesis* 349-361.

³⁹"Die Komposition der Joseph-Geschichte," *ZDMG* N.F. 1 (1922) 61. The same type of analysis and the same view of the results of source criticism are evident in Gressmann's "Ursprung und Entwicklung der Joseph-Sage," *Eucharisterion* (ed. Hans Schmidt; Göttingen: Vandenhoeck & Ruprecht, 1923) 1. 1-55. Eissfeldt's rejoinder to Gunkel's article, reasserting the necessity for careful source criticism, appears in the same volume, 56-77.

⁴⁰Volz-Rudolph, *Elohist als Erzähler* 148-149.

⁴¹*Ibid.*, 149-150.

⁴²*Ibid.*, 151-175.

⁴³G. von Rad, "The Joseph Narrative and Ancient Wisdom," *The Problem of the Hexateuch and Other Essays* 292-300; L. Ruppert, *Die Josepherzählung der Genesis* (Munich: Kösel-Verlag, 1965).

⁴⁴D. B. Redford, *A Study of the Biblical Story of Joseph*, VT Sup 20 (Leiden: Brill, 1970) 252-253.

⁴⁵An attack has also been made on source analysis of the Joseph story by R. N. Whybray in "The Joseph Story and Pentateuchal Criticism," *VT* 18 (1968) 522-528. Whybray points up difficulties and inconsistencies which he sees in such analysis, particularly in the light of von Rad's emphasis on the story as a unity with strong wisdom themes, but Whybray offers no alternative analysis or solution of his own.

⁴⁶See, for example, the summary of Skinner, *Genesis* 148-150.

⁴⁷Volz-Rudolph, *Elohist als Erzähler* 152-155.

⁴⁸Bentzen, *Introduction* 2. 46.

⁴⁹This is the conclusion of most critics; cf. Wellhausen, *Composition* 54-55; Skinner, *Genesis*

443; Gunkel, *Genesis* 354-356; von Rad, *Genesis* 349-355. Gunkel attempted a further division of the sources in 37:1-20 through an analysis of the dominant narrative motifs. One strand (vss. 5-11, 19-20, 28a, 29-30) is dominated by the themes of the dream, the cistern, and the Midianites who steal Joseph. The other strand (vss. 3-4, 23, 25-27, 28b, 32-33) is dominated by the themes of the coat and the sale to the Ishmaelites. In addition, the dream-Midianites-Reuben strand uses "Israel." In Gunkel's analysis, the former strand (vss. 5-11, 19-20, 28a, 29-30) is E; the latter is J (*Genesis* 356). There is, however, some doubt as to the possibility of such detailed analysis; cf. the remarks of Bentzen, quoted above.

[50] Chs. 40-41 have long been regarded as basically Elohistic; cf. Wellhausen, *Composition* 57; Carpenter and Harford-Battersby, *Hexateuch* 1. 274; von Rad, *Genesis* 369-379. Traces of J have been found in ch. 41, especially in vss. 34a, 35b, 40-45a, 46b, 49, 55; so Noth, *Traditions* 30. The contradictions and repetitions which led to these divisions include: the two different terms for Joseph's master ("the Egyptian," 39:2, 5; "Potiphar, an officer of Pharaoh, the captain of the guard," 39:1; cf. 40:50); the recommendation by Joseph for the appointment of a single official over all Egypt (41:33), as compared with the appointment of a group of overseers in 41:34; the state's taking one-fifth of the harvest (41:34) as compared to the exacting of the entire harvest (41:35); the twice-repeated report of Joseph's appointment (41:40, 41, 42-43); of his trip of inspection (vss. 46b, 47), and of the coming of the famine (vss. 54, 55). Cf. von Rad, *Genesis* 377; Skinner, *Genesis* 464-466.

[51] E.g., the use of *pātar* and derivatives in 40:5, 8, 12, 18, 22; 41:8, 11, 12, 13, 15. The report that the recipients of the dreams were troubled: (40:6; 41:8) and the description of the awakening in 41:7 (cf. 1 Kgs 3:15) follow standard dream-report patterns. See E. L. Ehrlich *Der Traum im AT* 54-85; Oppenheim, *Interpretation of Dreams* 184-245.

[52] See above, n. 50. Skinner (*Genesis* 485) remarks that "some of these differences may, no doubt, prove to be illusory; but taken cumulatively they suffice to prove that the passage is composite, although a satisfactory analysis cannot be given."

[53] von Rad, *Genesis* 381.

[54] I am here following the source analysis proposed by B. W. Anderson in Noth, *Traditions* 266.

[55] Only in vs. 14 is Simeon mentioned. The use there of *El Shaddai* suggests a harmonizing redaction, since neither J nor E ever uses this term elsewhere.

[56] Cf. n. 46, above.

[57] The use of *Elohim* in Judah's speech is not ground enough for assigning the passage to E. Again we must reckon either with redaction or with stylistic variation on the part of the J school. No text-critical problems arise; throughout the Joseph stories the LXX and other major versions agree closely with the MT where *Elohim* appears.

[58] This is basically the division of Noth (*Traditions* 30, 36), who regards vss. 1, 4, 5a, 16-28 as J; and vss. 2, 3, 5b-15 as E.

[59] Skinner, *Genesis* 468.

[60] Carpenter and Harford-Battersby (*Hexateuch* 1. 274) call vss. 6, 8-27 "P." Gunkel (*Genesis* 433-35) indicates that vss. 6a,7 are P; vss. 8-27 are secondary. This analysis is essentially that of Rudolph (*Elohist als Erzähler* 165) and Noth (*Traditions* 18).

[61] See above, pp. 21-22, 24-26.

[62] B. W. Anderson in *The Oxford Annotated Bible*, (ed. H. G. May and Bruce Metzger; New York: Oxford, 1962) 59.

[63] E.g., the phrase ויפרו וירבו מאד (vs. 27) and the connection of vs. 30 with the P traditions of Gen 23; 49:29-33; 50:13. Cf. Gunkel, *Genesis* 436; Noth, *Traditions* 17-18.

[64] I.e., אל שדי (vs. 3); מפרך והרביתך; נתתי לקהל עמים (vs. 4); פדן (vs. 7); see Skinner, *Genesis* 502.

[65] Noth, *Traditions* 36, n. 137.

[66] Noth rightly comments, "The 'blessing of Jacob' is framed by P elements. To attribute it to J, as is usually done, cannot be proven literarily any better than the assignment of the 'blessing of Moses' to E. It survives as special material, and it is absolutely impossible to know at which stage of the process of Pentateuchal development it was incorporated into the present context."*Ibid.*, 18, n. 54.

67 Wolff, "Elohistic Fragments" 161.
68 On the use of wisdom motifs, see von Rad, *Genesis* 433-439.
69 Ruppert, *Josepherzählung* 219-223.
70 Wolff, "Kerygma of the Yahwist" 151-152.
71 JB translation.
72 von Rad, *Genesis* 431.
73 Cf. *ibid.*, 432.
74 Wolff, "Elohistic Fragments" 168.
75 Wellhausen, *Composition* 24; Carpenter and Harford-Battersby, *Hexateuch* 2, 22-23; Eissfeldt, *Synopse* 23; Procksch, *Elohimquelle* 7; Skinner, *Genesis* 276-277. Skinner typifies the reaction of most scholars when he comments, "The analysis is beset with peculiar, and perhaps insurmountable difficulties."
76 So in Wellhausen, *Composition* 24.
77 Noth, *Traditions* 28, 35. The verses in parentheses are considered secondary. Gunkel's analysis (*Genesis* 156) is similar.
78 Noth, *Traditions* 28, n. 85.
79 "Sehr bezeichnend für J und charakteristisch für die ganze Originalität und Kühnheit dieses grossartigen Erzählers ist auch hier das Nebeneinander zweier so gänzlich verschiedener Erzählungen" (*Elohist als Erzähler* 33).
80 Cf. Carpenter and Harford-Battersby, *Hexateuch* 1. 190; Martin Noth, *Überlieferungsgeschichtliche Studien: Die sammelnden und bearbeitenden Geschichtswerke im AT* (Darmstadt:Wissenschaftliche Buchgesellschaft, 1963: first pub. 1943) 29-30.
81 The first expression is used frequently in Jer (cf. Jer 1:2, 4, 11, 13; 2:2; 13:3, 8; 16:1, etc.) and in the editorial introductions to earlier prophets; cf. Hos 1:1; Mic 1:1; Zeph 1:1. It appears several times in the Deuteronomistic history (e.g. 1 Sam 15:10; 1 Kgs 16:1, (both with ויהי instead of היה), and in exilic and post-exilic prophetic and apocalyptic writings (e.g., Zech 1:1, 7; Dan 9:2). The second expression is found nowhere else in the Pentateuch. In the entire OT it only occurs twice; both passages are from the Deuteronomistic history: Judg 3:20; 1 Kgs 19:9.
82 Kilian, "*Abrahamsüberlieferungen*" 306-307. See also Kilian's more detailed study of Gen 15, "Der heilsgeschichtliche Aspekt in der elohistischen Geschichtstradition," *ThGl* 56/4 (1966) 369-384.
83 Cf. Ronald Clements, *Abraham and David: Genesis 15 and its Meaning for Israelite Tradition*, SBT, 2d series, 5 (London: SCM Press, 1967) 15-22. Clements sees a fundamental break between vss. 7-21 (J) and vss. 1-6, but he does not think that an E substratum for vss. 1-6 can be detected.
84 Gunkel, *Genesis* 258.
85 *Ibid.*, 257, 270 ascribes 25:9-34 to E, and finds E interwoven with J in ch. 28.
86 Cf. von Rad, *Genesis* 276; Noth, *Traditions* 29. Wellhausen (*Composition* 32) long ago noted that in ch. 28 "die beiden Fäden, aus denen JE zusammengewirkt ist, reissen hier nicht ab, sondern setzen sich fort aber in so enger Verschlingung, dass an eine reinliche Sonderung durchweg nicht zu denken ist. Am besten gelingt die Scheidung in 28:10-22."
87 Gunkel (*Genesis* 279-283) considers vs. 14 redactional, but the evidence for this sort of minute division here is slight. He also suggests that vs. 21*b* is redactional (so also Noth, *Traditions* 35), both because of the appearance of Yahweh in this E context, and because the substance of the vow, centering on the sacred pillar, is complete without the mention of *Yahweh* as Jacob's God (vs. 21*b*). Certainly it is possible to regard the vow as a whole as substantially E, and to regard vs. 21*b* as a later expansion. In vs. 20 LXX reads ’Εὰν ᾖ κύριος ὁ θεὸς μετ' ἐμοῦ; MT has אם יהיה אלהים עמדי; it is possible that κύριος arose here by a misreading of יהיה.
88 Cf. von Rad, *Genesis* 286.
89 Cf. Gunkel, *Genesis* 324-329.
90 Noth, *Traditions* 29.
91 Noth attempts such a source division: *ibid.*, 29-30.
92 By contrast, *Yahweh* is used in the preceding and partly parallel section, 30:25 — 31:3. The

Samaritan text reads *Yahweh* instead of *Elohim* in 31:7, 9, 16a; the Syriac reads *Yahweh* in 16b. This is not sufficient ground for denying the narrative to E, especially since other constants are present; the agreement of LXX and MT is good evidence that the *Elohim* reading is to be preferred as original.

[93] *Genesis* 307.

[94] Von Rad, *Genesis* 307.

[95] Cf. Noth (*Traditions* 29) who attributes only vss. 1, 3, 17, 18aα, 19a, 20, 21aαb, 22, 23 to J. Skinner is representative of the critics in the older literature, holding that "1-16 is an almost homogenous (though perhaps not continuous) excerpt from E ... while in 17-54 E still preponderates, though J is more largely represented than some critics ... allow." *Genesis* 394.

[96] Cf. Gunkel, *Genesis* 310-311; Skinner, *Genesis* 399. Procksch (*Elohimquelle* 27-29), however, exactly reverses this analysis, attributing these verses to J.

[97] So Skinner, *Genesis* 399.

[98] In addition to the use of *Elohim*, there are several allusions to the E narrative of 31:4-16, the tendency to exonerate Jacob of any blame, and the emphasis on the divine protection which surrounds Jacob in his wanderings (vs. 42; cf. 28:20-21). Cf. von Rad, who remarks that "the Elohistic narrative ... is dominant here and in what follows as far as v. 45." *Genesis* 309.

[99] The use of *Elohim* in 32:28, 30, is a necessary part of the explanation of the names Penuel and Israel, and shows nothing about the regular usage of the tradition involved.

[100] The LXX and other major versions support the MT's *Elohim* in this section. 33:18-20, in whole or in part, is attributed by many commentators to E; e.g., Carpenter and Harford-Battersby, *Hexateuch* 2. 52; Skinner, *Genesis* 412; Gunkel, *Genesis* 326-327. The main basis for this identification is the apparent connection of the account with Josh 24:32, which has been assumed by most to stem from E. But in view of the difficulty of assigning any part of Joshua to E (see below, pp. 60-63), we cannot accept this argument.

[101] Von Rad, *Genesis* 330. Noth, for example, regards the chapter as composed of a Yahwist base and a number of secondary expansions (*Traditions* 30, n. 99). Skinner sees two parallel narratives, but refuses to identify either as J or E (*Genesis* 418).

[102] Cf. von Rad, *Genesis* 334-335.

[103] "Die Wallfahrt von Sichem nach Bethel," *Kleine Schriften zur Geschichte des Volkes Israel* (Munich: C. H. Beck, 1959) 1. 87.

[104] *Ibid.*, 86-88.

[105] As claimed, for example, by Carpenter and Harford-Battersby, *Hexateuch* 2. 358.

[106] Cf. G. E. Wright, "Book of Exodus," *IDB* 2. 192-194.

[107] Wright, "Book of Exodus" 194. Cf. Noth, *Exodus: A Commentary* (trans. J. S. Bowden; Philadelphia: Westminster, 1962) 15.

[108] Vs. 22 is assigned to J by Carpenter and Harford-Battersby, *Hexateuch* 1. 81; and by Noth, *Traditions* 30.

[109] Rudolph's explanation of the use of *Elohim* here is that the midwives are Egyptians, and hence cannot be expected to fear Yahweh. This necessitates reading למילדת העבריות in vs. 15 as "the midwives of the Hebrews" rather than "the Hebrew midwives." Such a proposal suggests the amount of strained interpretation which is necessary if one is determined to eliminate an Elohistic tradition from the Pentateuch (*Elohist von Exodus bis Josua* 3).

[110] Cf. Carpenter and Harford-Battersby, *Hexateuch* 2. 81-83; cf. S. R. Driver, *Introduction* 22. This is essentially the conclusion of most commentators, although there have been attempts to find E in vss. 8-12; Procksch, *Elohimquelle* 60-62, designates vss. 11-12 as E.

[111] See Wolff, "Fragments" 165.

[112] Noth, *Exodus* 23-24.

[113] See Wolfgang Richter's recent and thorough study of the parallel strands of Exod 3-4 in *Die sogenannten vorprophetischen Berufungsberichte*, FRLANT 101 (Göttingen: Vandenhoeck & Ruprecht, 1970) 57-133; and N. Habel's excellent earlier study, "The Form and Significance of the Call Narratives," *ZAW* 77 (1965) 297-323.

[114] The use of חרב for "Sinai" has long been regarded as a mark of E style; cf. the tables of Carpenter and Harford-Battersby, *Hexateuch* 1. 186, showing "Horeb" as a consistent feature of the style of Deuteronomy as well. Recently, however, Noth has denied the force of this usage as a criterion, pointing out the decidedly secondary position of the term "Horeb" in the three E passages in Exodus where it appears, Exod 3:1; 17:6; 33:6 (*UGS* 29; cf. Noth, *Traditions* 60, n. 186). I find Noth's analysis convincing. If these passages are to be assigned to E, we must do so on other grounds than the use of "Horeb." In Exod 3:1*b*, it should be mentioned, LXX omits אלהים and reads simply τὸ ὄρος Χωρηβ. Other E constants are, however, clearly present, as noted below.

[115] This form of address in a revelation scene is one of the most important marks of E; cf. the comments above, pp. 21-22, 30-31, 24-26, on the occurrences of the formula in Genesis.

[116] Note the conjunction of *Elohim* with the motif of fear; cf. pp. 21, 25-26 above.

[117] Cf. the analogous explanation of Yahweh's name in P, Exod 6:2-3.

[118] So Carpenter and Harford-Battersby, *Hexateuch* 2. 83. Noth earlier took the opposite view and assigned vs. 14 to E, vs. 15 to a later editor (*Traditions* 36), but in a later writing he modified this view as follows: "We should regard the simple giving of the name in vs. 15 as an original answer to the question at the end of vs. 13, in the same way as the sentence in vs. 15*b*, 'this is my name forever,' will then take up the question 'What is his name?' in vs. 13. Verse 14*a* would then have been added subsequently as an explanation of the name Yahweh and would have been inserted into the context because of 14*b* which verbally anticipates the following clause." *Exodus* 43.

[119] Cf. Noth, *Traditions* 36 (E = 4*b*, 6, 9-14); Richter, *Berufungsberichte* 70-71, (E = 1*bβ*, 4*b*, 6*a*, 9-15). On the other hand, Habel sees vss. 1-6 as a section having considerable unity and many signs of E style and theology, including the appearance of God in a light or fire which cannot be approached, rather than in "the bold human form typical of the Yahwist narratives." On the basis of his analysis, including the fact that the Samaritan text has *Elohim* instead of *Yahweh* in 3:4*a*, Habel concludes that there is very likely an E basis for the whole narrative of vss. 1-6. "Call Narratives," 302.

[120] Noth, *Exodus* 40-41.

[121] Richter, *Berufungsberichte* 133.

[122] See the literature cited in *ibid*. and Habel, "Call Narratives."

[123] *Berufungsberichte* 180.

[124] *Ibid*., 170.

[125] *Ibid*., 173-174.

[126] *Ibid*., 181.

[127] Cf. *ibid*., 132-133; Noth, *Exodus* 40-41.

[128] Noth, *Exodus* 47.

[129] So Carpenter and Harford-Battersby, *Hexateuch* 1. 275; 2. 88-89. This analysis is typical of older critics; cf. Holzinger, *Exodus*, HKAT (Tübingen: J. C. B. Mohr, 1900) xvi-xvii, assigning to E Exod 7:15*b*, 17*b*, 20*aβb*, 21*a*, 23; finding "traces" in 8:8-10; 9:22, 23*a*, 24*a*, 35*aαb*; 10:12, 13*a*א, 14*aα*, 21-23, 24*αβ*, 25, 27; 11:1-3.

[130] J. L. Mihelic and G. E. Wright, "The Plagues in Exodus," *IDB* 3. 823-824; cf. Noth, *Exodus* 67-70.

[131] Noth (*Exodus* 70) denies any E passages in these sections. Wright concludes, "It must be admitted, however, that in themselves the passages in question are too fragmentary, and the criteria for distinguishing them too imprecise, to make it entirely certain that a third document (E) is definitely to be distinguished in the plague narratives" ("Plagues," *IDB* 3. 824.)

[132] *The Book of Exodus*, Cambridge Bible for Schools and Colleges (Cambridge: The University Press, 1911) 105-161.

[133] *Ibid*., xvii.

[134] *Traditions* 36.

[135] Cf. the tradition in Josh 24:32 that the bones of Joseph were finally buried in a tomb at Shechem.

¹³⁶Cf. the other occurrences of this apparently rare expression, always in this form, in Josh 1:14; 4:12; Judg 7:11. It is also often conjectured as an emendation for חמשים in Num 32:17; cf. F. Brown, S. R. Driver, C. A. Briggs, *Hebrew and English Lexicon of the OT* (Oxford: Clarendon Press, 1955) 332; Driver, *Exodus* 112.

¹³⁷Noth, however, believes that the statement that the Hebrews fled from Egypt (14:5a) can be attributed to E, and that this is an important fragment of "what is doubtless a very old form of the Exodus tradition . . ." (*Exodus* 112). Cf. E. W. Nicholson, *Exodus and Sinai in History and Tradition* (Richmond: John Knox Press, 1973) 55-56.

¹³⁸See F. M. Cross, Jr. and D. N. Freedman, "The Song of Miriam," *JNES* (1955) 237-239. See also the recent treatment by Patrick D. Miller, Jr., in *The Divine Warrior in Early Israel* (Cambridge: Harvard University Press, 1973) 113-117, 168-170, for a discussion both of the antiquity of this poem and of its significance for the formation of Israelite religious conceptions.

¹³⁹So Artur Weiser, *Introduction to the OT* (London: Darton, Longman & Todd, 1961) 106.

¹⁴⁰So Cross and Freedman, "Song of Miriam" 238.

¹⁴¹Cf. Carpenter and Harford-Battersby, *Hexateuch* 2. 104; Driver, *Exodus* 143.

¹⁴²Noth, *Exodus* 128-129.

¹⁴³Cf. Georg Beer, *Exodus* (Tübingen: J. C. B. Mohr, 1939) 86.

¹⁴⁴E.g., "hearken to the voice," Deut 15:5; 28:1; "Yahweh thy God," Deut 1:21, 31, *et passim*; "that which is right," Deut 6:18; 22:25, 28; "give ear," Deut 1:45; "commandments and statutes," Deut 4:40; 6:17, 10:13; *et passim*. See the vocabulary tables in S. R. Driver, *Deuteronomy*, ICC (New York: Scribners, 1895) lxxvii-xcv.

¹⁴⁵Carpenter and Harford-Battersby assign a fragment of the quails and manna story (16:4) to E on the following basis: (a) There seem to be two accounts of Yahweh's promising food, in 16:4 and in 16:11; (b) vs. 11 is part of the P account (cf. vs. 10), and therefore vs. 4 is either E or J; (c) vs. 4 is E because of the theme of testing, which also appears in Gen 22:1; Ex 15:25b. *Hexateuch* 2. 104-105. But in the absence of any stronger evidence than this, we cannot identify the fragment as E. Noth assigns this verse, along with vss. 29-31, to J (*Exodus* 132); so also Driver, *Exodus* 146.

¹⁴⁶We may, with Noth (*Exodus* 137-139) regard 2c, 7c, and "Massah" in 7a as additions to the original narrative, explaining the place name "Meribah" by the verb *rîb*. This would mean that another tradition about the spring which is called "Massah" in Exod 15:25b has been secondarily introduced here.

¹⁴⁷Exod 3:17. Against Noth, who thinks "Horeb" is a later addition and that the rod is to be associated with the J plague story in Exod 7:17, 20a. *Exodus* 139-140. Hence, Noth would assign only vs. 3 to E. *Traditions* 36, n. 137. Driver (*Exodus* 157) assigns vss. 5-6 to E; Holzinger (*Exodus* xvii) designates the same verses as "JE."

¹⁴⁸But cf. G. W. Coats, *Rebellion in the Wilderness* (Nashville: Abingdon, 1968) 53-71, 249-254, where only J is claimed as a source. Coats admits that Exod 17:3-4 are "difficult to control," but ends up assigning them to J on grounds which are not literary-critical (p. 250).

¹⁴⁹So Holzinger, *Exodus* 60. But contrast Noth (*Exodus* 141-142) who thinks "rod of God" is an addition to the original narrative, which he thinks may be J.

¹⁵⁰Cf. the brief discussion by Noth in *Traditions* 35, n. 138, and in *Exodus* 145-150. See also W. F. Albright, "Jethro, Hobab, and Reuel in Early Hebrew Tradition," *CBQ* 25 (1963) 1-11.

¹⁵¹See Noth's discussion, *Exodus* 144-150.

¹⁵²*Ibid.*, 148-149.

¹⁵³*Ibid.*, 146.

¹⁵⁴*Ibid.*, 148-149. 18:2b, which speaks of the "sending away" of Moses' wife, would thus be an explanatory gloss which harmonizes the disparate traditions of J and E on this point.

¹⁵⁵Wolff, "Fragments" 165.

¹⁵⁶Murray Newman has preferred to tie this tradition to the Wilderness narratives, and has identified the site of the meeting in Exod 18 with Kadesh: *The People of the Covenant* (Nashville: Abingdon, 1962) 83-90. As Newman emphasizes, Exod 18 has long been a major passage cited in support of the Kenite hypothesis, precisely because vs. 12 depicts the Kenite or Midianite priest offering sacrifice to Yahweh. *Ibid.* 25-26.

[157]J. M. Schmidt, "Erwägungen zum Verhältnis von Auszugs- und Sinaitradition," *ZAW* 82 (1970) 15-16.

[158]*Exodus and Sinai* 67-70, 79-81.

[159]See C. H. W. Breckelmans, "Exodus xviii and the origins of Yahwism in Israel," *OTS* 10 (1954) 215-224; F. C. Fensham, "Did a Treaty between the Israelites and the Kenites Exist?", *BASOR* 175 (1964) 51-54.

[160] Cf. Pfeiffer, *Introduction* 189; Driver, *Introduction* 37; Carpenter and Harford-Battersby, *Hexateuch* 1. 276; Eissfeldt, *Synopse* 100; Noth, *Traditions* 18; Walter Beyerlin, *Origins and History of the Oldest Sinaitic Traditions* (Oxford: Basil Blackwell, 1965) 1-4. These sources show substantial agreement in attributing the following passages to P: 19:1-2a; 24:15b-18a; 25:1 — 31:17; 31:18a; 34:29-35; 35 — 40.

[161]Procksch (*Elohimquelle* 88-89) puts forward typical arguments in which the E tradition is related to eighth-century prophecy and the Decalogue is viewed as a reflex of this prophetic movement. Carpenter and Harford-Battersby (*Hexateuch* 2. 111) state: "The Ten Words . . . are almost unanimously assigned in the present redaction to E." Cf. the opinion of Pfeiffer (*Introduction* 230): "No, the Ten Commandments do not represent the prophetic teaching in its inspired purity, but rather a Deuteronomic compromise between the prophetic religion of right motives and the priestly religion of ritual observances." See also the discussion by Eissfeldt (*Introduction* 215), who argues: ". . . Notwithstanding the great similarity which otherwise exists between E and J, E does nevertheless undertake marked emendations of the religious and moral attitudes which are presupposed by J. . . . With this would accord well the fact that E has substituted for J's cultic decalogue an ethical decalogue which clearly deliberately passes over agricultural festivals, just as we may observe that Deuteronomy, which in many respects builds upon E, does not seem originally to have taken account of agricultural festivals in its festival laws (xvi, 17)." See also the discussion by Bentzen, *Introduction* 2. 54.

[162]Cf. Mendenhall, *Law and Covenant* 31-44; Baltzer, *Covenant* 1-41; Hillers, *Covenant* 25-71.

[163]See H. H. Rowley, "Moses and the Decalogue," *BJRL* 34 (1951) 81-118; and, more recently, J. J. Stamm and M. E. Andrew, *The Ten Commandments in Recent Research*, SBT, Second Series, 2 (London: SCM, 1967). Albrecht Alt's article, "Die Ursprünge des israelitischen Rechts," *Kleine Schriften* 1. 278-332 (now in English in *Essays on OT History and Religion* (Oxford: Blackwell, 1966, 79-132) paved the way for modern re-evaluation of the Decalogue. Cf. the comments of Albright, *Stone Age to Christianity* 257-272; Bentzen, *Introduction* 2. 54-55.

[164]Cf. Mendenhall's discussion of the new orientation in the study of Israel's religious development in "Biblical History in Transition," *The Bible and the Ancient Near East* 32-49.

[165]Noth, *Exodus* 154. Recently, however, some have argued that the Decalogue (in a pre-Priestly form) fits well into E's narrative if (a) 20:18-21 is placed before 20:1-17; and (b) Exod 24:3-8 is ascribed to E, the *sēper habbᵉrît* and the *dᵉbārîm* of 24:3, 4, 7, 8 being understood as references to the Decalogue; cf. Beyerlin, *Sinaitic Traditions* 36-48; Eissfeldt, *Introduction* 212-219. In addition to the literary considerations, Beyerlin emphasizes the parallels with the Hittite treaties, arguing that such a covenant formula as is reflected in the E narrative would naturally include some form of commands, analogous to the treaty stipulations. The repeated use of *Yahweh* in 24:3-8, however, precludes our assigning it to E, and we cannot argue that E *should* have and therefore *did* include a series of commands, knowing as little as we do about the actual history of the Sinai traditions. The E narrative which we propose below, including only 19:2b-3a, 4-6, 16-17, 19; 20:18-21; 24:1-2, 9-15a, 18b, is all that we can with certainty attribute to the Elohist.

[166]Noth, *Exodus* 175-176.

[167]*Ibid.*, 198-199. I am disagreeing here with Newman, *People of the Covenant* 40-51, who designates 24:3-8, as well as the Decalogue and Covenant Code, as E.

[168]*Hexateuch* 2. 113.

[169]Alt, "Ursprünge des israelitischen Rechts" 294-295; Pfeiffer, *Introduction* 215.

[170]Among the most interesting sections of the Covenant Code, and the most significant for a study of E, is the concluding exhortation, 23:20-33, which may be compared with the hortatory

conclusions of Deuteronomy and of the Holiness Code (so Driver, *Exodus* 247). If we could identify this passage as the contribution of the E tradition, this would indicate an extremely close relationship between the E school and the Deuteronomic circles, for points of contact with Deuteronomic style and phraseology have long been noted in the passage (cf. Carpenter and Harford-Battersby, *Hexateuch* 2. 168; Beyerlin, *Sinaitic Traditions* 5). The obviously complex history of this passage, like that of the other "proto-Deuteronomic" passage in 19:3-8, cannot be pursued at this point (see below, pp. 117-124ff.).

[171] See Wilhelm Rudolph, "Der Aufbau von Exodus 19 — 34," *Werden und Wesen des AT,* BZAW 66 (1936) 41-48.

[172] A detailed listing of the inconsistencies is given by Driver in *Exodus* 168; cf. Noth, *Exodus* 153-155).

[173] *Hexateuch* 2. 109-111.

[174] *Introduction* 30-32.

[175] "Der Aufbau von Exodus 19 — 34," 41-42, 48.

[176] *Ibid.*, 41. Similarly, Noth, *Exodus* 154, 160. Noth also includes vs. 25 in this secondary material.

[177] Rudolph, *Elohist von Exodus bis Josua* 41. Beyerlin concurs in this judgment, although he is inclined to include vs. 20 also as part of the expansion. *Sinaitic Traditions* 7-9.

[178] Vss. 3a and 3b are clearly doublets; note the use of *Elohim* in 3a and *Yahweh* in 3b.

[179] Noth, *Exodus* 157-159.

[180] James Muilenburg, "The Form and Structure of the Covenantal Formulations," *VT* 9 (1959) 351-357.

[181] See Driver, *Exodus* 170. Among the parallels noted are: "eagle wings" (על כנפי נשרים), cf. Deut 32:10; "hearken to" (אם שמוע תשמעו), cf. Deut 11:13; 15:5; 28:1; "a peculiar possession" (סגלה), cf. Deut 7:6; 14:2; 26:18; "a holy nation" (וגוי קדוש), cf. Deut 7:6; 14:2, 21; 26:10.

[182] So Noth, *Exodus* 157; Beyerlin, *Sinaitic Traditions* 10-11.

[183] See Driver, *Exodus* 171; Muilenburg, "Form and Structure of Covenantal Formulations" 351-353.

[184] On the separateness of the Tetrateuch from the Deuteronomistic history, see Noth, *Überlieferungsgeschichtliche Studien* 180-216. Cf. G. Ernest Wright, "Deuteronomy," *IB* 2.320: "The view that there was a thorough Deuteronomic redaction of JE appears increasingly subjective and difficult to prove." Chr. Brekelmans has reviewed this topic in "Die sogenannten deuteronomischen Elemente in Gen-Num: ein Beitrag zur Vorgeschichte Deuteronomiums," VTSup 15 (1965) 90-96, and has concluded — very much as we do here — that such a passage as Exod 19:3-8 is *proto*-Deuteronomic rather than post-Deuteronomic, and represents the extent to which the Deuteronomic theology and style drew upon Elohistic elements.

[185] Wright, "Deuteronomy," *IB* 2. 320; Muilenburg, "Form and Structure of Covenantal Formulations" 351; Breckelmans, "Sogenannten deuteronomischen Elemente" 94-96.

[186] See below, Chapter III.

[187] See Carpenter and Harford-Battersby, *Hexateuch* 2. 190-211; cf. Newman, *People of the Covenant* 39-55.

[188] So Noth, *Exodus* 197-199; but contrast Eissfeldt, *Introduction* 212-219; Beyerlin, *Sinaitic Traditions* 36-67.

[189] Noth, *Exodus* 197-199. But Rudolph ("Aufbau von Exodus 19 — 34" 46-48) is also incorrect in ascribing the passage to J. J's covenant narrative is found in Exod 34. Cf. *ibid.*, 198, 260.

[190] Cf. Num 24:4, 16 (also E); Isa 1:1; 2:1; Amos 1:1; Mic 1:1.

[191] Beyerlin, *Sinaitic Traditions* 36-48; Nicholson, *Exodus and Sinai* 68.

[192] Beer, *Exodus* 128. Rudolph (*Elohist von Exodus bis Josua* 48) identifies vss. 16-18a as P, as does Driver, *Exodus* 251.

[193] Cf. the related tradition of Exod 18:12, where only Aaron appears, together with "all the elders of Israel" to share the sacred (covenant?) meal with Jethro. In that passage Moses himself is not mentioned.

[194] Wellhausen, *Composition* 194; Holzinger, *Exodus* 108; Carpenter and Harford-Battersby, *Hexateuch* 2. 130-132.

[195] See the summary of Carpenter and Harford-Battersby, *Hexateuch* 2. 130-131 and, more fully, Noth, *Exodus* 243-252.

[196] This interpretation was first suggested by H. Th. Obbink, "Jahwebilder" *ZAW* 47 (1929) 264-71. This view was further developed and defined by Albright, *Stone Age to Christianity* 199; R. DeVaux, *Ancient Israel* (New York: McGraw-Hill, 1961) 332-336; and W. Eichrodt, *Theology of the OT* (Philadelphia: Westminster, 1961) 1. 117. See also, most recently, Cross, *Canaanite Myth and Hebrew Epic* 73-75, 89 n. 23. Cross observes, however, that there were indeed grounds for the accusation in Exod 32 and 1 Kgs 12 that the bulls were worshipped: "a god and his animal 'participate in each other,' and while the god may be conceived as enthroned or standing on the bull in Canaanite mythology and iconography, he also is immanent in his animal so that the two may be confused" (p. 73, n. 117).

[197] Cf. the parallel formulas in 1 Kgs 12:28 and Neh 9:18. While the 1 Kgs 12 formula (הנה אלהיך ... אשר העלוך) does not necessarily indicate a plurality of gods — the plural verb appears with *Elohim* in Gen 20:13; 31:53; 35:7; Exod 22:8 (EV 22:9), and with a plural adjective in Josh 24:19 — the use here of אלה forces us to translate *Elohim* as plural. Still, the Elohist is undoubtedly thinking here of the two images and not of two distinct gods.

[198] See the excellent summary of the extraordinary number of parallels between Exod 32 and 1 Kgs 12 in M. Aberbach and L. Smolar, "Aaron, Jeroboam, and the Golden Calves," *JBL* 86 (1967) 129-140.

[199] We are opposing Noth, *Traditions* 142-145, who seems to be arguing that Exod 32 is dependent upon the 1 Kgs 12 tradition.

[200] R. Dussaud, *Les origines cananéenes du sacrifice israélite* (Paris: Leroux, 1921) 244, argues for a basis in an old non-critical tradition. Cf. Eissfeldt, "Lade und Stierbild," *ZAW* 63 (1940/41) 190-215, and the more recent detailed treatment by Beyerlin, *Sinaitic Traditions* 126-133, and also the works cited in n. 196.

[201] See F. M. Cross, "Yahweh and the God of the Patriarchs," *HTR* (1962) 257-259; and *Canaanite Myth and Hebrew Epic* 74.

[202] "Since the act of Jeroboam I was an outrageous repetition of that original apostasy at Sinai which occurred in immediate connection with the fundamental revelation of God, it therefore falls likewise — so Ex. 32 intends to be understood, of course — under the condemning judgment, curse, and punishment of God which hovers now, as at that time, threateningly over the faithless." Noth, *Traditions* 143.

[203] *Canaanite Myth and Hebrew Epic* 74.

[204] *Ibid.*, 74.

[205] Cf. Noth, *Traditions* 31, although Noth regards the nucleus of the narrative as Yahwistic.

[206] See below, pp. 103-105.

[207] Cf. Rudolph, *Exodus bis Josua* 53-58; Beer, *Exodus* 157-159; Noth, *Exodus* 253-258.

[208] Noth, *Exodus* 253-258.

[209] *Sinaitic Traditions* 25-26.

[210] Noth, *Exodus* 253-258.

[211] *Exodus bis Josua* 54-55.

[212] See the discussion in Cross, *Canaanite Myth and Hebrew Epic* 198-200.

[213] Beyerlin, *Sinaitic Traditions* 111-112.

[214] *Ibid.*, 125.

[215] *Ibid.*, 124-126.

[216] As Cross puts it (*Canaanite Myth and Hebrew Epic* 199), Jeroboam I is actually attempting to "out-archaize" David by selecting the ancient Bethel shrine with its archaic bull-image, whereas David had "only" the Ark of the Covenant to use in his new central sanctuary at Jerusalem.

[217] See Ch. III.

[218] G. B. Gray, *Numbers*, ICC (New York: Scribners, 1903) 103.

[219] Cf. Carpenter and Harford-Battersby, *Hexateuch* 1. 277; Procksch, *Elohimquelle* 98.

[220] Cf. Gray, *Numbers* 99-100.

[221] I am here sharply disagreeing with Murray Newman, *People of the Covenant* 93-95, in his attempt to attribute Exod 33:1-7, as well as these key passages in Num 11 — 12 which deal with Moses' role and authority, to the J epic. Newman then relates these passages to "southern priestly circles" (p. 94). This is part of his total attempt to arrive at a historical reconstruction of the early cultus and of two different covenant ideologies, represented by the J and E traditions. To these he connects, respectively, the Tent of Meeting and the Ark. In my opinion, the Tent of Meeting and the Ark were associated together from the very start (see Beyerlin, *Sinaitic Traditions* 114-120 for a good statement of some of the main arguments for associating Ark and Tent with the central sanctuary — probably first Shechem and then Shiloh — of pre-monarchical days). See also Cross, *Canaanite Myth and Hebrew Epic* 185-186, where the divine activity associated in a general way with the Ark ("Yahweh as Divine Warrior at the Sea and River") and with the Tent ("Yahweh as head of the Divine Council and giver of decrees") are traced back, respectively, to "Baal" and "El" motifs found in Israelite religion and literature at the most primitive level. In short, I think Newman has been led to attribute the "Tent of Meeting" and "authority of Moses" passages to J because of an incorrect historical reconstruction which separates the Ark from its Tent-shrine. I hold with Beyerlin and Cross, as well as the majority of the older critics, that these passages are Elohistic because of clear connections with other E passages.

[222] Against Noth (*Traditions* 36), who follows earlier scholars (e.g., Carpenter and Harford-Battersby, *Hexateuch* 2. 221-223) in ascribing the substance of 20:14-18; 21:21-31 to E. The stylistic criteria cited by Gray (*Numbers* 264-265) and by Carpenter and Harford-Battersby in support of such identification are inconclusive. Driver (*Introduction* 66) more cautiously designates these passages as "JE."

[223] Accepting the opinion of Albright ("The Oracles of Balaam," *JBL* 63 [1944] 207-233) and of previous commentators (e.g., Carpenter and Harford-Battersby, *Hexateuch* 2. 227), that the poems themselves are of independent origin and were taken up into the prose sources and furnished with a narrative framework. It is interesting to note, however, that the four poems (23:7-10, 18-24; 24:3-9, 15-19) use *Elohim* as the "A-word" and *Yahweh* or *El-Shadday* as the "B-word": cf. 23:8, 19, 22, 23, 24:4, 8, 16. Furthermore, "Jacob" is always the A-word and "Israel" the B-word: 23:7, 21, 23; 24:5, 17.

[224] *Hexateuch* 2. 224.

[225] Gray, *Numbers* 313; Noth, *Traditions* 32, 36.

[226] *Exodus bis Josua* 127-128. See Eissfeldt's summary, "Die Komposition der Bileam-Erzählung," *ZAW* 57 (1939) 218-220.

[227] So Albright, "Oracles of Balaam" 207.

[228] *Exodus bis Josua* 104-106. Cf. Eissfeldt's critique of Rudolph's method, "Bileam-Erzählung" 213-215.

[229] *Exodus bis Josua* 105-106.

[230] "Bileam-Erzählung" 232.

[231] See the attempt of L. M. von Pákozdy to establish the precise theological intentions of redactors in "Theologische Redaktionsarbeit in der Bileam-Perikope (Num 22 — 24)," *Von Ugarit nach Qumran*, BZAW 77 (Berlin: Töpelmann, 1958) 161-176, especially pp. 164-168.

[232] Gray, *Numbers* 313, attributes vss. 6, 7, 11, 17-18, 22-35, 37, to J. Similarly, Carpenter and Harford-Battersby, *Hexateuch* 1. 177.

[233] Cf. Rudolph's treatment of the chapter, *Exodus bis Josua* 106-119.

[234] Wolff, "Elohistic Fragments" 171.

[235] In agreement with Noth, *Traditions* 32-33, nn. 126, 127; 36-37, n. 142. Noth's earlier treatment, in *UGS* 27-28, 39-40, postulated the use of the old epic sources in Deut 1-4, 21-24, though he maintained that we cannot distinguish the sources in detail. Wolff ("Elohistic Fragments" 171) calls the Balaam pericope "the last major account in the Pentateuch which can with certainty be assigned to the Elohist."

[236] *Hexateuch* 2. 229; similarly, Gray, *Numbers* 380-383.

[237] So Rudolph, *Exodus bis Josua* 128, who argues "Während der letzte Lagerort der Israeliten

bei J auf der moabitischen Hochebene gelegen war (21:20; 23:[14], 28), sind sie mit 25:1 (Sittim) in die Jordansenke gelangt, die bei P schon in 22:1 erreicht war. 25:1 führt also die vorausgehende geographische J-Situation weiter und erweist sich damit als die Fortsetzung in J."

[238] With Rudolph, *Exodus bis Josua* 128-129. Rudolph argues in addition that אלהיהן in vs. 2 means "their god."

[239] Cf. John Marsh, "Numbers," *IB* 2. 263.

[240] *Hexateuch* 2. 239-241.

[241] *Numbers* 426.

[242] *Elohimquelle* 119; cf. 111-112.

[243] *Traditions* 36-37, n. 142.

[244] For example, Carpenter and Harford-Battersby (*Hexateuch* 1. 278) ascribe ch. 33 to E, but designate ch. 32 as an addition to D. Eissfeldt (*Introduction* 226-232) attributes ch. 32 to E, but describes ch. 33 as an ancient poem which, like the Blessing of Jacob in Gen 49, is not to be attributed to one of the Pentateuchal sources. Procksch (*Elohimquelle* 120-127) relates ch. 33 to E, but attributes ch. 32 to a Deuteronomic source. Among recent writers, Weiser (*Introduction* 117-119) still argues that both chs. 32 and 33 were transmitted within the E tradition.

[245] On Deut 32, see especially G. E. Wright, "The Lawsuit of God: A Form-Critical Study of Deuteronomy 32," *Israel's Prophetic Heritage* 26-67, with the bibliography cited there. On Deut 33, see F. M. Cross, Jr., and David N. Freedman, "The Blessing of Moses," *JBL* 67 (1948) 191-210.

[246] So G. E. Wright, *IB* 2. 315, 511-537.

[247] Wright, "Deuteronomy," *IB* 2. 516.

[248] Cf. Driver, *Deuteronomy* 333-344.

[249] *Hexateuch* 2.295.

[250] So Rudolph, *Exodus bis Josua* 159-160, who designates all these passages as "J supplements."

[251] Wellhausen, *Composition* 115-116; Carpenter and Harford-Battersby, *Hexateuch* 2. 301. The latter call ch. 34 "an amalgam of all the chief documents of the Hexateuch." Cf. Procksch, *Elohimquelle* 127-128; Rudolph, *Exodus bis Josua* 162-164.

[252] Cf. Rudolph, *Exodus bis Josua* 164: "Bei v. 10-12 erinnert v. 10 stark an Ex 33:11, Num 12:8, so dass man an dieselbe Hand wie dort denken könnte." Wright (*IB* 2. 511) regards the editor as the author of the Deuteronomistic history, as in Noth's theory.

[253] Noth, *UGS* 3-110; *Das Buch Josua*, HAT (2nd ed., Tübingen: J. C. B. Mohr [Paul Siebeck], 1953), 7-16. See also Cross, *Canaanite Myth and Hebrew Epic* 274-289.

[254] John Bright has argued that the J and E traditions must have concluded with an account of the conquest, "Joshua," *IB* 2. 544.

[255] *Josua* 7-16. Cf. Bright's excellent summary of Noth's position, *IB* 2. 541-542. Cross (*Canaanite Myth and Hebrew Epic* 274-289) accepts Noth's main thesis as to the fundamental distinction to be drawn between the Deuteronomistic historian and the Pentateuchal sources, but strongly argues for a pre-Exilic dating of that historian's work. Engnell also argued — independently of Noth's work, apparently — for the independence of the Deuteronomistic work from the "Tetrateuch" (Gen through Num). See *A Rigid Scrutiny* 58-67.

[256] Noth, *UGS* 39-40, 211-216.

[257] *Josua* 20-21. Noth acknowledges the earlier studies to which he is indebted in this matter, especially Albrecht Alt's "Josua," *Werden und Wesen des AT* 13-29.

[258] *Josua* 11-16.

[259] *Introduction* 241-257.

[260] *Introduction* 143-147.

[261] *IB* 2. 543-545.

[262] *Ibid.*, 544.

[263] E. M. Good, "Book of Joshua," *IDB* 2. 990.

[264] See the discussion of doublets and inconsistencies in Carpenter and Harford-Battersby, *Hexateuch* 2. 304-306. There are doublets and other signs of composition in Joshua, but these

only demonstrate variation between ancient traditions on which the Deuteronomistic historian drew, not the presence of J and E.

[265] *Ibid.*, 309, 320-359.
[266] *Introduction* 145.
[267] *Ibid.*, 132.
[268] *Ibid.*, 146.
[269] Oslo: Jacob Dybwad, 1937.
[270] *Die sogenannte Paradieserzählung: Aufbau, Herkunft und theologische Bedeutung* (Gütersloh: Verlagshaus Gerd Mohn, 1968).
[271] *Two Sources* 7-43.
[272] *Ibid.*, 44-50.
[273] *Ibid.*, 50-72.
[274] *Ibid.*, 72-84. Mowinckel follows Hölscher in tracing E through the Deuteronomistic history, and dates its composition after the fall of Jerusalem in 587 B.C. (*ibid.*, 78, n. 1). See also Mowinckel's *Tetrateuch-Pentateuch-Hexateuch: Die Berichte über die Landnahme in den drei altisraelitischen Geschichtswerke*, BZAW 90, 1964.
[275] *Composition* 15-16.
[276] Gunkel, *Genesis* 1-140; see especially the summary on pp. 1-3.
[277] Mowinckel, *Two Sources* 9.
[278] *Ibid.*, 42 (emphasis in original).
[279] *Ibid.*, 68-69 (the * indicates that only part of the verse is attributed to the source named).
[280] *Traditions* 237-238.
[281] Mowinckel, *Two Sources* 46.
[282] Albright, in his review of Mowinckel's book, *JBL* 57 (1938) 103. Mowinckel and Albright later exchanged views in "The Babylonian Matter in the Predeuteronomic Primeval History (JE) in Gen 1 — 11," *JBL* 58 (1939) 87-103.
[283] Cf. George Mendenhall, "Biblical History in Transition," *The Bible and the Ancient Near East* 38-40.
[284] The methods and finding of Werner Fuss in the work mentioned in n. 270 are similar to those of Mowinckel. Fuss finds fine differences of style and language and attributes them to J and E — though his stylistic features do not, in my opinion, tie in very convincingly with the acknowledged constants of J and E (see Fuss, *Paradieserzählung* 85-87 for a listing of some of these major stylistic features). Fuss also tries to match up the conceptualities of the sources on which he thinks the Gen 2 — 3 narrative draws, attributing these to the theological differences between J and E. For example, he compares the strand of Gen 2 — 3 in which man must be kept away from the tree of life with E passages in which man is told to "keep his distance" from God or the Sacred, such as Exod 3:5 and 19:12-13. The fundamental difficulty here, as in Mowinckel's work, is that stylistic "constants" are separated from theological constants so that no control can be maintained by the analyst. We have emphasized throughout our analysis of literary passages that we must rely upon the *conjunction* of *major* linguistic and theological constants in our determination of literary sources. These constants, moreover, must be as *specific* as possible. The theme of reverence for the sacred is not specific enough to be valuable in determining sources. On the other hand, the occurrence of the specific phrase "fear of God," together with other constants, might be sufficient to indicate an Elohist passage.
[285] The passages here included represent the substance of our findings in the foregoing discussion. Such a list, of course, cannot show the varying degrees of certainty with which we assigned passages to E, or the fact that some passages are undoubtedly part of the original Elohist epic while others are secondary additions. For such nuances the reader must consult the appropriate sections in Chapter II, above.

CHAPTER III

The E Tradition and Early Northern Prophecy

Having characterized the E tradition in the Pentateuch and delimited its scope, our next task is to ascertain the date and provenance of this tradition. In accordance with the methodology which we discussed in Chapter I and used in Chapter II, we shall not argue in terms of isolated geographical and historical references or minute matters of style and diction. Instead we shall examine the history of the traditions with which E has the closest affinities, and then attempt to determine the relative date of E as compared with these other Old Testament traditions. This will lead us into a discussion of the Samuel and Elijah traditions and then, in the last chapter, of Hosea and Deuteronomy.

(A) The Prophetic Traditions Concerning Samuel

Before we are able to discuss the affinities of the E tradition with the prophetic traditions concerning Samuel we must establish a critical basis by discussing these Samuel traditions in themselves. The most influential efforts to resolve the problems presented by them must be evaluated.

(1) History of Criticism

Since the beginning of modern Old Testament criticism scholars have recognized that the Books of Samuel are composite.[1] Commonly, the critics have resorted to a literary analysis which breaks down the present narrative into its original components, which are regarded as fragments of originally separate and continuous sources. In this type of analysis, two main sources have been recognized.[2]

Not only has the method thus employed been very similar to that used in Pentateuchal studies, but the results of Pentateuchal criticism have often been marshalled to sustain the analysis. As a result, some influential scholars have held that the two main sources are actually identical with J and E.[3] While we do not agree with this solution in detail, we believe that the Samuel traditions which have been identified as "E" do have close affinities with the Elohist source of the Pentateuch, and may have been produced by a northern prophetic-levitical school associated with the E circle.

The body of traditions in question here has been variously designated by those scholars who do *not* identify it with E as "the late source,"[4] "the prophetic traditions,"[5] and "the Samuel source."[6] The main passages generally assigned to this corpus of tradition are: 1 Sam 1:1-4:1*a*; 7; 8; 10:17-27; 12; 13:8-15; 15; 16:1-13.[7] They are characterized by (1) the centrality of Samuel in the events surrounding the beginning of the monarchy (cf. especially 1 Sam 7); (2) the negative judgment passed on the institution of monarchy. Israel's desire for a king is condemned as an implied rejection of the kingship of Yahweh over his chosen people (1 Sam 8; 10:17-27; 12:12, 19).

How reliably does this "Samuel source" reflect attitudes and events of the early monarchy? According to many literary critics we cannot rely on these traditions for accurate depiction of history. H. P. Smith describes the source as "less concrete" than the other source, which is "earlier and more primitive." The Samuel source "idealizes persons and events," being "dominated by a theological idea." Its design and method indicate "a comparatively late date — perhaps in or after the Exile."[8] Pfeiffer's similar judgment is more colorfully expressed:

> With the supercilious indifference to facts typical of some theologians, the authors of the late source glibly proceed to concoct stories and speeches glorifying Samuel and David and vilifying Hophni, Phinehas, and Saul, suppressing when possible or disguising when necessary Saul's noble acts, Samuel's obscure position as a village clairvoyant, and David's detestable actions, which are honestly reported in the old source. . . . The mist of legend and the compelling authority of dogma conspire to produce in the late source an atmosphere of make-believe and the illusion of a mirage.[9]

Thus, the literary critics of a past generation solved the problems of 1 Samuel by assigning the contradictory narratives to two sources. The earlier and more reliable of these sources viewed the kingship as a divine gift, intended to save Israel from the Philistines (1 Sam 9:16), and put Samuel in his proper place as an obscure country seer (9:1 — 10:16). The later and scarcely credible "Samuel source" reflected Israel's bitter experience with the monarchy and showed the bias of prophetic groups who created legends to glorify their revered hero, Samuel.

Nor have most modern critics deviated greatly from the older solution. Martin Noth's work is very similar to that of the older critics, especially Wellhausen, both in the treatment of literary-critical problems and in the question of historicity.[10] While admitting that there was a body of prophetic "Samuel traditions" available to the Deuteronomistic historian, Noth maintains that the historian greatly altered and supplemented these older traditions. This is especially the case, in Noth's view, in 1 Sam 7:2 — 8:22; 10:17-27; 12:1-25.[11] In these chapters the Deuteronomistic historian presents the ministry of Samuel as the last act in the period of the judges, hence the statement that Samuel "judged Israel" (7:6, 15-17). The historian closes this period with the farewell scene in ch. 12, which is obviously modeled on Joshua's farewell in Josh 23 - 24.[12]

By contrast to this we may note the much more conservative views of Eissfeldt, in his monograph *Geschichtsschreibung im Alten Testament*. The leading themes of the Deuteronomistic history — idolatry, defeat through enemies, repentance, divine grace and assistance — are much older than the Deuteronomistic historian of the Exilic period. These themes are inherent in Israelite traditions as early as the tenth century B.C.[13]

It is clear that the contradictions between the scholarly opinions described above cannot be resolved without a fresh analysis of the historical and literary problems involved. Through this analysis, brief as it must be, we hope to show: (1) that the "prophetic traditions concerning Samuel" are indeed ancient, and reflect early attitudes and events near the beginning of the monarchy; and (2) that there is a close affinity between these traditions and the E traditions.

(2) *The Age and Character of the "Samuel Source"*

First of all we can quickly dispose of the claim that the anti-monarchical tone of these Samuel traditions must reflect a *post facto* evaluation of the monarchy, stemming from Israel's later experience. In an article published in 1956, I. Mendelsohn demonstrated that this anti-monarchical bias can be entirely historical in eleventh-century Israel:

> ... On the basis of the new data from Alalakh and particularly from Ugarit, dating from the 18th to the 13th century B.C., there is good reason to assume that the Samuel account [1 Sam 8:4-17] is an authentic description of the semi-feudal Canaanite society as it existed prior to and during the time of Samuel and that its author could conceivably have been the prophet himself or a spokesman of the anti-monarchical movement of that period.[14]

Not only does the passage accurately reflect Canaanite kingship in the Late Bronze Age, it represents a critique of kingship which has its roots in the very early tribal-league period in Israel. The theocratic pattern of life in the tribal league meant that Yahweh's rule over his people was to be expressed through charismatic leaders whom Yahweh empowered for a given task.[15] The desire of the Hebrews for a king, seen in terms of this ancient ideology, constituted rebellion against the divine ruler of Israel (cf. also Judg 8:23).[16]

This ideal of charismatic rule remained a powerful element in the northern kingdom long after dynastic succession had been accepted in Judah, as shown by the many occasions on which a northern king was designated by a prophet. Jeroboam I, Baasha, Elah, Zimri, and Jehu all received some degree of prophetic backing; the house of Omri did not. With this custom of prophetic designation, maintaining in another form the older pattern of charismatic leadership, Israel was naturally prevented from developing a firm principle of dynastic succession.[17]

The anti-monarchical attitude of the Samuel traditions can thus be illustrated from the Old Testament and from extra-biblical literature. But what was the relation of this attitude to the role of Samuel? As suggested by G. Ernest Wright, Samuel's creative contribution was a "compromise" whereby the old office of the charismatic judge was to be expressed through two persons, the prophet and the king, with the prophet retaining the direct charismatic authority of Yahweh, and the king playing a subordinate role as *nāgîd* or military leader.[18]

In other words, the tribal-league form of theocracy proved unworkable under constant Philistine military and economic pressure. Samuel, acting as judge, responded to the crisis by instituting a "limited monarchy" which would exist at the will and word of Yahweh, as revealed through the prophets. Only so could Israel's true relation to her divine king be preserved. Saul and many a later king fell, according to this prophetic point of view, because they refused to stay within the strictly prescribed bounds delimited by Samuel and his successors. Samuel thus laid the groundwork for the view of the monarchy in the northern kingdom. The "Samuel traditions" which represent him in this highly significant transitional role are themselves ancient and historically credible.

What of the remaining contradictions in the titles and roles attributed to Samuel? Here again much light has been shed on difficult problems, once the traditions themselves have been taken seriously, as in recent studies by Albright[19] and Weiser.[20]

(3) Samuel and the Cult

Seldom has it been recognized sufficiently that all of the traditions concerning Samuel, whatever their source or date, depict him in the closest association with the cult or with some public assembly of the league of tribes. The traditions which show Samuel in some cultic role may be outlined as follows:

1 Sam 1—3	Samuel's parentage, birth, and rearing at the Shiloh sanctuary, where he receives a prophetic call in the presence of the Ark.
1 Sam 7	Samuel issues the command to "put away the foreign gods" and calls "the house of Israel" together at Mizpah, where he prays and offers sacrifice, "judges" Israel, and leads in holy war.
1 Sam 8	Samuel meets with the "elders of Israel" at Ramah, and warns of the nature of the kingship which they are requesting.
1 Sam 9:1—10:16	Samuel, as a "man of God," presides over the local cultus at Ramah; here he is called a "seer" and appears in association with ecstatic group prophets.
1 Sam 10:17-27	Samuel calls the people together at Mizpah and chooses Saul as king.
1 Sam 11:12-15	Samuel assembles the people at Gilgal where they "renew the kingdom" and "make Saul king before

	Yahweh at Gilgal."
1 Sam 12	Samuel presides over an assembly at an unspecified place, and leads in a ceremony which has marked parallels with Old Testament covenant ceremonies, particularly the one depicted in Josh 24.
1 Sam 13:8-15	Samuel is expected by Saul to offer sacrifice at Gilgal. When Saul offers sacrifice himself, he is reproved for disobedience.
1 Sam 15	Samuel enforces the holy-war ban and executes Agag "before Yahweh at Gilgal."

The clear implication is that the involvement of Samuel in the cultus of the amphictyony is no creation of the Deuteronomistic historian, but is witnessed in every stratum of tradition which we possess. In Weiser's words,

> That the appearance of Samuel in the different Samuel traditions is almost without exception depicted in the framework of assemblies of all Israel or its representatives must, consequently, go back to historically reliable tradition. The understanding of this tradition does not necessitate as a preconception the supposed Deuteronomic pattern of judges.[21]

The many circumstantial narratives of Samuel's role in public assemblies support the summary given in one part of the tradition:

> Samuel judged Israel all the days of his life. And he went on a circuit year by year to Bethel, Gilgal, and Mizpah; and he judged Israel in all these places. Then he would come back to Ramah, for his home was there, and there also he administered justice to Israel. And he built there an altar to the Lord. (1 Sam 7:15-17; RSV)

The solution which most commends itself is that of Albright, which is supported in detail by the independent literary studies of other scholars, notably Artur Weiser. Albright proposes that Samuel was indeed reared at the Shiloh sanctuary in the last period of that shrine's existence as the sanctuary of the tribal league. Samuel, as is now supported by a 4QSam text, was a "Nazirite" (נזיר), and perhaps was jealous of the elevated status of the Levitical priests of the sanctuary. In the confused and desperate period following the fall of Shiloh, Samuel gained control of Israel as a result, we may suppose, of the prominence he had gained as a "seer" and a "man of God." Making no effort to restore a single sanctuary or a Levitical priesthood, Samuel instead encouraged charismatic leadership, carried on by the prophets and by a military leader or נגיד under his own direction.[22]

This reconstruction shows that "all the public roles ascribed to Samuel were probably correct — each in its proper time and place."[23] As one vowed to God he was a נזיר. The titles "judge" (שפט), "seer" (ראה), and "prophet (נביא) are also explicable:

> As charismatic leader of Israel he was automatically also a "judge," that is, a recognized arbitrator because of his inter-tribal role in the amphictyonic confederation of Israel. But as leader and patron of the ecstatic prophets, who had carried on their ancient functions as oracular diviners, he was also a *roʾeh*, a "seer." Furthermore, continuing ancient West-Semitic and specifically Hebrew custom, he was a *nabiʾ*, one called directly by God to his

service, outside hereditary office and royal appointment.[24]

Weiser's analyses of 1 Sam 7 — 12 and 1 Sam 15 tend to support Albright's reconstruction from the standpoint of tradition-criticism, and demonstrate that the Deuteronomistic historian had at his disposal an already fixed cycle of Samuel traditions, transmitted through cultic and prophetic channels, which were not greatly altered by the historian. These traditions bear the marks, as we have seen, of definite historical and geographical settings, and have as their primary *Sitz im Leben* the tribal-league assemblies carried out under Samuel's aegis.

The tradition of 1 Sam 12 is particularly interesting for the evidence it gives of Samuel's involvement in a covenant ceremony. The parallels with other covenant texts are many, including: the rehearsal of Yahweh's saving acts toward Israel in the past (vss. 8-13);[25] the announcement of curses in typically formulated antithetical conditions (vss. 14-15; the expected blessing formula is not fully represented);[26] the apodictic command for obedience (vss. 20-21);[27] and the concluding threat of curse if this obedience is not rendered (vs. 25).[28] Baltzer remarks, "the schema of the covenant renewal is preserved almost intact."[29] Samuel is depicted as "covenant representative, covenant mediator, and covenant intercessor."[30]

Another important text which illuminates Samuel's relation to the Israelite cultus is found in the story of his call, 1 Sam 3:1 — 4:1*a*. This tradition depicts Samuel's call to be a prophet in terms which specify that he succeeded the Shiloh priesthood in religious leadership, after being given the message of doom for that priesthood.

> And Samuel grew, and Yahweh was with him and let none of his words fall to the ground. And all Israel from Dan to Beersheba knew that Samuel was established as a prophet of Yahweh. And Yahweh appeared again at Shiloh, for Yahweh revealed himself to Samuel at Shiloh by the word of Yahweh. And the word of Samuel came to all Israel. (3:19 — 4:1*a*)

This tradition of a nocturnal revelation, undoubtedly preserved by prophets who looked to Samuel as their founder, explains and justifies a revolutionary transfer of authority from priest to prophet — a shift soon made absolutely necessary by the fall of Shiloh and the loss of the Ark. Thus, Samuel's involvement in covenant ceremonies and other cultic assemblies is given its ground in a call to exercise charismatic leadership as a *nābîʾ*. At the same time the priestly modes of revelation are expressly replaced by the prophetic "word of Yahweh."[31]

We conclude that when all the traditions in 1 Samuel are taken seriously, there stands out one group of narratives in which Samuel is the key figure, and in which a peculiarly northern and prophetic view is taken of the institution of monarchy. While these traditions do not represent any single continuous narrative sources, as was once thought, they are very similar in their basic emphases and motifs. We should doubtless look to northern prophetic or prophetic-levitical circles of the early monarchic period for the bearers of these traditions, for in such circles we would expect to find those who looked back to Samuel as their founder, and who stubbornly maintained the Samuelic attitude toward kingship — a view which had its roots in the tribal-league theocracy. Thus we are justified, as Weiser points out, in calling these texts "the prophetic traditions."[32] These traditions are certainly capable of exaggerating Samuel's role because of their peculiar *Tendenz*,[33] but the picture given of Samuel's part in the transition to monarchy is fundamentally historical.

(4) E and the Prophetic Traditions of 1 Samuel

The literary critics who ascribe the traditions of 1 Samuel to the Pentateuchal sources J and E have always identified the prophetic or "Samuel source" which we have been discussing as E.[34] This is no accident, for there are in fact many striking affinities between E and these traditions. The affinities are mainly theological; the occasional affinities in vocabulary and style are almost always associated with the theological motifs.

(a) Prophecy and the Prophet. — The outstanding feature of these traditions, as we have seen, is the way prophecy and the prophet stand in the center of events. This is true even though Samuel is expressly called a *nabi'* in only one tradition, the story of his call at the Shiloh sanctuary (1 Sam 3:1 — 4:1a).

The narrative of Samuel's call displays remarkable affinities with similar traditions in E, particularly the story of Moses' call, Exod 3:1, 4b, 9-13, 15. The parallel between Exod 3:4b and 1 Sam 3:4b is especially striking:

Exod 3:4	1 Sam 3:4
ויקרא אליו אלהים מתוך הסנה	ויקרא יהוה אל שמואל
ויאמר משה משה ויאמר הנני	ויאמר הנני

Like Moses, Samuel is called to exercise leadership over the people (Exod 3:10; 1 Sam 3:19 — 4:1) and to save them from a former oppression (Exod 3:9; 1 Sam 3:11-14). As is common in the E tradition, Samuel's prophetic revelation takes place at night (3:3, 15; cf. Gen 20:6; 28:10-22; 31:11; 46:2); the same motif appears in another Samuel tradition (1 Sam 15:10, 16).

Like the call of Moses, the call of Samuel stresses the auditory rather than the visual phenomena, even though the conventions of prophetic expression still call for the use of visionary terminology. Thus in 1 Sam 3:1, "vision" (חזון) and "the word of Yahweh" (דבר יהוה) are parallel, and in 3:15 Samuel's experience is called a "vision" (מראה), yet what is related in the narrative is the *word* which Samuel hears (vss. 10-14). Similarly the E tradition of Exod 3 emphasizes the word spoken to Moses, in contrast to the J emphasis on what he sees (cf. Exod 3:2-3 [J] and vs. 4b [E]).[35]

The prophetic role of Samuel is further defined in later passages in which he intercedes for the people (7:5; 8:6; 19:19, 23). The Hebrew word used for his prayer, התפלל, is the same as that used by E in speaking of Abraham's intercession (Gen 20:7). The role of Moses in E also involved his intercession, as in Num 11:2.

What is the significance of the emphasis upon the prophet as intercessor, in both E and the prophetic traditions of 1 Samuel? The most common answer has been that this intercessory role comes from an early phase in the prophetic movement — "from a phase," von Rad says, "in which this movement was connected much more closely with the sanctuary and the cult than at the time of the major prophets. Their office at that time was less the proclamation of eschatological messages than of authorized intercession."[36]

In the case of the Samuel traditions we can be more specific than this. Samuel's role as judge and revered seer would naturally entail his acting as intercessor for the tribes before Yahweh. Such action, as Weiser suggests, may be the basis for the tradition of Samuel's involvement in holy war,[37] although some kind of actual military leadership against the Philistines may well have been involved also. If Samuel's attempt at reform included the encouragement of charismatic leadership by local prophetic bands, we may assume that these $n^eb\hat{i}^{\,}\hat{i}m$ also came to share in the cultically connected function of intercession. This would explain Samuel's intercession, and would suggest that the E traditions stem from a period in the prophetic movement when this remained a major part of the prophet's role.

The prophet in the prophetic traditions concerning Samuel, like the prophet in E, has, therefore, these characteristics: he receives the divine word in nocturnal auditory revelations; he delivers this power-filled word to the people; he represents the people toward God as their intercessor. As the designated messenger of Yahweh he stands above the king; he is not only independent of the political order, he may be called to direct and order it by virtue of his own charismatic authority. Samuel, at any rate, had such authority, and we assume that the circles which preserve these traditions believed that the prophets were always intended to have it.

As F. M. Cross has observed, it is no accident that the office of the prophet, conceived in this way as a structure which limits the monarchy, should have arisen precisely at the time it did in Israel. Prophecy, as Samuel seems to have understood it, was a continuation of the charismatic order which prevailed in the period of the judges, but adapted to meet the situation in which monarchy becomes necessary for military and other reasons. In short, prophecy and monarchy in Israel began together and ended together hundreds of years later in the Exile.[38]

When we compare Samuelic prophecy with the prophetic role ascribed by E to Israel's ancestors we find striking similarities even in the depiction of Abraham. But the outstanding model and pattern of the prophet in E was Moses. In a pre-eminent sense Moses is the Lord's representative to Israel and to the great king of Egypt. He brings the people forth from Egypt; he judges them and leads them in holy war; he concludes the covenant between the people and their God; he intercedes for them in their apostasy. To him God speaks "face to face" and "mouth to mouth" and because of the certainty and power of this revelation Moses can rule the people by his word.

It would be difficult to escape recognizing that this E portrait of Moses is almost identical with the portrait of Samuel drawn by the prophetic traditions of 1 Samuel. In every respect Samuel fulfills the prophetic office of Moses, even to being covenant-mediator, holy-war leader, and judge. Both Samuel and Moses are distinguished by a prophetic role which is primarily one of acting rather than one of speaking; they do not deliver oracles only, but plunge themselves deeply into events by asserting their authority over the people of God.[39]

The most likely reason for the marked similarity in the depictions of Moses and Samuel is that the traditions were preserved in the same or related circles. Perhaps the historical figure of Samuel, as remembered by his followers, actually served as the *Vorbild* for the figure of Moses among the closely related E circle. At any rate such a relationship between the tradents of the Elohist materials and the tradition-school responsible for the prophetic traditions of 1 Samuel would explain the fact that the prophet in E is like Samuel, but is not like the classical *nābî'* of later times.

(b) Prophecy and History. — The affinities between E and the prophetic Samuel traditions extend beyond a mere mutual interest in and emphasis upon prophecy. The very understanding of historical events is influenced in both cases by prophetic conceptions.

The simplest way to state this is by comparing two accounts drawn respectively from E and from the Samuel traditions: Gen 20 and 1 Sam 15.

We have already pointed out in our discussion of Gen 20 that in E the whole narrative turns on questions of guilt, sin, and punishment.[40] Abimelech's taking of Sarah is not viewed as mere lust, or even primarily as a threat to the fulfillment of God's promise to Abraham, but as a sin against God and against his prophetic representative. Even though done in innocence (Gen 20:4-6), the act endangers the very lives of the king and his people. Only by Abraham's intercession can the king and his subjects be restored to health (20:7, 17-18).

The categories of sin and guilt thus resolve into the categories of obedience and disobedience. The king can be saved through the prophet's intercession if he now renders obedience. The contrast of this profoundly religious understanding with J's more "worldly" presentation (Gen 12:10-20) is evident.[41]

In 1 Sam 15, the whole history of the people of Israel is made to turn on precisely the same factor, the obedience or disobedience of the king. The issue — the *ḥerem* or holy-war ban — is itself significant, for this marks Samuel as an upholder of the ancient league traditions of sacral battle over against the encroachments of a secularizing monarchy. Nevertheless, the central point of the narrative is that God demands absolute obedience from the king, for he has sent the king on a mission as his representative (1 Sam 15:2-3, 18). The word of Yahweh through his prophet is that which will enforce this obedience through punishment, for the prophet also acts as Yahweh's appointed messenger.[42] To his commanding word no disobedience can be tolerated; Saul's sin is punished by the loss of his kingship.

Thus in both narratives we have a theological presentation of history. The categories of historical understanding are provided by Israel's covenant faith, as mediated through the prophet. The key issue is that of obedience to Yahweh's word. The words which conclude 1 Sam 15 read like a commentary on this major theme of the Elohist, as expressed most tellingly in the Abraham narratives, and above all in Gen 20 — 22, climaxing with the offering of Isaac:

> Has Yahweh as great delight in burnt offerings and sacrifices,
> As in obeying the voice of Yahweh?
> Behold, to obey is better than sacrifice,
> And to hearken than the fat of rams![43]

(5) Conclusions

The picture of prophecy which is drawn in the prophetic traditions of 1 Samuel is in every important respect identical with that given in the E traditions. The correspondences between the figures of Moses and Samuel are exceedingly close. In general, the two traditions use the same language of revelation, speaking in terms of visions and dreams, but emphasizing the auditory aspect of the revelation, the word of Yahweh. The primary time of revelation in both traditions is the night.

Both E and the prophetic traditions concerning Samuel show the prophet in a wide range of functions: he is not only the recipient of revelations and the messenger of Yahweh's word as thus revealed; he is also covenant mediator and intercessor for the people as they gather "before Yahweh."

In both traditions the charismatic leader is the prophet who, at least in the cases of Moses and Samuel, exercises also the authority and functions of holy-war leader and arbitrating judge. Both king and priest are pushed into the background by this prophet-judge, and the related charisma of the group prophets is simultaneously being brought under his control.

The understanding of history which arises in both traditions is distinctively prophetic, based upon the covenant categories of obedience and disobedience. We have already seen in a number of cases how this theological context enables the Elohist to see events in terms of clear categories of meaning and how he is even able, in a remarkable way, to formulate an overview of events to such an extent that the Elohist's thematic linking of events was noted by Wolff as an important stylistic feature.[44]

Weiser has commented upon the very similar ability to grasp events in a coherent pattern which is visible in the prophetic Samuel traditions:

From the point of view of the history of tradition and of literature a new manner of presenting and interpreting history is being worked out here which undertakes to explain what has happened and to render it intelligible from the religious point of view. In the background there stands the conflict between worldly and divine power, the clash between king and prophet or judge which brought strong feelings into this manner of regarding history.... The specially high esteem in which Samuel is held as a prophet in these passages shows that this form of the tradition was developed in the circles of the prophets who regarded Samuel as their ancestor. This is the reason too for the spiritual relationship with the E strand of the Hexateuch, which likewise, though only later on, arose out of the interpretation of history in these circles.[45]

Going beyond Weiser's suggestion, we would posit not only an extremely close thematic affinity, but a very close relation in time between the prophetic traditions of 1 Samuel and the Pentateuchal E traditions. Indeed, the parallels which we have noted indicate that the circles in which the two bodies of tradition developed were all but identical. If so, we must look for the origin of the tradition very early in northern Israel, among prophetic schools who looked back to Samuel as their founder and hero.

(B) The Elijah-Elisha Traditions

We have suggested an intimate relationship between E and the early prophetic traditions concerning Samuel, emphasizing especially the close similarity in the way the role of the prophet is described. In our consideration of the Elijah-Elisha traditions we shall note some of the same similarities with E in the standing of the prophet and in matters of prophetic theological emphasis. Above all, the evidence is very clear that the Elijah-Elisha traditions, like the traditions concerning Samuel as prophet and judge, were developed and passed on in northern prophetic circles.

We shall see, however, that the Elijah-Elisha traditions definitely reflect a somewhat different type of prophetism and a later historical context than the E epic. Our dating of E will depend in part on its relationship to both the Samuel and the Elijah-Elisha traditions.

(1) Literary Criticism

That the Elijah-Elisha traditions represent the deposit of independent northern prophetic traditions has long been recognized by most Old Testament scholars.[46] The Deuteronomistic historian's editing seems to consist of juxtaposing these older traditions with his other sources (e.g., the prophetic narratives of 1 Kgs 20; 22; which are thus placed in the context of Elijah's ministry and Ahab's reign), together with occasional comments and summaries which give the traditions their desired significance in the Deuteronomistic historian's over-all plan.[47] The traditions could not have received thorough and detailed reshaping at the hands of the later historian, as Nielsen suggests especially of the Elijah cycle,[48] in view of their magnificently vivid narrative style, the obvious signs of folkloristic embellishment through oral transmission, and the occasional lack of agreement with the Deuteronomistic aims and ideals. For example, it is difficult to imagine the Deuteronomistic historian, with his constant polemic against extra-Jerusalem worship, composing the story of Elijah's sacrifice upon the Carmel altar (1 Kgs 18).[49]

Most scholars conclude that the Elijah-Elisha narratives reached a fixed form long before the fall of the northern kingdom, and were put in writing by *ca.* 800 B.C. According to Albright,

> The Elijah stories cannot have been handed down long by tradition, since they bear a very close relation to the facts of external history as we know them from other sources, and since they are written in the purest classical Hebrew, of a type which can hardly be later than the eighth century.[50]

Fohrer states that "The formation and development of the Elijah tradition began shortly after the events around which it centers, and certainly reached a first conclusive stage by the close of the ninth century."[51] Pfeiffer dates the writing of the Elijah stories about 800 B.C., and that of the Elisha narratives about 750.[52]

The traditions of Elijah and Elisha which are embedded in 1-2 Kings cannot be made into biographies of the prophets, and it is even doubtful whether these narratives existed in the sequence in which they are now found before the Deuteronomistic historian's work. Instead, it is probable that the separate stories of the prophets were first passed on orally in the ninth-century circles of their followers, and were only later worked into cycles which give the appearance of continuity.[53] Thus Noth speaks of "certain narrative cycles which formed around each prophetic figure and which came to be transmitted in the circles of the *homines religiosi.*"[54]

The Elijah cycle as we now find it in the Deuteronomistic historian's work includes 1 Kgs 17 — 19; 21 — 22; 2 Kgs 1 — 2. The Elisha cycle, partly entwined with the Elijah narratives, begins at 1 Kgs 19:19 and continues to 2 Kgs 9, concluding with a postscript, 2 Kgs 13:14-21.[55] The close and complex relation between the two bodies of tradition, together with the obvious differences in the way the two prophets are represented, constitutes one of the standing puzzles of Old Testament study. Elijah figures mainly in dramatic events in which the rule of Yahweh is threatened, like the great scene on Mt. Carmel (1 Kgs 18), or the incomparable confrontation with Ahab in Naboth's vineyard (21:17-24). Yet the prophet himself is not the hero or the real center of interest: that place is reserved for Israel's divine Lord.[56] In the Elisha narratives the folkloristic element is much stronger, and Elisha himself takes the center of the stage as miracle-worker and mover of political events.[57] His pastoral role is much more fully elaborated by the tradition than Elijah's, and he appears in close association with the prophetic guilds. Yet, in spite of all differences, the two figures are very closely related in the traditions concerning them (e.g., 1 Kgs 19:15-18).

In addition to the complex relationship between the two traditions, which indicates that narratives "wandered" between Elijah and Elisha in the oral stage of transmission, there is a fascinating series of parallels between the Elijah-Elisha traditions and the traditions of the ministry of Moses. The most obvious allusions to Mosaic traditions include: Elijah's receiving bread in the morning and meat in the evening (1 Kgs 17:6, LXX; cf. Exod 16:8, 12); his conflict with the Baal prophets (18:20-40), reminiscent of Moses' conflicts with the Egyptian magicians (Exod 7:8-13, 20-22, etc.); Elijah's journey to Mount Horeb, where the Mosaic theophany seems to be recapitulated and reinterpreted (1 Kgs 19; cf. Exod 3; 19; 33-34); the passing of Elijah's authority to Elisha, reminding one of the Moses-Joshua relationship (1 Kgs 19:16-21; 2 Kgs 2; cf. Deut 31:14; 34:9); the manner of Elijah's death in an unknown place beyond the Jordan (2 Kgs 2; cf. Deut 34:1-8).[58] As suggested by these references, Elisha seems to play "Joshua" to Elijah's "Moses"; this is true especially in 2 Kgs 2, in which Elisha, after the death of his master, returns to Jericho after miraculously parting the water of the Jordan with the prophetic mantle which he has received (cf. Josh 3 — 4).[59]

The many parallels with the traditions of Moses' life indicate that the Elijah-Elisha circles kept alive the Mosaic traditions, doubtless in conjunction with the covenant traditions with which the memories of Moses' ministry were so closely bound up. This suggests a kinship with the Deuteronomic tradition, which likewise represents a northern circle which kept alive the covenant tradition in conjunction with the traditions of Moses' ministry.[60]

(2) Historical Background

The single most important fact in Israel's external affairs during the time span of the Elijah-Elisha narratives was the military threat from Aram. This threat, never absent as a ruling factor in the Elisha narratives, is also prominent in the Elijah traditions (cf. 1 Kgs 19:15-18) and in the prophetic traditions joined with them in 1 Kgs 20 and 22. From the time of the accession of Ben-Hadad I of Damascus (*ca.* 880 B.C.), the northern kingdom had lived under this constant military and economic pressure. In the time of Ben-Hadad II, Israel was for a time almost wholly occupied by Aram. Samaria itself was not taken, and the Aramean attempt to take it was repelled in a significant victory ca. 856 B.C. (1 Kgs 20).[61] Still Aram remained the strongest state in the Syro-Palestinian area. The defense of Israel against the Arameans became the crucial task of Omri (876-869 B.C.) and his immediate successors.

The shrewd policy by which Israel defended herself against the Aramean threat led, however, to very grave internal problems for the kingdom. Omri's solution was the marriage of his son, Ahab, to Jezebel, daughter of Itto-baʾal of Tyre (1 Kgs 16:31), and the result was the intrusion into Israel of the worship of Baʾal Melqart and Ashera.[62]

The toleration of foreign cults under Ahab was, on the face of it, little different from what had taken place under Solomon. Even the building of a temple to Baʾal Melqart in the newly-founded capital (1 Kgs 16:32-33) must have seemed a perfectly natural way for an alien consort to maintain ties with her gods. What was new was the vigorous persecution of Yahwism which arose, being especially directed against the prophetic groups (1 Kgs 18:3; 19:1-3; 21:25). It may be that the prophets themselves gave Ahab grounds for this persecution by their refusal to allow him the Solomonic policy of toleration. At all events the state was set for a furious struggle between the monarchy and the prophets.

Thus the Elijah-Elisha traditions are permeated with the dual threat of Aram and Baalism. Against these forces the prophets stood as champions and servants of Yahweh, addressing the people in judgment and challenge against Baal, while leading them in holy war against the Arameans.

(C) Prophecy and the Prophet in the Elijah-Elisha Traditions and in the E Tradition

A comparison of the description of prophecy and the prophet's role in the Elijah-Elisha traditions with that in E shows up many parallels, but also some important differences. Our discussion can best be carried out under headings which separate the complex functions of northern prophets in the ninth century.

(1) Relation to the Monarchy. — Like the E traditions and the prophetic traditions of 1 Samuel, the Elijah-Elisha traditions presume the prophet's priority over the Israelite king, and even over a foreign king. The absolute authority of prophets over the nation's political affairs was expressed by the use of royal symbols in describing their relation to Israel's divine King. That Elijah presented himself to Ahab and to all Israel as the court herald of Yahweh is suggested by the wording of 1 Kgs 18:15: יהוה צבאות אשר עמדתי לפניו ("Yahweh Sabaoth before whom I stand as servant/messenger"). In the famous encounter with Ahab in Naboth's vineyard, Elijah declares the divine "No!" which answers Jezebel's ironic query to the king, "Do you now govern Israel?" (1 Kgs 21:7)

The very specific involvement of Elijah and Elisha in the political affairs of the northern kingdom is evidenced above all by the part which the prophets played in the Jehu revolution. Jehu is anointed by a prophet dispatched by Elisha (2 Kgs 9:3, 6, 12), and then accepted and proclaimed king by the army, acting as representatives of the people. This is exactly the pattern of kingship which Samuel attempted to establish, and the ceremony has the same outline as that performed at the accession of other northern kings, notably Jeroboam I. Popular acclamation follows upon prophetic anointing, preserving the pattern of charismatic leadership inherited from pre-monarchical times.

The engagement of both Elijah and Elisha in military affairs, and the prominence of holy-war motifs in the traditions, show how deep this adherence to ancient theocratic ideals went among the prophets. Elijah, earlier protected by divine fire from the soldiers of Ahaziah (2 Kgs 1:1-17), is swept away from Elisha by chariots and horses of fire, and is acclaimed by his successor as the "chariot of Israel and its chargers" (רכב ישראל ופרשיו; 2 Kgs 2:12, *JB*).

Elisha, who received the same accolade at his death (2 Kgs 13:14), was even more deeply involved in holy war, as in the account of the battle with the Moabites (2 Kgs 3:9-27) and in the story of the prophetic instigation of the Jehu revolt, which took on the shape of a holy war against the Baal worshipers (cf. 2 Kgs 9:7-13). The holy-war ideology permeates the tradition of the siege of Samaria (2 Kgs 7), in which Yahweh gives victory through four lepers rather than through the king and his military establishment.[63] In the prophetic narrative of 1 Kgs 20, the unnamed prophet, like Samuel before him, enforces the *ḥerem* or holy-war ban against the Aramean captives whom the king intended to release (cf. 1 Sam 15). The tradition of Micaiah's oracle in 1 Kgs 22 shows the royal custom of obtaining prophetic oracles before battle, though Micaiah refuses to give the favorable answer expected.

We may conclude that the ninth-century prophets, like Moses in E and Samuel in the prophetic traditions of 1 Samuel, adhered to the traditions of holy war and to the ideal of charismatic rule implied in the holy-war ideology. The king ruled at the behest of the prophet, who stood as the servant and herald of Israel's God.[64]

(2) Prophetic Revelation. — That the Elijah traditions were preserved by circles which had reflected deeply on the nature of revelation is shown by the powerful narrative of Elijah's sojourn at Mount Horeb in 1 Kgs 19:9-18. This concern with prophetic revelation and a desire to see such revelation as continuing the task and role of Moses — these shine through clearly, even though the narrative as a whole remains opaque to modern interpreters.

In the key passage, vss. 9-15, difficulties abound. The traditional elements of early Israelite theophanies seem to be explicitly rejected as vehicles of revelation. Wind, earthquake, and fire occur, but Yahweh is not in them (vss. 11*b*-12*a*).[65] Finally there comes — nothing! Surely this is the meaning of קול דממה דקה.[66] In this silence the Lord speaks to his prophet with commands, "Go! Return!" The implication is surely that traditional forms of theophany, even the Sinai and holy-war images, are rejected, since these theophanic images are so closely bound up with the storm-god imagery of Baalism. What stands in their place is prophetic revelation.[67]

It could be argued, on the other hand, that the wind, the earthquake, and the fire precede the divine word precisely in order to mark the prophetic revelation as theophanic and as a sequel to the Mosaic revelation. The traditional theophanic imagery would thus be used in a positive manner, emphasizing Elijah's succession to the office of Moses. This would accord with the many other passages in the Elijah-Elisha traditions in which the events and patterns of Israel's Mosaic period are recapitulated in a new prophetically oriented setting.[68]

It must be admitted that the exact meaning of the passage remains enigmatic. The account is doubtless polemical or propagandistic, but the point of it is no longer clear.[69] Nevertheless, the general theological concerns of the narrator are transparent. The circle responsible for the tradition identifies the role of the prophet with that of Moses and is acutely concerned with the nature and authority of divine revelation for ninth-century Israel.

At a less exalted level, prophetic revelation takes place also through the time-honored means of the "angel of Yahweh" (2 Kgs 1:3), and through the ecstasy induced by music (2 Kgs 3:15; cf. 1 Sam 10:5). In no passage, however, does a night dream (חלום) or vision constitute the medium of revelation to a prophet.[70] This is significantly different from the language of E and from the prophetic traditions concerning Samuel; in both of the latter streams of tradition dreams played an important part. By contrast, the most frequent form of revelation in the Elijah-Elisha traditions is simply, "And the word of Yahweh came to him" (ויהי דבר יהוה אליו).[71] As we have seen, this expression is generally associated with the Deuteronomistic school and with Jeremiah, only appearing in the Pentateuch in Gen 15:1, a chapter which displays signs of later editing.[72]

We may conclude, then, that the three bodies of traditions under discussion all show their prophetic associations by the intense interest accorded the question of revelation. All three traditions present history as the fulfillment of the divine word communicated to prophets. In the E traditions and in the prophetic traditions of 1 Samuel, these revelations took the form of dreams or visions, even though the auditory aspects of the experience were usually stressed. In the Elijah-Elisha traditions dreams and visions are replaced by the formula, "And the word of Yahweh came to him."

(3) The Prophet and the Cultus. — In our previous discussion of Samuel's role, we postulated a prophetic attempt to control the league cultus after the fall of Shiloh, in the early years of the monarchy. We saw Samuel continually appearing in various cultic roles, and denouncing the king for attempting to displace him in the offering of sacrifice. We assume that the followers of Samuel would have continued to adhere to the "Samuel compromise" as an ideal, and thus would try to maintain charismatic control over the cultus, independent of the king.

There are signs in the Elijah-Elisha traditions that a prophet could still act as cult leader in the ninth century, though there is no indication that this was a permanent and regular prophetic function. In the contest with the prophets of Baal on Mount Carmel, Elijah certainly acts in a cultic role as an offerer of sacrifice and, in the present text, as covenant mediator.[73] The assembly of "all Israel" (18:19, 20) is like a gathering of the league of tribes; like Joshua at Shechem (Josh 24), Elijah challenges the people to choose the god whom they will serve, and to declare their loyalty.[74] Therefore, even if vss. 31-32a are, as many think, a secondary doublet,[75] Elijah is acting as covenant mediator in his capacity as herald of the covenant God; we have already seen this motif in the 1 Kings 19 narrative of the visit of Elijah to the site of Moses' theophany and covenant.

In other passages, both Elijah and Elisha act as intercessors, but there is no implication that this is thought to be an important constituent of their prophetic role. Their intercession for the widow in the parallel stories of 1 Kgs 17:17-24 and 2 Kgs 4:18-37 is a private matter and pertains to the traditional functions of men of God.

We may conclude that Elijah at least could act as a covenant mediator in the crucial period of conflict with Baal, and that another tradition represents him as concerned with the broken covenant (1 Kgs 19:10, 14) and perhaps as a second Moses. Otherwise there is no evidence that the prophets or the prophetic guilds had any clear-cut cultic functions in the ninth century. In this respect the Elijah-Elisha traditions distinguish themselves from the prophetic traditions concerning Samuel and from E: both of the latter portray the prophet in important cultic functions.

(4) The Prophet versus Israel. — Far more important for the history of prophecy than the still debatable relation of early prophets to the cult is a shift in the direction of the prophetic address; this change can be dated approximately to the time of Elijah. Whereas earlier prophets, from Samuel on, had addressed themselves primarily to the king, often announcing the divine judgment upon his acts, the prophet now steps into a new role as the proclaimer of the judgment of Israel's God against the whole nation. Where Samuel castigated Saul's disobedience (1 Sam 13; 15) and Ahijah denounced the sins of Solomon (1 Kgs 11), Elijah challenges *all Israel* to be faithful to the covenant. The ancient covenant relation thus received a fresh and profound interpretation under the impact of the Aramean wars and the crisis produced by the introduction of Baalism.

> The proposition that Israel belonged to Jahweh and to him alone, a belief deriving from the people's earlier days, no doubt found in Elijah a champion such as it had never had before, but at the same time he also was to say something about this relationship between Jahweh and Israel which went far and away beyond the nation's whole experience with Jahweh up to this time — Jahweh is resolved not to tolerate the apostasy of his people, but is about to rise up against them.[76]

G. Ernest Wright has stated that "The story of the prophet Micaiah in 1 Kgs 22 (vv. 17-22) furnishes the first documented and datable portrayal of the heavenly *rîb*" — the sentence of divine judgment pronounced in the heavenly assembly.[77] With this declaration of judgment Wright associates Elijah's address to all Israel upon Mount Carmel and the plaint that the whole people of Israel have forsaken the covenant, torn down Yahweh's altars, and killed his prophets (1 Kgs 19:14). Wright then concludes that "the same thematic interpretation of the Aramean defeats of Israel appears in the Elisha cycle of tradition (e.g. 2 Kgs 8:12-13), and, of course, this in turn is used by the Deuteronomistic historian (e.g., 2 Kgs 13:3-6)."[78]

This points up something new and profoundly important in the development of northern prophecy in the ninth century. The close relation to the monarch which was the common pattern in earlier prophecy now gave way to a new conception in which the prophet stood as the Lord's messenger of judgment against all Israel, including the king. To a certain extent this shift represents a break with the unworkable Samuel compromise, a turning to the entire people of God in the face of the monarchy's failure to obey and to live in the covenant relationship. Perhaps this shift was facilitated by the association of prophets with the league cultus, beginning with Samuel, which may well have been paralleled and continued as later prophets took a role in covenant renewal ceremonies. Certainly these ceremonies maintained, from earliest times, this direct address of God to all Israel. Under the pressure of Israel's ninth-century defeats the prophets are probably responsible for taking this form of address out of the cultic context and for adapting it to prophetic discourse.

When we examine the Pentateuchal materials which can be assigned to E, we do not find any reflection of this covenant-lawsuit or *rîb* pattern which Wright noted in Deut 32 and in later prophetic passages. The only E text in which there is a suggestion of Israel's breaking the covenant is the narrative about Aaron's golden bull in Exod 32. But this narrative implies, as we have seen, a polemic against Jeroboam's cultus and against an Aaronic priesthood, not a prophetic indictment of "all Israel" for breaking the covenant. The terrible seriousness of the Deuteronomistic literature and associated earlier literature (e.g., Deut 32) is lacking in the Elohist tradition. In E, hope still remains for Israel's obedience to the covenant. The defeat of Israel for abandoning the covenant is not yet in sight.

(D) The Relation of E to the Elijah-Elisha Traditions

In our very rapid survey of some central features of the ninth-century prophetic traditions we have seen both similarities and differences as compared with E. Certainly the Elijah-Elisha traditions, like E, reflect their prophetic provenance by their interest in revelation and by their emphasis on the office of the prophet as Israel's charismatic leader, superior even to the king. The exact means of revelation, however, were described differently; not once in the Elijah-Elisha traditions is there mention of prophetic revelation in a night dream or vision.

In both bodies of tradition the prophet could stand in close relation to the cultus as covenant mediator, as was also true of the prophet in the 1 Samuel traditions.

Most important of all, the Elijah-Elisha traditions, and the associated narrative of Micaiah ben-Imlah, displayed a much deeper emphasis on the divine judgment pronounced against all Israel. In a corollary development, the prophet stood forth as Yahweh's messenger to the entire people, in contrast to the earlier prophets whose audience and object of attack was primarily the king.

This lack of the prophetic *rîb* or lawsuit in E is paralleled by what we may deduce about the historical background of that tradition. The two great conflicts which faced ninth-century Israel — the conflict with Aram and the conflict with Baalism — are nowhere clearly reflected in the E traditions. In these, as we have seen, there is some indication that relations with Aram are still capable of peaceful settlement.[79] At the same time, no sign exists of the massive prophetic struggle with Baalism. The command, "Put away the foreign gods which are in your midst" in Gen 35:2 has nothing to do with Baalism. The almost verbatim recurrence of this command in a covenant renewal context in Josh 24 and in the ritual context of 1 Sam 7 shows that this is an old northern cultic formula used in preparations for covenant renewal and perhaps for holy war; the apodictic form suggests covenant-renewal as its original *Sitz im Leben*.[80] There remains no passage which implies the struggle against paganism which beset Israel from the ninth century until the nation's downfall.[81]

We conclude that the E tradition finds closer parallels, both in the historical background and in the development of prophecy which is reflected, in the prophetic traditions of 1 Samuel. The Elijah-Elisha traditions, while they show themselves to be part of the same stream of northern prophetic literature, display important differences which indicate that they spring from a later situation than the 1 Samuel traditions or E. In the next section we shall develop an argument for a more precise dating of E in the period between Samuel and Elijah.

(E) The Date and Provenance of E

(1) The Political Context

We have proposed that the origin of the E traditions must be sought in the period between Samuel and Elijah, and that there is evidence of closer connections with the situation of prophecy in Samuel's time and after (the eleventh and tenth centuries) than with Elijah's era. Hence we are led to consider the century following Samuel's ministry as the most probable time for the origin of the E tradition. At what point in the tenth century might this epic have been put into a more or less fixed form? What historical circumstances would call forth such a distinctively prophetic and North-Israelite molding of the common epic tradition?

Our first line of evidence is analogical. A number of scholars now accept as established the close connection of the Yahwist's writing with the revolutionary changes which brought Israel into being as an empire with a dynastic monarchy and a royal cultic establishment in Jerusalem. These vast changes culminated in the reign of Solomon, and it is to the reign of Solomon that the first Israelite historiography is attributed. The established monarchy, Israel's new place as a world power, the great economic success of the new kingdom, a splendid temple and a brilliant court: all these combined to produce a new atmosphere in which Israel sought an understanding of herself in her own sacred-historical traditions. Hence the composition, probably during Solomon's reign, of the J epic.[82]

By analogy we may assume that the composition of the E epic was also called forth by some important and profound change in the people's life and place in history, this time in northern Israel. Such a change occurred after the death of Solomon, *ca.* 922 B.C., when the northern section of the Kingdom broke away and established itself as an independent state with Jeroboam I as its king (1 Kgs 11:16 — 12:33). Just as David had "brought Shiloh to Jerusalem" by transferring the Ark to the seat of the monarchy,[83] so Jeroboam established his own rival royal sanctuary at Bethel, with another at Dan in the far north. The Bethel sanctuary had ancient associations with the tribal league and even a tradition of patriarchal founding. The capital of the new kingdom was Shechem, also a city with ancient cultic associations. Thus the new state was established with a rival cultic and political order which had its own claim to venerable precedent. These developments might well have provided the context for the composition in the new kingdom of a rival version of the old common epic tradition.

If we pursue the implications of the analogical argument, a new and more direct line of evidence presents itself. The division of the kingdom, according to ancient tradition (1 Kgs 12:1-20),[84] was the result of northern opposition to the oppressive policies of Solomon, and had its roots in a hostility to the Davidic dynasty. This is indicated by the repetition, "like a national anthem,"[85] of the outcry of earlier rebels against David:

> What portion have we in David?
> We have no inheritance in the son of Jesse.
> To your tents, O Israel!
> Look now to your own house, David!
>   (I Kgs 12:16; 2 Sam 20:1)

The rebels rejected the Solomonic pattern of kingship and returned to the earlier form of monarchy instituted by Samuel.[86] Jeroboam was first designated king by a prophet (1 Kgs 11:29) and then accepted as ruler by all of the people in an assembly at Shechem (1 Kgs 12:20).

Thus the northern monarchy in its inception was backed by northern prophets and was intended to follow the pattern of rule established between Samuel and Saul. This movement would provide a perfect situation for the composition of a northern version of the common epic tradition by members of a prophetic circle who adhered to the Samuelic compromise and viewed Israel's past in prophetic categories.

One element in the E tradition serves to tie its composition even more closely to the division of the kingdom and the reign of Jeroboam I. This is the polemical account of the making of the "golden bulls" in Exod 32. The text is clearly to be understood in relation to the new king's cultic establishment at Bethel.

(2) The Cultus of Jeroboam I

In an act parallel to Solomon's founding of the Jerusalem temple, Jeroboam set up his own royal sanctuary at the ancient shrine of Bethel, thus providing for the new nation an official cult center.

The details concerning Jeroboam's establishment are preserved by the Deuteronomistic historian in 1 Kgs 12. The tradition reports the setting up of altars at Bethel and Dan, and the staffing of these holy places with Jeroboam's own priesthood. The narrative further reports the king's designation of a pilgrim festival (חג) in the eighth month, over which he himself presided at Bethel (12:31-33).

The horrified interest of the historian focuses on the "calves of gold" which Jeroboam introduced into the worship of his kingdom, proclaiming,

(vs. 28) הנה אלהיך ישראל אשר העלוך מארץ מצרים.

Clearly the historian is concerned to condemn Jeroboam's action; he views the "calves" as idols to be worshipped as Israel's gods.

As is now recognized by a number of scholars, this interpretation completely misses the point of Jeroboam's action. What was involved was not an introduction of new gods or a return to paganism, but simply the introduction of a new type of cultic imagery, parallel to the cherubim of the Jerusalem temple. The bulls[87] themselves were not intended as representations of the Deity, but were the pedestals upon which Yahweh invisibly stood, just as he was said to be enthroned upon the cherubim.[88]

> In the primitive religions of Asia Minor, Mesopotamia, and Egypt, the sacred animal is not the god and is not confused with the god; it merely embodies his attributes, is an ornament of his throne or a support for it, or a footstool for his use. The Temple of Jerusalem had the Ark, and the Cherubim above it formed the throne of Yahweh; Jeroboam needed something similar for the sanctuaries he founded and he made the "golden calves" as the throne for the invisible godhead.[89]

The orthodoxy of Jeroboam's intention is shown by the very firmness with which Yahweh is identified as the God who brought Israel out of Egypt. The plural form of the verb in 12:28 does not necessarily mean that "your gods" is the correct translation of אלהיך, since *Elohim* can and frequently does take the plural verb. In any case, the singular verb in the same expression in Neh 9:18 establishes the meaning of the formula.[90]

The particular relevance of the bull symbol at Bethel, "the House (sanctuary) of El," is explained by the use of the bull as the symbol of El in Canaanite iconography and literature.[91] Hence, it appears that Jeroboam was by no means a paganizer or even an innovator, but was returning to an ancient El-symbol. The acceptability of an El symbol in the cult of Yahweh was made possible by the very early identification of Yahweh with or appropriation of the attributes of El. As a result, the most orthodox circles in Israel used symbols and language relating to El with no embarrassment, although they could never use Baal motifs in the same casual manner.[92] In any case, we can view the cultic establishment of Jeroboam as an orthodox attempt to rival

Jerusalem in every respect; possibly what was involved was a revival of very ancient symbols and practices current at Bethel and related to a patriarchal El cultus at that place.

We have stated, however, that the Exod 32 tradition preserved by E is presented in the form of a polemic against Jeroboam's cultus and against its Aaronic priesthood.[93] What would be the basis for such a negative judgment by the prophetic group who had supported the new monarch at his accession?

Plainly, Jeroboam did not adhere to the Samuel compromise once he was in power. The old struggle between prophet and king must have been promptly renewed; Jeroboam had the clear intention of reigning on the pattern with which he himself was most familiar — the Jerusalem (and Canaanite) pattern. This is demonstrated by his establishment of an official royal sanctuary, later described in Amos 7:13 as "a royal shrine and a national temple."[94] It is precisely this establishment, with its bull symbol and allegedly illegitimate priesthood which the E tradition of Exod 32 castigates.

As Frank M. Cross has recently argued, the polemic against Jeroboam and his establishment in both Exod 32 and 1 Kgs 12 could only come from the North. Moreover, it must stem from a northern group which has a special animosity towards Bethel, its priesthood (which clearly must have prided itself on its Aaronic ancestry) and its bull iconography. The most reasonable source of such a polemic is the Mushite (Gershonite) priesthood, also Levitical, of the ancient league shrine of Shiloh, whose iconography and priesthood had been inherited by the Jerusalem Temple.[95]

We are therefore attributing the Elohist epic to a group which we can best term "prophetic-levitical" which had close relations with or included members of the Shilonite priesthood and which also associated itself with the prophetic movement which had its origins in the time of Samuel.[96] This group continued to idealize Samuel's political and religious compromise — his vision of a "limited monarchy," with the chief limiting factor being prophetic spokesmen of Yahweh. Ahijah of Shiloh, the prophet who designated Jeroboam king in accordance with this ancient ideal, may have represented the very circle which is responsible for the Elohist epic. If so, he and those associated with him must have soon been disappointed in Jeroboam. The Elohist source as it stands might be said to represent both the ideal of limited or conditional monarchy under prophetic leadership, and disapproval of the way in which Jeroboam's new establishment failed to reflect this ideal, succeeding only in breaking the divinely ordained unity of Israel and putting in its place a rather pale imitation of the Solomonic establishment against which he and his supporters had once rebelled.[97]

It appears likely, therefore, that the E epic arose and received its peculiar stamp in a north-Israelite prophetic-levitical circle during the eleventh and tenth centuries, with the lifetime of Samuel being the period in which the process of formulation began. The clear polemic against Jeroboam I and his Bethel sanctuary suggests the late tenth century as the *terminus ad quem* of this process, since the site of Bethel soon passed into the control of Rehoboam and was held by the southern Kingdom of Judah for more than a century afterwards.[98]

(3) E as a Tenth-Century Collection

We have proposed as a context for the final formulation of the Elohist epic the northern kingdom, shortly after the division of the kingdom in *ca.* 922 B.C., and have identified the tradition-circle responsible as a prophetic-levitical school in the North descending from the era of Samuel.

Such a dating of E contrasts so sharply with most earlier works that we must state how this date explains commonly accepted characteristics of E more satisfactorily than the previously almost universal eighth-century date.

The literary-critical argument for the eighth-century dating of E proceeded in two stages. First, E was dated as relatively later than J. Then an appropriate date was sought for E, in accordance with some evolutionary scheme of the development of Israel's religion.

In both stages of this argument, four characteristics of E were appealed to: (1) the interest in prophecy; (2) the lack of anthropomorphism in representations of the Deity, gross features of earlier theophanies being replaced by the appearance or speaking of God in a dream or vision; (3) a higher ethical sensibility than that apparent in J, since the E traditions attempt to exculpate the patriarchs when their actions are morally dubious (e.g., Gen 20:12; 31:1-16); (4) a more developed and reflective view of history than J's. These characteristics were almost unanimously thought to point to a date in the eighth century, in the beginnings of classical prophetism.[99]

Even if we accept the above description of E's characteristics, tendentious as it may be, we can explain these characteristics more pointedly in a tenth-century prophetic-levitical context, once it is granted that the basic faith and institutions of Israel were already established long before the prophetic movement of the eighth century.[100]

In the tenth-century prophetic milieu there would naturally be great interest in the problems of revelation, and a natural tendency to picture the great figures of Israel's past as prophets. The common device of the dream or vision in revelations of the Deity — which is certainly extremely ancient in Near Eastern religions[101] — is the result of this prophetic milieu, not of a higher degree of theological sophistication than J displays. In other words, the dream or vision as a device of the narrator has nothing to do with "anti-anthropomorphism"; it simply reflects the prophetic categories in which a circle close to early prophecy would think.[102]

The same can be said for the view of history which is taken in E. The Elohist's understanding of history is not more "advanced" than J's; it is more unified and simple because it is the product of a specific prophetic milieu. In fact, the scope of E's understanding, like the scope of the epic itself, is narrower, less cosmopolitan, less subtle than J's, precisely because in the

Elohist everything is brought captive to prophetic categories.

The tenth-century date for E, then, can explain its peculiarities more simply and more credibly than an eighth-century date, and can explain them in a way which is less bound up with nineteenth-century historiographical and philosophical ideas. In addition, the tenth-century date makes the prophetic emphasis of E come through in a more pointed and sharply focused way. E's stress on prophetic categories and on the role of the prophet in events is now seen to reflect a definite polemic — a polemic which has a particular context and situation which is discernible in other north-Israelite traditions. In every depiction of a past hero as a prophet, in other words, there is an implied rebuke to the northern monarchy, precisely parallel to Samuel's rebuke of Saul and to Ahijah's castigation of both Solomon and Jeroboam I. Perhaps this polemic is specifically directed against Jeroboam's royal establishment at Bethel immediately after the division of the kingdom; there seems to be strong evidence for such a specific date and context. At any rate the prophetic emphasis long noted in the Elohist epic reflects the tense situation in the early days of the northern kingdom, when king and prophet vied for control of Israel and her destiny.

---

[1] The composition of the Books of Samuel was first analyzed critically by J. G. Eichhorn in his *Einleitung ins AT* (Leipzig, 1787), 3. 499-533. See Eissfeldt, *Introduction* 269-271 and Fohrer, *Introduction* 215-227 for surveys of critical treatments since Eichhorn.

[2] Cf. Wellhausen, *Composition* 238-266; Otto Thenius, *Die Bücher Samuelis* (ed. Max Löhr, Leipzig: S. Hirzel, 1898); H. P. Smith, *A Critical and Exegetical Commentary on the Books of Samuel*, ICC (New York: Scribners, 1929). Cf. Norman Snaith, "The Historical Books," *OT and Modern Study* 97-102.

[3] First by Karl Budde, *Die Bücher Samuel*, KHCAT vol. 7 (ed. Karl Marti, Tübingen: J. C. B. Mohr, 1902). So also in Carl Cornill's *Introduction to the Canonical Books of the OT* (New York: Scribners, 1907). The relation of the sources of 1-2 Samuel to the Pentateuchal sources is still maintained by Eissfeldt in his *Introduction* (pp. 271-280) and by Gustav Hölscher, *Geschichtsschreibung in Israel* (Lund: C. W. K. Gleerup, 1952).

[4] So Pfeiffer, *Introduction* 359-61.

[5] So Weiser, *Introduction* 166-170.

[6] So H. P. Smith, *Samuel* xv-xvii.

[7] Weiser, *Introduction* 166-167. Cross refers to most of these passages (he excludes 1 Sam 1 — 3 and 13:8-15 from his list) as "source B," calling it "the younger northern source" (*Canaanite Myth and Hebrew Epic* 220, n. 4).

[8] Smith, *Samuel* xviii.

[9] Pfeiffer, *Introduction* 363.

[10] Noth, *UGS* 54-61; cf. Wellhausen, *Composition* 238-248.

[11] Noth, *UGS* 54-56.

¹²*Ibid.*, 47, 55, 59-60.

¹³Otto Eissfeldt, *Geschichtsschreibung im AT* (Berlin: Evangelische Verlagsanstalt, 1948) 43. Noth himself ordinarily maintains that the Deuteronomistic historian follows the traditions which he employs, limiting his own work to arrangement and editorial comments and summaries; see *UGS* 100. Only in regard to the Books of Samuel does Noth suppose that the historian actually composed lengthy narratives out of his own imagination, or from very scanty older traditions. Cf. the criticisms of Noth by Weiser in *Samuel: seine geschichtliche Aufgabe und religiöse Bedeutung*, FRLANT 81 (Göttingen: Vandenhoeck & Ruprecht, 1962). See also Cross, *Canaanite Myth and Hebrew Epic* 274-289 for a recent study of the way in which the Deuteronomistic historian uses his materials to communicate his major themes.

¹⁴Isaac Mendelsohn, "Samuel's Denunciation of Kingship in the Light of the Akkadian Documents from Ugarit," *BASOR* 143 (1956) 17-18.

¹⁵Cf. Martin Noth, *Das System der zwölf Stämme Israels*, BWANT 4:1 (1930); Noth, *History of Israel* (rev. ed., New York: Harper & Row, 1960) 85-109.

¹⁶See Cross, *Canaanite Myth and Hebrew Epic* 219-229. Cross uses the terms "limited monarchy" and "conditional monarchy" in preference to "charismatic monarchy" or the like.

¹⁷The distinctive understanding of kingship which prevailed in the northern kingdom has been studied in detail by Albrecht Alt in "Das Königtum in den Reichen Israel und Juda," *Kleine Schriften* 2. 116-134 (translated in *Essays* 239-259). Cf. also "The Formation of the Israelite State in Palestine," *Essays* 194-205, and Cross's essay noted above (n. 16).

¹⁸See Wright's remarks in "The Lawsuit of God," *Israel's Prophetic Heritage* 63. Cf. W. F. Albright, *Samuel and the Beginnings of the Prophetic Movement* (Cincinnati: Hebrew Union College, 1961); Cross, *Canaanite Myth and Hebrew Epic* 219-222; John Bright, *A History of Israel* (2nd ed.; Philadelphia: Westminster, 1972) 181-190.

¹⁹*Samuel and the Beginnings of the Prophetic Movement*. See also Albright's *Yahweh and the Gods of Canaan* (London: Athlone Press, 1968) 180-185.

²⁰*Samuel: seine geschichtliche Aufgabe und religiöse Bedeutung*; also "1 Samuel 15," *ZAW* 54 (1936) 1-28; *Introduction* 166-170.

²¹*Samuel* 10.

²²Albright, *Samuel* 12-18.

²³*Ibid.*, 14.

²⁴*Ibid.*, 13.

²⁵Cf. Josh 24:2-13; Exod 19:4; 20:2. In spite of the many parallels with the ceremony of Josh 24, which lead Noth to think the Deuteronomistic historian is here simply copying that tradition, there are enough concrete references to a particular situation in the 1 Sam 12 text to indicate an independent witness to the same basic covenant form as that found in Josh 24. See J. Muilenburg, "Form and Structure of Covenantal Formulations," *VT* 9 (1959) 361-363. Von Rad ("Das formgeschichtliches Problem des Hexateuch," *Gesammelte Studien* 16-17, 63-64) had already pointed out the significance of 1 Sam 12 as an important summary of the *heilsgeschichtliche* tradition, though he had not analyzed, as Muilenburg did, the covenantal structure of the passage.

²⁶Baltzer, *Covenant* 66-67.

²⁷Cf. Josh 24:14, 23; Exod 20:3-17. On the analysis of the entire chapter as a covenant form, see especially *ibid.*, 66-68, and the Muilenburg article cited above (n. 25).

²⁸Cf. Josh 24:19-20; Deut 27.

²⁹Baltzer, *Covenant* 67.

³⁰Muilenburg, "Covenantal Formulations" 361.

³¹See Murray Newman, "The Prophetic Call of Samuel," *Israel's Prophetic Heritage* 86-97.

³²In concluding his analysis of 1 Sam 15, Weiser comments, "Kap. 15 bildet somit die logisch notwendige und darum auch geschichtlich wahrscheinliche Voraussetzung für die spätere Ausgestaltung der Tradition in den Kreisen der Propheten und auch der Kampf für die Durchführung und Reinheit der Jahwereligion, den der Prophetismus in Nordreich gegen das Königtum selbst in die Hand genommen hat, baut auf den Erfahrung und Erkenntnissen weiter,

die uns in Kap. 15 auf der ersten Königszeit überliefert sind." "I Samuel 15," *ZAW* 54 (1936) 26-27.

[33] E.g., the statement that it was Samuel who routed the Philistines from Israelite territory, 1 Sam 7:13-14. According to other evidence, it was David who finally eliminated the Philistine threat (2 Sam 8:1). Cf. Noth, *History* 187-189; Bright, *History*, 177-179; Weiser, *Samuel* 19-21. Weiser proposes that the report of Samuel's involvement in victory over the Philistines may be historical to the extent that Samuel, in his charismatic capacity as holy-war leader, declared the divine judgment against the Philistines, and interceded for Israel in its hour of threat. Surely Samuel's role as "judge" would involve some kind of war with the Philistines, in order to preserve Israel from becoming Philistine territory after the fall of Shiloh, ca. 1050 B.C.

[34] See Snaith, "The Historical Books," *OT and Modern Study* 97-99.

[35] The prominence of speaking and hearing in E may be a result of the emphasis on prophecy, as opposed to the theophanic pattern in J. Cf. Newman, *People of the Covenant* 47-49.

[36] von Rad, *Genesis* 228.

[37] Weiser, *Samuel* 19-21; cf. n. 33 above.

[38] Cross, *Canaanite Myth and Hebrew Epic* 223.

[39] von Rad, *Theology* 1. 292-294.

[40] See above, pp. 21-22.

[41] Cf. von Rad's discussion of the J passage in *Genesis* 167-170.

[42] 1 Sam 15:1 (אתי שלח יהוה למשחך עתה שמע לקול דברי יהוה) For a discussion of the type of *Botensformel* underlying this verse, see Claus Westermann, *Basic Forms of Prophetic Speech* (Philadelphia: Westminster, 1967) 90-128.

[43] Weiser (*Samuel* 10-12) points out that this prophetic pronouncement has nothing to do with a general condemnation of cultic sacrifices, but refers to the immediate situation, in which Saul has taken it upon himself to save some of the captured animals for sacrifice, thus disobeying Samuel's directive. Contrast Albright's remarks, identifying Samuel with a general prophetic condemnation of sacrificial ritual. *Samuel* 17-19.

[44] Wolff, "Elohistic Fragments," 167-170.

[45] Weiser, *Introduction* 167.

[46] J. A. Montgomery, *The Books of Kings*, ICC (New York: Scribners, 1951) 40-41; Pfeiffer, *Introduction* 403-408; Noth, *UGS* 78-80; Weiser, *Introduction* 176; Albright, *Stone Age to Christianity* 306-307; John Gray, *I & II Kings: A Commentary* (Philadelphia: Westminster, 1963) 335-337.

[47] Cf. Georg Fohrer, *Elia* (Zürich: Zwingli-Verlag, 1957) 45-47.

[48] Eduard Nielsen, *Oral Tradition: A Modern Problem in OT Introduction* SBT 11 (London: SCM, 1954) 77.

[49] This fact led Pfeiffer to postulate that the original Deuteronomistic author of Kings must have omitted these chapters, which were added later by another hand (*Introduction* 406). Surely it is more reasonable to suppose that the traditions were fixed before the time of the historian and that he, in accordance with his usual method, did not perform any basic alterations in them.

[50] *Stone Age to Christianity* 307.

[51] Fohrer, *Elia* 42.

[52] *Introduction* 403-405.

[53] Cf. Fohrer, *Elia* 45.

[54] *UGS* 78-80.

[55] Montgomery, *Kings* 41.

[56] von Rad, *Theology* 2. 24.

[57] *Ibid.*, 2. 27-28.

[58] Cf. Fohrer's list of parallels in *Elia* 48-50; see also R. P. Carroll, "The Elijah-Elisha Sagas: Some Remarks on Prophetic Succession in Ancient Israel," *VT* 19 (1969) 400-415; and Cross, *Canaanite Myth and Hebrew Epic* 190-194.

[59] See Carroll, "Elijah-Elisha Sagas" 404-405, 408-412.

[60] Cf. the suggestion of H.-J. Kraus, *Worship in Israel* 101-112, that the prophets inherited the

Mosaic role ("mosäisches Amt") through Samuel, the judges, and Joshua. Although it is still doubtful whether covenant-mediators or covenant messengers constituted an actual sacral office in Israel, it is interesting that E and the related northern traditions of Samuel and Elijah seem concerned to establish the relation of prophetic figures to Moses, and at the same time picture these figures in covenantal contexts: cf. Exod 19:3; 20:18-21; Num 12:6-8; 1 Sam 3:20; 1 Kgs 18:31; 19:8-10. Cf. Julien Harvey's arguments in support of Kraus in "Le 'Rib-Pattern,' requisitoire prophétique sur la rupture de l'alliance," *Biblica* 43 (1962) 172-196. See also Carroll, "Elijah-Elisha Sagas" for a defense of the position that Deut 18:15-18 explicitly refers to a "Mosaic succession" in prophecy and that the Elijah-Elisha tales are shaped to show that these prophets stood in the line of succession which reaches back to Moses.

⁶¹See Benjamin Mazar, "The Aramean Empire and its Relations with Israel," *BA* 25 (1962) 98-120, especially pp. 105-109, where Mazar takes issue with Albright's solution (*BASOR* 87 [1942] 23-25), and plausibly separates Ben-Hadad I and II. See also Bright, *History* 236-243.

⁶²On the identification of Baal Melqart, see Albright, *Archeology and the Religion of Israel* (4th ed., Baltimore: Johns Hopkins, 1956) 156-157, 229.

⁶³Gerhard von Rad, *Der heilige Krieg im AT* (Göttingen: Vandenhoeck & Ruprecht, 1958) 53-55.

⁶⁴See Cross, *Canaanite Myth and Hebrew Epic* 222-229.

⁶⁵With Montgomery (*Kings* 313) omitting vss. 9b-11a as secondary.

⁶⁶Cf. the translation of von Rad: "Die Stimme eines feinen Schweigens" (*Theology* 2. 33). Cross (*Canaanite Myth and Hebrew Epic* 194) says, "Yahweh passed in a 'thin whisper of sound' ... that is to say, imperceptibly, in silence."

⁶⁷Cross, *Canaanite Myth and Hebrew Epic* 190-194.

⁶⁸This interpretation was suggested to me by Prof. G. Ernest Wright.

⁶⁹Cross (*Canaanite Myth and Hebrew Epic* 192-193) resolves the problem by treating vss. 9b-14 as a doublet "which has obscured the interpretation of the climax of the legend." In this case the basic narrative is one of a visit of Elijah to Horeb to experience a theophany like that of Moses, after which Yahweh does indeed "pass by." Into this story has been inserted another tradition which has as its goal the denial of the expected theophany, since that would involve imagery of Yahweh as a Baal figure.

⁷⁰Unless this is implied by Elijah's "incubation" in the cave at Horeb, as affirmed by Cross, *ibid.*, 193.

⁷¹E.g., 1 Kgs 17:2, 8; 18:1, 31; 19:9; 21:17, 28. Cf. Fohrer, *Elia* 46.

⁷²See above, pp. 33-35.

⁷³Cf. Murray Newman, "The Prophetic Call of Samuel," *Israel's Prophetic Heritage* 95-97.

⁷⁴Cf. Josh 24:14-15, parallel to 1 Kgs 18:21.

⁷⁵Cf. Montgomery, *Kings* 304.

⁷⁶von Rad, *Theology* 2. 25.

⁷⁷"The Lawsuit of God." *Israel's Prophetic Heritage* 64.

⁷⁸*Ibid.*

⁷⁹Commenting on Gen 31:43-55, von Rad remarks, "It apparently goes back to a very old boundary agreement, which was made between Israelites (settlers east of the Jordan) and an Aramean tribe "Laban," and it must derive from the time of the first fairly peaceful encounter with the Arameans in Gilead. It was, therefore, a harmless affair in contrast to the deadly Aramean wars in which Israel was involved in the ninth and eighth centuries." *Genesis* 312.

⁸⁰Cf. Albrecht Alt, "Die Wallfahrt von Sichem nach Bethel," *KS* 1. 79-88.

⁸¹Even if an E tradition of the worship of Baal-Peor can be distinguished in the fragmentary narrative of Num 25:1-5, which is doubtful, the passage is not significant at this point. What is reflected here is not the great conflict with Baalism of the ninth and eighth centuries, but a fragment of an ancient tradition about early rebellion during the wilderness period — a tradition that once must have existed in fuller form, to judge from the many allusions to it in the OT; cf. Num 31:16; Hos 9:10; Deut 4:3; Josh 22:18; Ps 106:28. I am here disagreeing with Wolff, who is inclined to date the Elohist in the period between Elijah and Hosea, when the northern kingdom

faced the problem of syncretism in its most acute form ("Elohistic Fragments" 172-173). As will be seen below, I see a much more definite context for E in the struggles over the nature of monarchy and the founding of the northern kingdom in the 11th-10th centuries.

[82]Noth, *History* 220; Weiser, *Introduction* 92; von Rad, *Theology* 1. 49; G. E. Wright, *God Who Acts*, SBT 8 (London: SCM, 1952) 73, n. 1; John Bright, "The Modern Study of OT Literature," *The Bible and the Ancient Near East* 18.

[83]Otto Eissfeldt, "Siloh und Jerusalem," VTSup 4 (1957) 142; cf. von Rad, *Theology* 1. 42-43; Bright, *History* 193-197; Cross, *Canaanite Myth and Hebrew Epic* 229-237.

[84]The antiquity of this tradition is indicated by the remark in 12:19, "So Israel has been in rebellion against the house of David to this day." The tradition must have been fixed before the fall of the northern kingdom. According to Noth (*UGS* 79), it is part of an ancient and unified prophetic tradition concerning the reign of Jeroboam I, found in 1 Kgs 11:29-31; 12:1-20, 26-31; 14:1-18.

[85]Montgomery, *Kings* 250.

[86]Alt, "The Formation of the Israelite State," *Essays* 297-303, 318-321; Bright, *History* 220-229; Cross, *Canaanite Myth and Hebrew Epic* 222-223. A view of the split which very convincingly emphasizes economic and military factors which accompanied the ideological differences between North and South is found in Baruch Halpern, "Sectionalism and the Schism," *JBL* 93 (1974) 519-532.

[87]The word עֵגֶל could be used of a young bull, as in Ps 106:19-20, where it is parallel to שׁוֹר אֹכֵל עֵשֶׂב. Cf. Albright, *Stone Age to Christianity* 300, n. 33. In Ugaritic, the plural is used in one text for "year-old bullocks" (ʿglm dt snt); see C. H. Gordon, *Ugaritic Handbook* (Rome: Pontifical Institute, 1948), Text 51: VI: 42; cf. Glossary, No. 1449.

[88]Ps 80:2 (English 80:1); 99:1; Isa 37:16.

[89]Roland de Vaux, *Ancient Israel* (New York: McGraw-Hill, 1961) 333-334. See, in addition to the references cited above on pp. 50-52, O. Eissfeldt, "Lade und Stierbild," *ZAW* 58 (1940-41) 190-215; G. E. Wright, *Biblical Archaeology* (rev. ed., Philadelphia: Westminster, 1962) 148-149; Walter Harrelson, "Golden Calf," *IDB* 1. 488-489.

[90]A plural form is used with אלהים in Gen 20:13; 35:7 (both E). See F. M. Cross, Jr., "Yahweh and the God of the Patriarchs," *HTR* 55 (1962) 257, n. 141; Cross, *Canaanite Myth and Hebrew Epic* 73-74.

[91]The expression ṯr ʾil, "Bull El," occurs several times in Ugaritic texts (Gordon, *Ugaritic Handbook*, Text 49: IV: 34; VI: 26-27; Text 51: III: 31). See Cross, "Yahweh and the God of the Patriarchs," 258; *Canaanite Myth and Hebrew Epic* 74-75; M. H. Pope, *El in the Ugaritic Texts*, VTSupl 4 (1955) 35-41.

[92]Cross, *Canaanite Myth and Hebrew Epic* 3-75, 147-194.

[93]The Deuteronomistic historian's claim (1 Kgs 12:31) that Jeroboam's priests were not Levitical must have been prompted by their claim to such descent, as suggested by Albright, *Archeology and the Religion of Israel* 110; *Stone Age to Christianity* 299. Aaron's place in Exod 32 confirms the association of the bulls with the Aaronic priesthood.

[94]מקדש מלך . . . ובית ממלכה, using Bright's translation, *History* 233.

[95]*Canaanite Myth and Hebrew Epic* 195-215; see also Halpern, "Sectionalism and the Schism," *JBL* 93, esp. 519-520.

[96]We use the admittedly awkward term "prophetic-levitical circles" in an attempt to define as closely as possible the circles to which our investigation has led. The related circles responsible for the whole stream of northern traditions which we trace from "the prophetic traditions concerning Samuel" through E, the Elijah traditions, the Elisha traditions and Deuteronomy to Hosea are clearly sympathetic to prophecy and indeed idealize great figures from Abraham to Moses and Samuel by ascribing to them prophetic functions. Yet these circles are Levitical and they show the prophets in a close relation to the cultus, carrying out such Levitical functions as intercession, teaching, and covenant mediation. Cf. von Rad's discussion of the northern Levitical circles which he identifies as the tradents of the Deuteronomic tradition, *Studies in Deuteronomy*, SBT 9 (London: SCM, 1953) 60-69; G. E. Wright, "Deuteronomy," *IB* 2. 325-336. Kraus has used the

term "levitisch-nebiistischen" in his discussion of the identity of the בני הנביאים whom he links with the preservation of the Mosaic traditions and the transmission of the traditions about Elijah and Elisha in the ninth century (*Worship in Israel* 103). See also Wolff's essay, "Hoseas geistige Heimat," *TLZ* 81 (1956) 83-94, in which Wolff analyzes the relation of the prophet Hosea to these "prophetic-levitical" traditions.

⁹⁷In the light of Ahijah's later condemnation of Jeroboam, reflected in 1 Kgs 14, Noth has suggested that Ahijah and his group approved of the political schism from Jerusalem but condemned the break from the Jerusalem cultus, with its ties to the Ark of the Confederacy (*The Laws in the Pentateuch and Other Studies* [Philadelphia: Fortress Press, 1967] 132-138). Bright raises the question whether Ahijah might not have hoped for the restoration at Shiloh of the tribal-league cultus. *History* 234, n. 32. Both suggestions are probably correct, in the sense that the Ark-centered cultus of Shiloh had been transferred to Jerusalem.

⁹⁸See F. M. Cross, Jr., and G. E. Wright, "The Boundary and Province Lists of the Kingdom of Judah," *JBL* 75 (1956) 202-226, esp. pp. 222-23, where the argument is based on 2 Chr 13:19.

⁹⁹I have here summarized and synthesized statements of many scholars from the classic period of OT literary criticism. See J. Wellhausen, *Prolegomena to the History of Ancient Israel* (New York: Meridian, 1957) 361; Carpenter and Harford-Battersby, *Hexateuch* 1. 112. Otto Eissfeldt still maintains the description of E as less anthropomorphic than J in *Die Genesis der Genesis* (Tübingen, 1958) 30.

¹⁰⁰This view, of course, is gaining increasing acceptance. See George Mendenhall, "Biblical History in Transition," *The Bible and the Ancient Near East* 32-49.

¹⁰¹See A. L. Oppenheim, *The Interpretation of Dreams in the Ancient Near East* (Philadelphia: Transaction of the American Philosophical Society, 1956).

¹⁰²In any case, one cannot distinguish the age of the narrative strands by the criterion of "anthropomorphism," since all (including P) have anthropomorphic features; cf. Bentzen, *Introduction* 2. 50.

CHAPTER IV

E and Later North Israelite Traditions

In the last chapter we argued for a tenth-century dating of E. Viewing the E tradition in the context of early northern prophecy, we attempted to show that the type of prophetic activity and theology reflected there falls in the period between Samuel and Elijah. The new royal establishment in the North following Solomon's death, we suggested, must have provided the context for the crystallizing into written form of this distinctively northern version of the old common epic tradition.

In any event, there are evident connections between E and the early northern prophetic traditions concerning Samuel, Elijah, and Elisha, and we have had occasion to discuss these connections in some detail. How does E compare with the northern traditions whose fixation in writing was somewhat later? We shall answer this by discussing Hosea and Deuteronomy in relation to E and in relation to the whole stream of early northern traditions of which E is a part.

We cannot pretend to do this study in all the completeness and detail which it deserves. Such an undertaking would demand a separate volume, especially if the equally important traditions of Jeremiah were included in the analysis. We shall merely suggest the relevance of our study of E and related early northern traditions to a broader study of all the north Israelite traditions, and we shall ask whether our reconstruction of the development of early Israelite prophecy finds support from the texts of Hosea and Deuteronomy. If it does, then our early dating of E will gain in plausibility.

(A) Hosea

Parallels and similarities between Hosea and the Elohist epic seem especially susceptible to analysis because of the profusion of Hosea's references and allusions to events in Israel's history.[1] I will discuss the most recognizable of these direct and indirect references thematically as follows: Jacob, Moses, the Covenant, the Golden Calf, the Wilderness, and Kingship.[2]

(1) Jacob, Hos 12:3-7, 13 (EV 12:2-6, 12)

Hosea's use of motifs drawn from the Jacob narratives of Genesis suggests a direct familiarity with them as living traditions rather than a secondary literary use of them in some written form. With great freedom the prophet mentions — but not in chronological order — Jacob's birth, his flight to Aram, his theophanic experience at Bethel, his service for Laban to procure a wife, and his wrestling with an angel.

The references are thus to every basic motif of the Jacob tradition as we have it, but not to specifically J or E versions of that tradition. Indeed, there are clear signs that Hosea has access to an independent stream of tradition, perhaps oral, which does not duplicate in detail the JE narratives as we have them. For example, 12:4a (EV 3a) has Jacob "heeling" his brother in the womb rather than after their birth, as in Gen 25:25a. Jacob's weeping and beseeching favor is not contained in the parallel Genesis narrative of the encounter with the angel at Penuel (Gen 32:24-32), generally attributed to J. Hos 12:5b (EV 4b) parallels the J account of Jacob's stay at Bethel in Gen 28 in which the familiar J promise of progeny and land is given. But Hos 12:7 (EV 6), apparently intended to convey the content of Yahweh's promise to Jacob, in no way resembles the speech of Yahweh found in the J tradition of Gen 28:13b-15.[3]

We must conclude that Hosea, while richly illuminating the tenacity and continued vigor of the patriarchal traditions — perhaps especially strongly in the northern kingdom[4] — in no way demonstrates a direct literary knowledge of our J or E. Those like Procksch who claim that Hosea shows undoubted and exclusive knowledge of E cannot produce convincing evidence of such dependence on the basis of the prophet's references to the Jacob legends.[5]

(2) Moses and the Exodus, Hosea 9:3; 11:5; 12:14 (EV 12:13)

Similarly, with respect to the Moses-Exodus traditions, we must differ with Procksch, who states decisively, "There is, then, no basis here for presuming any other source for Hosea than E."[6] In detail there are as many allusions to J narratives as to E, or (as in the case of 9:3; 11:5; 13:4-6) the references are simply too general to specify the exact referent.

In only one important respect are we able to establish a connection with E and other early northern traditions. This is in Hosea's explicit description of Moses as a prophet in 12:14 (EV 12:13): "By a prophet Yahweh brought Israel up from Egypt, and by a prophet he was preserved" (ובנביא העלה יהוה את ישראל ממצרים ובנביא נשמר). Here, surely we are encountering a later echo from the northern tradition circles which we have discussed, including those responsible for E. We are reminded of the E narrative of the call of Moses (Exod 3:1, 4b, 9-13, 15) and of the narrative of Samuel's call (1 Sam 3), which interprets his ministry as prophetic even though the call takes a different form.

The Elohist's view of Moses' prophetic role was also evident in Num

11 — 12, where the seventy elders prophesy when a portion of Moses' spirit is given to them, and Moses is designated as the one with whom Yahweh speaks "mouth to mouth, clearly, and not in dark speech" (Num 12:8). We saw the same tendency to view Moses' ministry as prophetic in the Elijah-Elisha narratives, with their network of allusions to the Moses stories which are clearly intended to depict Elijah as a second Moses.

Because of this similar interpretation of Moses' role and significance we may assume that Hosea stands in the same line of northern prophetic-levitical traditions which we found reflected in E. The same conception of Moses' role appears later on in Deuteronomy. In the words of J. L. Mays, "This identification of Moses as the first of the prophetic succession appears in Hosea and then recurs in Deut 18:15ff., another clue that Hosea was connected with the circles whose thinking and faith constitute the background of the Deuteronomic outlook."[7]

Nevertheless, so far we have found only theological similarities between Hosea and E, not direct literary dependence of any sort.

(3) The Covenant, Hos 4:2; 8:12

The allusion to God's writing of his laws for Israel (8:12) is such a general reference that we cannot determine what version of the Sinai tradition Hosea knows. There are references to the tablets of stone which contained the "words" written by God in both J and E contexts (Exod 32:15-20; 34:1-4, 27-29) and a reference to Moses' recording of God's "laws" in Deut 31. There is no basis here for asserting that Hosea had an exclusive knowledge of one tradition as opposed to another.

In 4:2 Hosea makes typically free use of the contents of the Ten Commandments, specifically paralleling Exod 20:7, 16, 15, 14. Older scholars — Procksch, for example — felt that this allusion established Hosea's dependence upon E, since it was generally agreed that Exod 20:1-17 contained the "E Decalogue."[8] As we have seen, the relation of Exod 20:1-17 to the E Sinai account is problematical; the Decalogue could well be a secondary insertion into that narrative. Moreover, James M. Ward shows, in a special additional note on "Hosea 4:2 and the Decalogue," that we cannot be at all sure that Hosea is actually making reference to the Decalogue in 4:2, since the literary parallels are not precise enough to make that determination.[9]

It is true, nevertheless, that Hosea's strong emphasis on the covenant places him in the same stream of northern tradition which is represented by the Elijah-Elisha narratives and, as G. Ernest Wright has shown, by the Song of Moses, Deut 32. Precisely as in Deut 32 and 1 Kgs 18 the covenant in Hosea's preaching is a broken covenant, and all Israel is charged by the prophet with the crime of destroying the covenant relation in which Israel was intended to live.[10] This somber view of Israel's apostasy and the prophetic address to all Israel reflect a later development, as we stressed in Chapter III, than the Samuelic-Elohist view of the prophet's role. Yet the affinity of E with the general theological circles in which the prophetic lawsuit or *rîb* developed is increasingly clear.

(4) The Golden Calf, Hos 8:5-6; 10:5-6

In both passages in Hosea which mention the making of a calf (עֵגֶל), the allusion is to the bull images installed by Jeroboam I rather than to the E narrative about Aaron's bull, Exod 32. This is suggested by the fact that both passages have as their immediate context a condemnation of Israelite kingship. In addition, there is in the "Beth-awen" (בֵּית אָוֶן) of 10:5 an obvious sarcastic reference to the royal sanctuary at Bethel. The direct connection of the calf with Samaria in 8:15 establishes this as the frame of reference beyond any doubt.[11]

It is clear, then, that Hosea shares in the same prophetic condemnation of Jeroboam I which we saw reflected in the E tradition of Exod 32 and in the narrative traditions of 1 Kgs 12 — 14. Jeroboam's cultic establishment and the continuation of it by later kings constitutes a direct affront to Yahweh.[12] On this important issue Hosea thoroughly agrees with the E tradition circle and with the generally anti-monarchical bias of the northern prophetic schools. Again, we can establish an important theological affinity, but no direct literary contact between Hosea and the E epic.

(5) The Wilderness, Hos 9:10; 11:1-4; 13:4-6

The latter two of the three passages cited here make free lyric use of the wilderness theme without any clear reference to a specific Pentateuchal narrative. It is true that 13:4-6 might refer to the tradition which we have in Num 11, and Hos 11:1-4 might allude to the Baal-Peor incident of Num 25:1-5 (see below), but no more than a general knowledge of these traditions is necessarily reflected in Hosea.[13]

In Hos 9:10, however, the prophet clearly refers to the Baal-Peor story which we know from Num 25:1-5 and from other scattered Old Testament passages (Num 31:16; Deut 4:3; Josh 22:18; Ps 105:28). But as we have seen we cannot go farther than to ascribe the Numbers narrative to JE (see above, pp. 58-59). We must conclude that Hosea refers to wilderness narratives and motifs which are common to both J and E.

If there is anything in Hosea's use of these themes which is peculiarly prophetic and northern, it is in the exceedingly somber negative judgment which he passes upon Israel by means of these allusions. As James Ward suggests, Hosea radically reinterprets the meaning of the Exodus event so that, instead of being a signal demonstration of Yahweh's power and graciousness it becomes almost a "non-event" — an occurrence which made no impression whatever on the Israelites (Hos 11:2-3). Hosea apparently has taken the negative side of the Wilderness experience — the ancient tradition of Israel's murmuring and rebellion there — and has thrown it like a dark pall over the whole of the period of Israel's first deliverance so that it becomes, simultaneously, the moment of Israel's first rejection of Yahweh.[14] This reinterpretation of the Exodus in terms of the wilderness rebellion stories enables Hosea to present the divine *rîb* against his people with striking poetic originality and intensity.

(6) Kingship Condemned, Hos 3:4; 7:3-7; 8:4, 10; 10:7, 15; 13:10-11

One of the most persistent themes in Hosea's invective against eighth-century Israel is his flat condemnation of kingship. It was this condemnation of monarchy which Alt identified as the first bond linking the prophet Hosea with the Deuteronomic traditions and with earlier northern tradition circles.[15] In the day of punishment which is coming, the prophet declares, there will be neither king nor prince in Israel (3:4; 8:10; 10:7, 15). Kingship shatters the intimate father-son relationship of God with Israel — the relationship which stands for the covenant[16] — and as a result Israel is given kings only through Yahweh's anger (13:10-11).

It is this last proposition which aligns Hosea in the most striking manner with the prophetic traditions concerning Samuel and with the E school's indirect polemic against the northern kingship, as expressed especially in Exod 32. Like the "Samuel source," Hosea attributes the existence of kingship to the petition of the people. "Having a court was their idea, and the quotation [in 13:10] sounds like an echo of the old anti-monarchical source in the early chapters of Samuel (I Sam 8:6)."[17]

Just as is the case in the prophetic condemnation of the northern monarchy which we meet in 1 Kgs 12 — 14, Hosea's attack lumps together the monarchy and the cultic establishment over which the kings presided — in this case the infamous Bethel sanctuary with its bull icons. This is clear both in Hos 8:4-10 and in the parallel poem, 10:1-15, and it helps to explain the radical disapproval with which Hosea views the monarchy. Standing as he does within a circle which views the king as inheriting the responsibilities of the old sacral order which prevailed in the tribal league period, Hosea condemns him for failing to save the people from their foes and for establishing violence and perversity in place of the right order of the community. But this ancient and disregarded order of things which was supported by Israel's archaic sacral laws had its focus in the cultus. Therefore it is no wonder that a ruler who maintains a perverse and idolatrous cultic establishment will fail to "judge" Israel in all other significant respects as well.[18]

The most remarkable feature of Hosea's view of kingship, in any case, is the extremely radical way in which he condemns it, reaching back (if that is the point of the allusion to "the days of Gibeah," 10:9) to the very inception of the monarchy in Saul's time to find the point at which corruption began. The prophet's treatment of kingship is thus precisely parallel to his interpretation of the Exodus: what had been viewed in all or most circles in Israel as a marvellous example of Yahweh's gracious power is seen instead as the first occasion for his anger against a rebellious people.[19]

(7) Conclusions

Surveying the results of our discussion of Hosea in relation to E, we cannot find any evidence for a direct literary knowledge of the E tradition on the part of this prophet. It appears instead that Hosea made free and frequent use of the common epic traditions, which were still vital and far richer than we would expect on the basis of our written Pentateuch alone.

Theologically and ideologically, however, Hosea displays striking similarities with E and with the whole stream of northern traditions of which E is a part. This similarity is especially marked in the emphasis placed on the prophet's role in Israel's history and in the negative evaluation of the monarchy.

Equally significant is the way in which Hosea takes over and deepens the declaration of the divine *rîb* or lawsuit against Israel. He thus betrays a date later than E and even than the Elijah traditions, for the threat of Baalism and the failure of Israel's political institutions have reached an acute stage.

Our discussion of Hosea thus provides a larger perspective for our description of the early northern prophetic-levitical circles to which we attribute E, demonstrating the continuing vitality, right down to the end of the northern kingdom, of those tradition circles. In the oracles of Hosea we find, in an intensified and, indeed, a radicalized form, those theological emphases and religious insights which we first encountered in the E tradition.[20] In the light of this analysis it seems quite impossible that E should have arisen in the eighth century as a reflex of the prophetic movement which Hosea represents. The Elohist source is far too mild in its moral judgments and far too optimistic about Israel's future to be a product of the eighth-century prophetic milieu!

(B) Deuteronomy

Before discussing the relationship between Deuteronomy and the E tradition it would be well to make clear the critical assumptions which will underlie this discussion. The first of these is the very generally accepted theory that the "book of the law" promulgated during Josiah's reign in the seventh century forms the core of Deuteronomy, but that the work then put forward was based on a body of very ancient traditions, and was by no means created *de novo* by some seventh-century Judean author.[21]

Secondly, we are accepting without detailed discussion the northern provenance of the Deuteronomic traditions. Independently proposed many years ago by Adam Welch and Theodor Oestreicher, the origin of this body of traditions in northern circles has been well supported by the work of Albrecht Alt, Gerhard von Rad, and G. Ernest Wright.[22]

Northern provenance is suggested by the marked affinities of Deuteronomic theology and language with known northern literature such as Hosea and Jeremiah. Furthermore, the tradition lacks the characteristic Jerusalem emphasis on the inviolability of Zion and the Davidic dynasty.[23] In place of these royal themes we find in Deuteronomy a resurgence of holy-war ideology and covenant theology dating back to the tribal league.[24]

The prominence of Shechem in the cultic observances mentioned makes it probable that the Deuteronomic tradition stems ultimately from the sanctuary at Shechem. The form and style suggest that the book comprises an anthology of Levitical preaching and teaching which was given there in liturgical contexts, perhaps in covenant-renewal ceremonies.[25]

If the scholarly reconstruction here accepted is correct, then it is evident that Deuteronomy can be described as a "later northern tradition" only if one refers to the final composition of the Deuteronomic code in the seventh century. In fact, the Deuteronomic traditions must have existed in some form from the period of the tribal league. This means that it is a stream of tradition parallel to those which we have discussed, including E, and that some of the same tradition circles may have been involved in the preservation and transmission of all these related traditions.

(1) Deuteronomy and the Contents of J and E

Our first and most obvious task is to discuss the significance of the Deuteronomic use of the content of the earlier epic traditions. The two main passages containing historical retrospect, Deut 1:6 — 3:9 and 9:8 — 10:11, make a host of allusions to and even direct citations of narratives which we find in the Tetrateuch. We here rely on the extremely helpful tables presented by S. R. Driver in his classic commentary on Deuteronomy, listing in footnote form the passages which according to our analysis of E in Chapter II are certainly or probably E.[26]

A glance at the number of passages listed as "E" in n. 26 shows immediately, when this modest list is compared with Driver's entire table, that Deuteronomy is by no means solely dependent upon the E traditions. As a whole, in fact, more of the Tetrateuchal passages cited are from J than from E. This observation supports Driver's conclusion that Deuteronomy is demonstrably dependent upon the earlier epic traditions which are commonly designated "JE," but exclusively dependent upon neither J nor E.[27]

This lack of dependence upon E is as true of the section 9:8 — 10:11, considered by most scholars to be part of the original Deuteronomic work, as it is of the first historical retrospect, 1:1 — 4:43, which can be viewed as the work of the later Deuteronomistic historian.[28] The unusually heavy use of E in Deut 9 results from the subject matter — the story of the Golden Calf, which is basically Elohistic — rather than from any peculiar affinity with the content of the E epic.

Much the same can be said of the Deuteronomic use of earlier legal materials. The legal matter of Deut 12 — 26 is almost entirely based on the "JE" laws of Exodus, particularly the Book of the Covenant, Exod

20:22 — 23:33.²⁹ This heavy use of the Covenant Code does not prove a necessary dependence on E, even for scholars who attribute the insertion of this legal corpus to E, for the Code must have had an independent existence and a fairly general dissemination before it could become part of the Sinai tradition.³⁰

We must conclude, then, that the relation of Deuteronomy to E is not to be argued in terms of content. In both the historical and the legal sections Deuteronomy is demonstrably dependent on earlier formulations of tradition, but not exclusively dependent upon either our J or our E. The relation to E and other northern traditions must be sought in the realms of theological emphasis and stylistic convention.³¹

(2) E and Deuteronomic Theology

Here the situation is quite different. The theological motifs which indicated the close relation of E to the prophetic Samuel traditions and to the later Elijah-Elisha traditions, as well as to Hosea, are evident also in Deuteronomy.

The most salient of these recurrent motifs, and the one which characterizes the E tradition most clearly, is the interest in prophecy and the tendency to depict Israel's heroic leaders as prophets. The Deuteronomic expression of the same prophetic interest is found in the well-known passage promising revelation and leadership for Israel through a prophet "like Moses," Deut 18:15-18. Here Deuteronomy explicitly states what was strongly implied in the Elohist depiction of Moses — that he was in fact a prophet. Deuteronomy goes further than this and defines the place and context of Moses' call: it was at Horeb in the midst of the Divine self-revelation in which Israel entered into the covenant with her Lord. The purpose of Moses' prophetic role was plainly that of "mediation": "You said, 'Let me not hear again the voice of the Lord my God, or see this great fire any more, lest I die'" (18:16).³²

Moses is thus for Deuteronomy the prophet *par excellence*, and his office is explicitly that of covenant mediator. This depiction of Moses' role suggests the very type of prophetic leadership which we postulated for Israel in the eleventh and tenth centuries, beginning with Samuel's assumption of judgeship and charismatic control over a monarchy that was understood in strictly limited terms. Samuel's leadership came into focus again and again in cultic contexts in which he played the part of covenant mediator.³³ The same task was taken up by Elijah in the ninth century. Hosea, in the eighth century, appears to have derived his understanding of tradition from a circle which kept alive the same idealization of Moses as prophetic covenant mediator.³⁴

There can scarcely be any question that the Deuteronomic school stands in the same line of tradition with its depiction of Moses and its elevation of the role of prophet at the expense of kingship. Whether there was in fact an actual succession of covenant mediators — represented by Samuel, Elijah and by many an unknown figure in addition — must remain an open question, though some rather convincing arguments have been presented that there was at least a theory concerning such a succession of Mosaic covenant-mediator-prophets in north Israel.[35]

It is relevant at this point to raise the question again about the identity of the tradition circles in which these "proto-Deuteronomic" traditions were kept alive. Von Rad has insisted on "Levitical" circles because of the legal and pedagogical character of Deuteronomy,[36] while Nicholson attributes Deuteronomy to "prophetic circles in northern Israel,"[37] and Weinfeld has pointed to scribal circles within the wisdom tradition.[38]

We prefer the same designation which was used in Chapter III to describe the circles responsible for preserving the Elohistic and prophetic traditions of the eleventh, tenth, and ninth centuries — "prophetic-levitical." This designation preserves what has been correctly stressed by a number of scholars about the cultic and covenant-renewal background of Deuteronomy and acknowledges the deep interest of Deuteronomic circles in the prophetic role and the prophet's task in relation to covenant. In other words, northern prophecy undoubtedly continued a lively interest in, and participation in, the cultus, particularly in relation to covenant renewal and covenant teaching. The term "prophetic-levitical" reminds us of this cultic relationship and accurately describes — we believe — the circles out of which both the Elohist and Deuteronomy came.

If Deuteronomy stands squarely in line with previous northern traditions in its treatment of Moses and the prophetic role, the same distinctively northern emphasis can be detected in its discussion of kingship. Albrecht Alt has remarked on the striking absence from the "law for the king" in Deut 17:14-20 of any truly positive evaluation of the king's role in Israelite life:

> Indispensable as he might be for the healthy development of the people's life, Deuteronomy allows no sort of positive function to be ascribed to the king. This is true both in the area of military leadership and in administration of law. Deuteronomy handles both of these functions as basic components of the people's ordering of society; as a result it treats them in relatively great detail.[39]

Deuteronomy here echoes the northern prophetic traditions of Samuel in viewing kingship as an assimilation to the surrounding pagan cultures — an adaptation which Israel made by concession rather than an ideal institution (17:4; cf. 1 Sam 8). In the face of the developing monarchy the Deuteronomic circles, like the followers of Samuel, can only hope to preserve a vestige of the old order by viewing the king as subordinate to covenant law — presided over, presumably, by "a prophet like Moses" — and by keeping alive the tribal-league institutions of holy war and Levitical teaching.[40]

The Elohist epic, as we have seen, implies the same view of the monarchy through its indirect polemic against Jeroboam I and his cultic establishment at Bethel, and through its exaltation of the prophet as leader. Deuteronomy and the other northern traditions express this bias openly whereas E, perhaps because of the limitations imposed by the epic materials, could only suggest it indirectly.

A close similarity between Deuteronomy and E can also be seen in the broader and more subtle elements which make up an understanding of history. Like E, Deuteronomy envisions the goal of Israel's life in deeply religious terms.[41] Like E, and to an even greater degree, Deuteronomy views the whole course of Israel's history in terms of specifically religious categories. The result is the strongly didactic presentation of history, the merging of narrative into exhortation, which so unmistakably characterizes the Deuteronomic traditions. We found this same tendency in E, for example, in its treatment of each of the major figures of patriarchal times — Abraham, Jacob, and Joseph — who in their revelations of God by dreams and visions received an understanding of events and of their place in God's plan which came to expression in sermon-like dialogues.[42] There is good reason to think that the Deuteronomic understanding of history, which is so similar, developed, through centuries of use in covenant-renewal and similar ceremonies, directly out of this Elohistic understanding of history.[43]

Almost equally important as a distinguishing mark of the E traditions in the Tetrateuch was the theme of the fear of God, expressed by the verb ירא. We find this also as a recurrent motif in Deuteronomy, appearing altogether in sixteen passages according to Driver's tables.[44] This usage is significant when we consider that "fear of God" does not occur in passages derived from J at all.

As Weinfeld shows in his study of the "fear of God" theme in Deuteronomy — a theme which he uses as a major way of linking Deuteronomy with the wisdom traditions — fear of God or of Yahweh connotes first of all covenant loyalty, observance of the covenant stipulations, as in the Akkadian treaties.[45] Secondly, however, fear of God can imply an obedience to precepts of humanity, justice and kindness which are not enforceable by law, and depend ultimately on man's conscience.

It is the second meaning which is most similar to the Elohist's use of "fear of God." This meaning is exemplified especially well by Deut 25:18, in which the Amalekites' attack on exhausted stragglers in the wilderness is explained by the failure of "Amalek" to fear God. Fear of God here and in related passages thus stands as the only source of protection for the weak and powerless — those who are not protected by the regular legal norms of a community.[46]

This conception of the fear of God is very similar to that which underlies several Elohist passages in which the expression appears. Abraham was afraid of what might happen in Gerar because he assumed there was no fear of God in that foreign place, and of course he was not protected by the laws of the local community (Gen 20:11). Joseph could have arrested his brothers in Egypt — like Abraham in Gerar they were not protected by community norms — but he did not do it because he feared God (Gen 41:18).[47]

Such passages clearly establish the Elohist background of this important Deuteronomic concept of the fear of God. In both traditions, as in wisdom teachings, this awe or fear defines man's relationship to God in a way which transcends national and covenant communities.

Parallel to "fear of Yahweh" in many Deuteronomic passages is the command that Israel "hearken to the voice of Yahweh," which surely is to be understood primarily in relation to the covenant relationship.

This characteristic Deuteronomic expression, often found as שמע בקול יהוה,[48] occurs in only a few Tetrateuchal passages (Exod 15:26; 19:5; 23:21-22; Num 14:22). Only one of these, moreover (Exod 19:5), can be assigned to E with any certainty. It is thus, in these exact words, a rare expression outside of Deuteronomy itself — not, as Weinfeld says, already a "cliche" in JE.[49]

Nevertheless, the conception which lies behind "hearken to the voice of Yahweh" in Deuteronomy — a conception which ultimately dovetails with the related concepts of "fear of Yahweh" and "love of Yahweh" (cf. Deut 6:5) — is found in the Elohist in a very striking form, above all in the story of the offering of Isaac in Gen 22. In that E narrative, utter obedience and "fear of God" (22:12) coincide as they do in the Deuteronomic idea of "love." In that story the Elohist tradition deepens and intensifies the covenant demand for obedience and loyalty to a new and unprecedented degree. God is depicted as claiming man's life in a way and to a level which is so comprehensive that only Hosea or the Deuteronomist, using their language of love, could equal it.

Thus two important characteristics of the Elohist tradition — fear of God and absolute obedience to his will — are found in a central position in Deuteronomic theology. Furthermore, Deuteronomy is seen to echo the Elohist way of depicting history as a divine plan which at crucial junctures is led toward fulfillment by God's designated prophetic leaders and spokesmen. Finally, both the E and the D traditions set the prophetic leader — above all, Moses — over against the king, and both view the ideal king as a ruler whose power is strictly limited because it is exercised within a framework of covenant and charisma.

At the same time, there is obviously no question here of a mechanical "borrowing." Deuteronomy and the Elohist traditions must be seen instead as descending from a common source in north-Israelite tradition circles.

(3) E and the Style of Deuteronomy

It has proved impossible in our discussion of the theological similarities between Deuteronomy and E to avoid stylistic features, especially characteristic vocabulary. This is understandable because, as we have tried to show, theological and stylistic features go hand in hand when we are dealing with the work of a school of traditions rather than productions of single authors.

It also happens to be the case that most of the similarities in style which are not theologically conditioned vanish or become dubious under analysis. The Deuteronomic use of "Horeb" for Sinai and of "Amorites" for the original inhabitants of Canaan illustrate this. Both have been claimed as stylistic features shared in common by Deuteronomy and the Elohist.[50] But we have accepted Noth's argument that the appearances of "Horeb" in E texts are probably secondary.[51] Similarly the use of "Amorites" outside of Deuteronomy appears in passages which we cannot identify as E.[52] This kind of argument, then, is not a strong basis for comparing E and Deuteronomy.

When we turn to stylistic features which have some connection with characteristic theological themes the case is different. Both Deuteronomy and E, for example, speak emphatically of the fear of God. The use of ירא in this context is significant, as has been shown, in pointing up the distinctive religious and ethical conceptions which lie behind both Deuteronomy and E. Such examples as this strongly suggest that E and Deuteronomy drew upon a shared stock of theological ideas which were often expressed in the same or similar language.

The use of the verb "to serve" (שרת) constitutes another interesting sign of contact between the two traditions. Deuteronomy uses the term several times in speaking of the ministry of Levites or priests (10:8; 17:12; 18:5; 18:7; 21:5). We find it elsewhere in the Pentateuch frequently in P,[53] only one time in J,[54] and four times in E, where the derived noun משרת is used to describe the service of Joshua.[55]

It is quite likely of significance for identifying the circles out of which both E and D came that this term is preponderantly used by E, D, and the Priestly traditions of the Pentateuch. Such a shared vocabulary item as this suggests the kind of close relationship between prophetic and Levitical groups which we have suggested by using the term "prophetic-levitical" to describe the tradition circles in question.

Of considerable theological similarity is another stylistic feature found in both E and D. This is the use of the verb נסה, "to test," with the Deity as subject. We saw earlier that the Elohist explains Abraham's ordeal at Mount Moriah in Gen 22 as God's "testing" of him to see whether he was a man who "feared God" (22:1, 12), and that God tested the Israelites in the wilderness. The underlying idea, as Wolff comments, is that Israel's history is understood on one level as a series of ordeals by which God tests his people's obedience — an obedience which, as we have seen, is understood in the most comprehensive way possible, precisely because the testing strains man's endurance and faithfulness to the breaking point.

In Deuteronomy precisely the same conception of "testing" underlies the depiction of the wilderness experience in 8:2, 16. There Israel's hardships were meant to drive home the knowledge "that man does not live by bread alone, but that man lives by everything that proceeds out of the mouth of the Lord" (8:3). This utter dependence upon Yahweh's mysterious word is clearly also what Abraham learns in the ordeal recounted in Gen 22. That the same tradition circles were involved in developing this theological understanding of events seems evident.[56]

Other stylistic similarities may be important, but are more difficult to explain on the theological side. The recurrent Deuteronomic phrase "God of my (thy, etc.) father" is also found in a number of E passages (Gen 31:5, 29, 42, 53; 46:1, 3; 50:17; Exod 3:13-16). In the E tradition this phrase may reflect a desire to make explicit the identity of the ancient El deity of the patriarchs whose cult was perhaps still alive in the northern kingdom at the time of Jeroboam I, with Yahweh, the God of the Exodus tradition.[57] The phrase also serves to impress the Elohist's peculiarly religious stamp upon even such a worldly rascal as Jacob.

In Deuteronomy, similarly, the phrase "God of your fathers" ties together the events of Israel's sacred history — above all, the promise of the land and the deliverance from Egypt — into one coherent cluster which the Israelites can grasp: the Yahweh of Abraham, Isaac, and Jacob is likewise the God of Moses and at the same time the God of Josiah's Judah. This drawing together of historical events into a theologically-shaped pattern is characteristic of both E and Deuteronomy. It is a "prophetic" understanding of history, though it almost certainly had its main roots in the covenant prologues.

Finally, we should mention Deuteronomy's use of the verb התפלל, "to pray, intercede," in the narrative about the golden calf (9:20, 26). At first glance two occurences of this word, which appears a few times in E (Gen 20:7, 17; Num 11:2), but not in J, would not seem to provide evidence of affinity with E. But the use of התפלל in Deuteronomy is very significant, for this word is introduced by the Deuteronomic writer into passages where it does not occur in the Exod 32 tradition which is being followed. This lays heavier stress on the intercessory function of Moses, thus agreeing with E's depiction of the prophetic leaders of Israel as intercessors (cf. also Samuel and Elijah).

In dealing with theological and stylistic similarities between E and Deuteronomy we have avoided basing the argument on Tetrateuchal passages which have been claimed for both E and D. Such texts as Exod 19:3-6 and 23:20-33 display such remarkable similarities to Deuteronomic style and interests that they have in the past been regarded as secondary expansions by Deuteronomic redactors.

The tendency now is to regard such passages as E, in view of the improbability of any thorough Deuteronomic revision of the Tetrateuch.[58] In our discussion of these texts we were inclined to designate Exod 19:3-6 as E, but to associate 23:20-33 with the Covenant Code, which we do not regard as E. If the passages are both E, then the theological and stylistic similarities between E and Deuteronomy are considerably more extensive than we have indicated. No certainty is possible, however, precisely because their language is so close to what we expect from the Deuteronomic school, and because we do not have sufficient independent evidence of the style of E. Indeed, such passages could be called either Elohistic or proto-Deuteronomic, since the tradition circles in question appear to be all but identical.

(4) Conclusions

The results of this last chapter and of our entire investigation can now be briefly summed up. There is no doubt that the Deuteronomic tradition has close affinity with the north-Israelite traditions concerning Samuel, Elijah, and Elisha, and with the E traditions in the Pentateuch, as well as with the northern prophet Hosea. All of these tradition-collections are characterized by an emphasis on prophecy and by a negative judgment on the monarchy. At the same time one can observe particularly in the E tradition, a rather clearly defined interest in the nature and modes of divine revelation.

The interest in prophecy which we have mentioned takes a very specific form in two ways. First of all, the great leaders of Israel's sacred-historical traditions are pictured as prophetic spokesmen, intercessors and — in the case of Moses, Samuel and Elijah — as covenant mediators. Secondly, the prophet is pictured as standing over against the king and deriving his authority from Yahweh, in the pattern which Albrecht Alt called "charismatic kingship." In short, prophecy is not simply idealized in an abstract fashion, but is viewed as the most potent and legitimate representation of Yahweh's ultimate lordship.

Closely related to this emphasis on the role of the prophet is an interpretation of history which puts the patriarchs and especially Moses in the center of *Heilsgeschichte* and which views that sacred history in terms of a series of revelations and ordeals through which man is tested and led forward to the goal which God has opened up to him through law and through promise. This theological understanding of history in terms of prophetic revelations, leaders, and ordeals is especially evident in Deuteronomy and Hosea but is also suggested in Elijah's attempt to recapitulate the Mosaic experience and covenant in a time of grave crisis, in Samuel's rehearsal of Yahweh's saving acts (1 Sam 12) and in the whole body of the Elohist epic.

Finally, as we have seen repeatedly, there is the Elohist emphasis on the fear of God which is echoed in Samuel's condemnation of the Shiloh priesthood and then of Saul's disobedience, Elijah's demand for Israel's renewed loyalty to her covenant Lord and his condemnation of the house of Ahab, Hosea's renewal of the same demand for justice in the context of a divine *rîb*, and Deuteronomy's deepening of "fear of Yahweh" to involve the total loyalty of every Israelite as expressed in the command to love Yahweh with all his heart, soul, and strength.

We have seen that this associated body of traditions does not always share a common style or vocabulary, though certain phrases and concepts continue to reappear. The Deuteronomic style is highly rhetorical, doubtless developing in prophetic-levitical circles in the North but shaped by the peculiar demands of a preaching and teaching context. Hosea's style is highly idiosyncratic, although he draws on themes and reflects attitudes common to the whole body of northern traditions. In neither E nor the prophetic traditions concerning Samuel, Elijah or Elisha could we distinguish a unified style, but only a related theological outlook and a few set expressions which are shared in conjunction with theological emphases. In the case of the traditions which are found in the Books of Samuel and Kings, of course, the Deuteronomic editing has doubtless leveled out many of the stylistic differences between the original sources. In the case of the Elohist epic, its fragmentary preservation and a number of editing processes probably conspire to eliminate — though not entirely — its peculiarities of style.

The results of our entire investigation have been mainly positive, however. We believe that we have met or profitably assimilated the negative criticisms presented by Volz, Rudolph, Engnell and others who would discard the entire hypothesis of an originally independent E epic. A definable body of E traditions has been isolated and studied in relation to the history and traditions of the northern kingdom. This examination shows that, far from being of less significance or value than the J tradition, the Elohist passages represent the remains of a major and very early formulation of the ancient common epic tradition — a formulation which can with great probability be dated about two centuries earlier than had been thought.

It is undoubtedly this early dating of E and the delineation of the probable setting and circumstances of its composition which are the most original and controversial proposals of this book. We believe that we have shown, however, that such a date and setting for the Elohist epic is highly probable when one studies the whole stream of events and traditions of which E is a part.

The Elohist source of the Pentateuch thus takes its place as one of the earliest expressions of Hebrew literary activity and religious faith. The attitudes and beliefs which find utterance in this early body of traditions reach their culmination in the prophetic address to all Israel of Elijah, Elisha, Hosea and Jeremiah, and in the powerful expression of Israel's covenant faith in Deuteronomy. Through these later prophets and covenant spokesmen as well as through the Pentateuch itself the E traditions live on to become a formative influence in all later thought and belief in the Jewish and Christian communities.

---

[1] Not as much detailed work has been done on the relation of Hosea to E and other northern traditions as on the problems of interpreting Hos 1-3 and on textual and translation problems in Hosea; cf. the recent bibliography cited by J. D. Smart in his article, "The Book of Hosea," *IDB* 2. 648-653 and H. H. Rowley's survey, "The Marriage of Hosea," *BJRL* 39 (1956-57) 200-233. Some of the most pregnant comments are those of Albrecht Alt in "Die Heimat des Deuteronomiums,"

KS 2. 250-275, and those of H. W. Wolff, "Hoseas geistige Heimat," *TLZ* 81 (1956) 83-94. See also the list of works dealing with Hosea's historical allusions in Wolff's *Hosea*, BKAT 14 (Neukirchen, 1961) xxx-xxxi and more recent bibliographies cited by James M. Ward, *Hosea: A Theological Commentary* (New York: Harper & Row, 1966) 259-254; and James Luther Mays, *Hosea: A Commentary* (Philadelphia: Westminster, 1969) 18-19; see also Fohrer, *Introduction* 418-425.

[2] *Hos 4:2* (cf. Exod 20:1-17) *8:4-5*; *10:5-6* (cf. Exod 32; 1 Kgs 12:25-33; 13); *8:12* (cf. Exod 31:18; 32:15-16; 34:1, 28; Deut 31:9-11); *8:13*; *9:3*; *11:5* (passim in Exodus) *9:10* (cf. Num 25:1-5); *11:1-4* (passim in Numbers); *12:3-7, 13* (cf. Gen 25:22-26; 27:43; 28:10-22; 29:18-20; 30:31-31:20; 32:22-32); *12:14* (passim in Exod 3-4; Num 12; Deut 34:10); *13:4-6* (cf. Exod 17:1-7; Num 11:4-6). In the above list, passages from Hosea are italicized to make them stand out. References are to the Hebrew text.

[3] See Mays, *Hosea* 162-165, though Mays is more inclined to attribute differences between Hosea and Pentateuchal traditions to free variation and embellishment on the prophet's part than to actual variant traditions (see for example Mays' comments on Hosea's possible embellishment of the Jacob story, p. 164).

[4] *Ibid.*, 162-163.

[5] Procksch, *Elohimquelle* 248-255.

[6] *Ibid.*, 252.

[7] Mays, *Hosea* 170.

[8] Procksch, *Elohimquelle* 252; cf. S. Spiegel, "A Prophetic Attestation of the Decalogue: Hosea 6:5," *HTR* 27 (1934) 105-144.

[9] Ward, *Hosea* 243-245.

[10] See especially Mays' comments on Hos 4, *Hosea* 60-79.

[11] Kraus (*Worship in Israel* 152) interprets this verse to mean that an actual calf image was set up in Samaria. Mays is probably correct, however, in interpreting Hosea to mean simply that the Bethel-Dan calves were set up under continuing royal patronage.

[12] Hosea, of course, flatly assesses the bull cult as idolatry, regardless of Jeroboam's possibly orthodox intentions; this puts the prophet in direct agreement with the Deuteronomistic assessment reflected in 1 Kgs 12 — 13; cf. Ward, *Hosea* 146; Mays, *Hosea* 118.

[13] As Ward comments, it is surprising that Hosea's use of the sacred-historical traditions is so "lacking in particularity," considering the prophet's profound concern for the lessons which Israel should draw from these traditions (*Hosea* 198-200).

[14] *Ibid.*, 199.

[15] Alt, "Die Heimat des Deuteronomiums," *KS* 2. 250-252. Contrast H. S. Nyberg's theory that Israel's crisis, as reflected in Hosea, is purely religious and that the references to kings, especially in such a passage as 10:7, are actually references to the god *melek* or *Malik*. This theory is impossible, in view of such obviously historical references as 8:4; 13:10-11. Cf. the criticisms of John Mauchline, "Hosea," *IB* 6. 555-556, and H. S. Nyberg, *Studien zum Hoseabuch* (Uppsala: Universitets Arsskrift, 1935).

[16] As F. C. Fensham has shown, the father-son imagery here and in many OT passages is drawn from treaty or covenant language; "Father and Son — Treaty and Covenant," *Near Eastern Studies in Honor of William Foxwell Albright* (ed. Hans Goedicke, Baltimore: Johns Hopkins, 1971) 121-135, esp. pp. 132-133.

[17] Mays, *Hosea* 178.

[18] Cf. von Rad, *Theology* 2. 143: "The apparent split between religion and politics in Hosea is a modern distinction. For Hosea himself, living more fully than any other prophet in the old sacral thinking which saw life as a whole, Israel's political experience was in no way on a different plane. We must again remind ourselves that the charismatic structure of monarchy in the Kingdom of Israel was actually dependent on the active co-operation of the prophets. Thus, in his keen participation in political affairs, particularly in the revolutions at the court of Samaria, Hosea acted the part of a genuine prophet of the northern kingdom, and continued the line of action already illustrated by Elisha." See also Mays, *Hosea* 140-141.

[19]See Ward, *Hosea* 181-188. Mays (*Hosea* 143) and Ward both acknowledge the problems of interpreting this passage, which could also refer, through the "Gibeah" image, to the Benjaminite's rape of the Levite's concubine (Judg 19 — 21). Ward is inclined to focus on the associations of Gibeah with Saul and therefore with the origins of the monarchy; Mays thinks the rape is the primary event alluded to, with the Saul-monarchy allusion secondary. As frequently in Hosea, the power of his poetry consists precisely in the rich range and depth of the associations aroused by his images.

[20]Cf. Alt, "Heimat des Deuteronomiums," 273; Wolff, "Hoseas geistige Heimat," *TLZ* 81 (1956) 83-94; E. W. Nicholson, *Deuteronomy and Tradition* (Philadelphia: Fortress, 1967) 73-76.

[21]See Wright, "Deuteronomy," *IB* 2. 320-322, with the bibliography cited there. See also Fohrer, *Introduction* 174-175; Nicholson, *Deuteronomy and Tradition* 58-82.

[22]In addition to the works cited in n. 21 above, see T. Oestreicher, *Das deuteronomische Grundgesetz* (Gütersloh: Bertelsmann, 1923); A. Welch, *The Code of Deuteronomy* (London: James Clarke, 1924); G. von Rad, *Studies in Deuteronomy*, SBT 9 (London: SCM, 1953); Alt, "Heimat des Deuteronomiums," *KS* 2. 250-275.

[23]Alt, "Heimat," 265-266.

[24]See especially von Rad, *Studies in Deuteronomy* 45-73.

[25]*Ibid.*, 60-69; Wright, "Deuteronomy," *IB* 2. 326, 488-490.

[26]*Deut 1:8* (cf. Gen 22:16-18); *1:12* (cf. Num 11:17b); *1:13a* (cf. Exod 18:21a); *1:15* (cf. Exod 18:25); *1:17b* (cf. Exod 18:22, 26); *4:10-12*; *5:2-4*; *18:16* (cf. Exod 19:3-6, 9, 17b; 20:18, 19, 20, 21b; 24:12-13); *6:16* (cf. Exod 17:7); *8:15* (cf. Exod 17:6); *9:9* (cf. Exod 24:12, 18b); *9:12* (cf. Exod 32:7-8a); *9:13* (cf. Exod 32:9); *9:14b* (cf. Exod 32:10b); *9:15* (cf. Exod 32:15); *9:16* (cf. Exod 32:19a); *9:17* (cf. Exod 32:19b); *9:21* (cf. Exod 32:20); *9:22* (cf. Num 11:1-3; Exod 17:7); *9:27* (cf. Exod 32:11b, 13); *9:28* (cf. Exod 32:12); *10:11* (cf. Exod 33:1); *24:9* (cf. Num 12:10) *25:17-19* (cf. Exod 17:8-16); *26:6-8* (cf. Exod 3:7, 9). The passages in Deuteronomy are italicized in the above listing for more convenient reading. The references, which are only to the E passages quoted or alluded to in Deut, are drawn from Driver, *Deuteronomy* xv-xvii, 10, 19, 24, 29, 33, 42, 46, 51, 66, 112.

[27]*Deuteronomy* xix.

[28]Noth, *UGS* 12-17; Wright, "Deuteronomy," *IB* 2. 314-318; Cross, *Canaanite Myth and Hebrew Epic* 274. See pp. 60-61, above.

[29]See Driver, *Deuteronomy* vii-xiv; cf. C. M. Carmichael, *The Laws of Deuteronomy* (Ithaca: Cornell University Press, 1974), esp. 53-67.

[30]Cf. Procksch, *Elohimquelle* 271. See also Fohrer, *Introduction* 133-137.

[31]While most scholars have assumed Deuteronomy's dependence upon JE, von Rad has challenged this assumption, postulating the use of a briefer and different compilation of ancient narrative materials than JE. In any case, the Deuteronomic use of earlier materials is so eclectic and creative that we surely cannot argue a one-sided dependence upon any particular early source. See G. von Rad, *Deuteronomy* (London, 1966); Driver's discussion of the problem in *Deuteronomy* xiv-xviii; Carmichael's brief but helpful and up-to-date discussion in *Laws of Deuteronomy* 25-33.

[32]See Wright's comments, *IB* 2. 449.

[33]See above, pp. 104-105; cf. Nicholson, *Deuteronomy and Tradition* 77-78.

[34]See especially Wolff, "Hosea's geistige Heimat," and Nicholson, *Deuteronomy and Tradition* 73-76.

[35]In addition to the works cited in n. 34, above, see R. P. Carroll, "The Elijah-Elisha Sagas," *VT* 19, 400-415. The original argument for the existence of a succession of covenant mediators in Israel is presented by Kraus, *Worship in Israel* 108-112.

[36]von Rad, *Studies in Deuteronomy* 60-69. Von Rad, of course, is aware of some prophetic influence upon Deuteronomy, but thinks that this influence is no more than would be expected because of the prevalence of prophetic ideas in the religious life of the whole period ("Deuteronomy," *IDB* 1. 836).

[37] *Deuteronomy and Tradition* 79-82.

[38]Moshe Weinfeld, *Deuteronomy and the Deuteronomic School* (Oxford: Clarendon Press, 1972).

[39] "Heimat des Deuteronomiums," *KS* 2. 264.
[40] Cf. Wright, "Deuteronomy," *IB* 2. 441-442; Nicholson, *Deuteronomy and Tradition* 105-106.
[41] For example, Gen 50:18-21; see above, pp. 32-33.
[42] E.g., Gen 20:10-13; 31:4-13; 50:19-21.
[43] Cf. Weiser, *Introduction* 125.
[44] Driver, *Deuteronomy* lxxviii-lxxxiv. See also the shorter tables and discussion in Wright, "Deuteronomy," *IB* 2. 318-320 and the extremely helpful lists in Weinfeld, *Deuteronomy* 320-365.
[45] Weinfeld, *Deuteronomy* 274-281.
[46] *Ibid.*, 274-276.
[47] *Ibid.*, 275; cf. Wolff, "Elohistic Fragments" 161-167.
[48] E.g., Deut 4:30; 27:10; 28:1, 2, 15. Deuteronomy also uses this expression several times in referring to the Israelites' hearing the voice of God at Mount Horeb (e.g., 4:12, 15, 33, 36). Deuteronomy thus plays on the relationship between literal "hearing" of Yahweh's voice and the kind of "hearing" which signifies obedience.
[49] Weinfeld, *Deuteronomy* 337.
[50] For example in Wright, "Deuteronomy," *IB* 319.
[51] See p. 75, n. 114.
[52] E.g., Gen 15:16; Num 13:29; Josh 24:8, 15, 18.
[53] E.g., Num 3:6, 31, 36 in describing the ministry of Levites in the sanctuary.
[54] Gen 39:4, of Joseph's serving Potiphar.
[55] The verb itself is used in Gen 40:4 by E; the derived noun "servant" appears in Exod 24:13; 33:11; Num 11:28.
[56] Both the Elohist and Deuteronomy also refer to the people's testing of Yahweh through their rebelliousness in the wilderness (Exod 17:7; Deut 6:16), and Deuteronomy introduces the idea of Yahweh's "testing" of Israel in a curious way into the passage about false prophets, 13:4, where it is used as an explanation of the existence of such misleading spokesmen of Yahweh. As we have seen, the idea of the people's disobedience and rebellion and the concern for true prophetic spokesmen are both major concerns of the Elohist. See Wright's exegesis of the passages mentioned, "Deuteronomy," *IB* 2. 376-377, 385-389, 418-419; see also 320, n. 28.
[57] See Cross, *Canaanite Myth and Hebrew Epic* 3-75.
[58] See Wright, "Deuteronomy," *IB* 2. 319-320.

Index of Biblical Passages

Genesis

Reference	Pages
1—11	13, 19, 63-66
2—3	64, 65, 82 (n. 284)
2:4b—3:24	64
2:7	64
3—4	63
3:18a, 19b	64
4	65
4:1, 1b	65
4:2-16	65
4:16-24	64
4:17, 17b	65
4:25	65
4:26	65
5	65
5:28b, 29	65
11:1-9	64
12—50	6, 38, 20-39
12	61
12:1-3, 7	61
12:2	24
12:2-3, 7	35
12:10-20	6, 21, 69 (n. 4), 91
13:14-17	61
14:17	43
15	33-34, 61, 73 (nn. 82, 83)
15:1	25, 34, 98
15:1a	34
15:1abα	34
15:1bα	34
15:1-6	33, 34, 67, 73 (n. 83)
15:2, 2a	34
15:3a, 3b	34
15:4	34
15:5	24, 34
15:5-6	34
15:6	34
15:6-12	34
15:7, 13-16	61
15:7-21	33, 73 (n. 83)
15:12-16	34
15:13	34
15:13a	34
15:13b	34
15:13-14	34
15:13-16	34, 61, 67
15:14abα	34
15:14bβ	34
15:15	34
15:16	34, 129 (n. 52)
15:17	34
15:18	34
15:19-21	34
16:1	22
16:1-14	21
16:2	70 (n. 13)
16:3	70 (n. 13)
16:4-14	22
16:5	22, 70 (n. 13)
16:6	22
16:8	20, 70 (n. 13)
16:10	24
16:11	22
16:12	22
16:17	22
16:19	22
16:20	22
17	69 (n. 3)
17:3	20
17:9	20
17:15	20
17:18	20
17:19	20
17:22	20
17:23	20
19:29	20, 69 (n. 3)
20	11, 21, 22, 24, 26, 29, 30, 44, 57, 69 (n. 4), 71 (n. 33), 91-92
20—21	33
20—22	26, 92
20:1-17	6, 21, 26, 29, 67, 70 (n. 13)
20:3	20, 21
20:3-7	37
20:4	21
20:4-6	91
20:5	21
20:6	20, 21, 22, 89
20:7	21, 26, 54, 90, 91, 124
20:8	22

20:9	21	23	72 (n. 63)
20:10-13	129 (n. 42)	24:3	69 (n. 1)
20:11	20, 21, 22, 26, 121	24:7	69 (n. 1)
20:12	26, 37, 105	24:12	69 (n. 1)
20:13	20, 79 (n. 197), 110 (n. 90)	24:27	69 (n. 1)
20:14	22	24:42	69 (n. 1)
20:17	20, 21, 26, 124	24:48	69 (n. 1)
20:17-18	54, 91	24:60	24
21	22, 26, 71 (n. 33)	25—35	34-38
21:2	20, 69 (n. 3)	25:9-34	73 (n. 85)
21:4	20, 70 (n. 12)	25:11	20
21:6	20, 70 (n. 12)	25:22-26	127 (n. 2)
21:8-20	21, 70 (n. 12)	25:25a	113
21:8-21	11, 22, 24, 39, 67	26:6-11	69 (n. 4)
21:8-34	26	26:12-25	23
21:10	70 (n. 13)	26:17-33	21
21:11	24	26:26-33	22
21:11-14	22	26:32	23
21:12	20, 22, 70 (n. 13)	27	35
21:13	70 (n. 13)	27:1	25
21:17	20, 22, 24	27:18	25
21:19	20, 22	27:28	20
21:20	20, 22	27:43	127 (n. 2)
21:21b	70 (n. 12)	28	35, 73 (nn. 85, 86), 113
21:22	20, 23	28:4	20
21:22-23	22	28:10	35
21:22-24	22	28:10-22	35, 73 (n. 86), 89, 127 (n. 2)
21:22-32	11		
21:22-34	21, 23, 67	28:11-12	35, 39, 67
21:23	20, 23, 70 (n. 16)	28:11-22	38
21:25-34	22	28:12	20
21:29-30	23	28:13	35
21:30	62	28:13-14	35
21:31	23	28:13-16	35
21:33	26	28:13b-15	113
22	25, 26, 30, 34, 67, 71 (nn. 28, 30, 33), 122, 123	28:14	73 (n. 87)
		28:16	35
22:1	20, 24, 25, 26, 34, 39, 43, 76 (n. 145), 123	28:17	20
		28:17-18	35, 67
22:1-14	24, 26, 33, 39, 67	28:17-22	39
22:1-18	69 (n. 7)	28:19	35
22:1-19	24-26	28:20	20, 38, 73 (n. 87)
22:3	20, 24	28:20-21	74 (n. 98)
22:8	20, 24	28:20-22	35, 67
22:9	20, 24	28:21b	73 (n. 87)
22:11	24, 25, 39, 70 (n. 21)	29:1-30	35
22:12	20, 24, 26, 40, 122, 123	29:18-20	127 (n. 2)
22:14	24, 70 (n. 21)	39:31	36
22:15	24, 70 (n. 21)	29:31—30:24	36
22:15-18	24, 70 (n. 21)	29:32	36
22:15-19	24	29:33	36
22:16-18	128 (n. 26)	29:35	36
22:19	24, 26, 67	30—31	47

Index of Biblical Passages

Reference	Pages
30:2	20, 36
30:3	70 (n. 13)
30:6	20, 36
30:8	20, 36
30:14-18	3
30:16	36
30:17	20, 36
30:18	20, 36
30:20	20, 36
30:22	20, 36
30:23	20, 36
30:24	36
30:25—31:3	73 (n. 92)
30:25—32:3	36-37
30:30	36
30:31—31:20	127 (n. 2)
31:1	74 (n. 95)
31:1-16	74 (n. 95), 105
31:1-24	37
31:2	11
31:3	74
31:4-13	129 (n. 42)
31:4-16	11, 36, 37, 39, 67, 74 (n. 98)
31:5	124
31:5b	36
31:7	20, 36, 74 (n. 92)
31:7b	36
31:7-8	36
31:9	20, 36, 74 (n. 92)
31:10-11	36
31:11	20, 25, 36, 89
31:12	36
31:13	36, 38
31:14	37
31:16	20, 36, 74 (n. 92)
31:17	74 (n. 95)
31:17-24	36, 67
31:17-54	74 (n. 95)
31:18a	74 (n. 95)
31:19a	74 (n. 95)
31:20	74 (n. 95)
31:21	74 (n. 95)
31:22	74 (n. 95)
31:23	74 (n. 95)
31:24	20, 36
31:25—32:3	37
31:25-42	37, 67
31:29	37, 124
31:32-33	36
31:33	70 (n. 13)
31:42	20, 36, 37, 74 (n. 98), 124
31:43-54	37
31:43-55	109 (n. 79)
31:45	37, 67, 74 (n. 98)
31:46, 46b	37
31:48, 48b	37
31:49	37, 67
31:49a	37
31:50	20, 36, 37, 67
31:51	37
31:52	37
31:53	37, 79 (n. 197), 124
31:53-54	67
31:54	37
32:1	37
32:2	20, 36, 37
32:3	20, 36
32:3—33:20	37
32:13	24
32:22-32	127 (n. 2)
32:24-32	113
32:28	74 (n. 99)
32:29	20
32:30	74 (n. 99)
32:31	8, 20
33:4-11	37
33:5	20, 37
33:5-11	37, 67
33:10	20, 37
33:11	20, 37
33:18-20	74 (n. 100)
34	37-38
34:4	37
34:6	37
34:8-10	37
34:11-12	37
34:13-29	38
34:19	37-38
34:25-26	38
34:27-29	38
34:30-31	38
35:1	20, 38
35:1-4	11
35:1-5	39
35:1-8	38, 67
35:2	38, 101
35:2-4	53
35:3	38
35:5	20, 38
35:7	11, 20, 38, 79 (n. 197), 110 (n. 90)
35:7-8	39
35:9	20
35:9-13	69 (n. 3)
35:10	20

35:11	20	41:12	72 (n. 51)
35:13	20	41:13	72 (n. 51)
35:15	20, 69 (n. 3)	41:15	29, 72 (n. 51)
35:16-20	38, 39	41:16	20, 29, 45
37	29, 33	41:18	121
37, 39	28-29	41:25	20, 41
37, 39—50	27-33	41:28	20, 41
37:1-20	72 (n. 49)	41:32	20, 41
37:3-4	72 (n. 49)	41:33	72 (n. 50)
37:5-11	72 (n. 49)	41:34, 34a	72 (n. 50)
37:11	25	41:35, 35b	72 (n. 50)
37:19-20	72 (n. 49)	41:38	20, 41
37:20	28	41:39	20, 41
37:21-23	28	41:40	72 (n. 50)
37:21-24	28, 29, 67	41:40-45a	72 (n. 50)
37:23	72 (n. 49)	41:41	72 (n. 50)
37:25-27	28, 29, 72 (n. 49)	41:42-43	72 (n. 50)
37:25b	28	41:46b	72 (n. 50)
37:26-27	28	41:47	72 (n. 50)
37:28	28	41:49	72 (n. 50)
37:28a	28, 29, 67, 72 (n. 49)	41:51	20, 41
37:28b	28, 29, 72 (n. 49)	41:52	20, 41
37:28-29	28	41:54	72 (n. 50)
37:29-30	28, 29, 67, 72 (n. 49)	41:55	72 (n. 50)
37:32-33	72 (n. 49)	42	29-30, 39
37:36	28, 29, 67	42:1a	29, 67
38	29	42:2-3	29, 67
39	27, 29, 71 (n. 24)	42:6-7	29, 67
39:1	28, 72 (n. 50)	42:11b	29, 67
39:1-23	29	42:13-26	30, 33, 67
39:2	72 (n. 50)	42:14-16	29
39:4	71 (n. 24), 129 (n. 54)	42:18	20, 40
39:5	72 (n. 50)	42:19	30, 32
39:6	71 (n. 24)	42:22	30
39:7	25, 71 (n. 24)	42:26-28	29
39:9	20	42:28	20
40—41	29, 31, 39, 67, 72 (n. 50)	42:28b-38	30, 33, 67
40:1	25	42:35	29
40:4	129 (n. 55)	42:37	30
40:5	72 (n. 51)	42:37-38	30
40:6	72 (n. 51)	42:38b	30
40:8	20, 40, 41, 72 (n. 51)	43—44	30
40:12	72 (n. 51)	43:3	30
40:15	28	43:3-7	30
40:18	72 (n. 51)	43:8-10	30
40:22	72 (n. 51)	43:14	72 (n. 55)
40:50	72 (n. 50)	43:29	20, 42
41	33, 72 (n. 50)	44	30
41—42	33	44:13	30
41:1	34	44:16	20, 30
41:7	72 (n. 51)	44:18-34	30
41:8	72 (n. 51)	45	30
41:11	72 (n. 51)	45:1, 4	30, 72 (n. 58)

Index of Biblical Passages

45:2-3	30, 33, 68, 72 (n. 58)
45:3-8	31, 32
45:4-5	28
45:5	20, 30, 32
45:5a	72 (n. 58)
45:5-8	30
45:5-15	30, 33, 68
45:5b-15	72 (n. 58)
45:7	20, 30, 32
45:8	20, 30
45:9	20, 30
45:9-15	30
45:10	42
45:16-20	30
45:16-28	30, 72 (n. 58)
45—50	30-33
46:1	124
46:1-2	30
46:1-4	30-31, 32, 33, 39, 68
46:2	20, 25, 39, 69 (n. 3), 89
46:3	124
46:6, 6a	72 (n. 60)
46:6-27	30
46:7	72 (n. 60)
46:8-27	72 (n. 60)
46:13—47:5	30
47:11	42
47:13-28	31
47:17-22	33
47:27	72 (n. 63)
47:27-31	31
47:30	72 (n. 63)
48	31
48:1	25, 31
48:1-2	33, 68
48:2	31
48:3	31, 72 (n. 64)
48:4	31, 72 (n. 64)
48:7	31, 72 (n. 64)
48:7-14	31, 33, 68
48:9	20, 31
48:11	20, 31
48:15	20, 31
48:15-16	31
48:17-22	31, 33, 68
48:20	20, 31
48:21	20, 31
49	31, 72 (n. 66), 81 (n. 244)
49:29-33	72 (n. 63)
50	31
50:12-26	32
50:13	72 (n. 63)
50:15-21	31
50:15-26	31-32, 33, 39, 68
50:17	62, 124
50:18-21	129 (n. 41)
50:19	31
50:19-20	20, 129 (n. 42)
50:20	20, 31, 32
50:22-26	31
50:24	20
50:25	20, 62
50:25-26	42

Exodus

1—3	40-41
1—6	42
1—15	5, 6
1—34	39-54
1:1-7	40
1:8-12	40, 74 (n. 110)
1:11-12	74 (n. 110)
1:12	40
1:13-14	40
1:15	43, 74 (n. 109)
1:15-21	40, 68
1:17	40
1:20, 20a	40
1:21	40
1:22	40, 74 (n. 108)
2:5	70 (n. 13)
2:22	44
3	40-41, 89, 95
3—4	127 (n. 2)
3:1	41, 68, 75 (nn. 114, 119), 113
3:1b	40
3:1-6	75 (n. 119)
3:2-3	89
3:4	40
3:4a	75 (n. 119)
3:4b	25, 41, 68, 75 (n. 119), 89, 113
3:5	82 (n. 284)
3:6	41, 68, 75 (n. 119)
3:6b	40
3:7	40, 41, 128 (n. 26)
3:8	40, 41
3:9	41, 89, 128 (n. 26)
3:9-13	41, 68, 89, 113
3:9-14	75 (n. 119)
3:10	40, 41, 50, 89
3:11a	41
3:12	41, 59
3:12-13	43
3:13	41, 75 (n. 118)
3:13-15	41

3:13-16	124	11:2	42
3:14	41, 75 (n. 118)	13—17	42-43
3:15	41, 68, 75 (n. 118), 89, 113	13:17-19	5, 42
3:15a	41	13:18	42
3:17	41, 76 (n. 147)	13:20-21	43
3:21	42	14	42-43
4—12	41-42	14:2-4	5
4:1-12	42	14:5a	43, 68, 76 (n. 137)
4:1-23	42	14:5b	43
4:17	42, 43, 68	14:5-7	5
4:18	42, 44, 68	14:7	42
4:19	42	14:10b	42
4:20	43	14:11	42
4:20a	42	14:15aβ	42
4:20b	42, 44, 68	14:16a	42
6:2-3	75 (n. 117)	14:19	5, 42
7—12	42	14:19a	42, 68
7:8-13	95	14:19b	43
7:15	42	14:20a	42
7:15b	75, (n. 129)	14:21	5
7:17	76 (n. 147)	14:21b	42
7:17b	42, 75 (n. 129)	14:22	42
7:20	75 (n. 129), 76 (n. 147)	14:23	42
7:20b	42	14:25a	42
7:20-22	95	14:26	42
7:21a	75 (n. 129)	14:27a	42
7:23	42, 75 (n. 129)	14:31	42
8:8-10	75 (n. 129)	15	15, 43
8:18 (EV 8:22)	42	15:1b-18	43
9:8-12	42	15:20-21	43, 68
9:19-23a	42	15:20-25	42
9:22	75 (n. 129)	15:25	25
9:23	42	15:25b	63, 76 (nn. 145, 146)
9:23a	75 (n. 129)	15:26	43, 122
9:24a	42, 75 (n. 129)	15:27	42
9:25a	42	16:4	25, 76 (n. 145)
9:26	42	16:10	76 (n. 145)
9:31	42	16:11	76 (n. 145)
9:35	42	16:12	95
9:35aαb	75 (n. 129)	16:29-31	76 (n. 145)
10:12	75 (n. 129)	17	43
10:12-13a	42	17:1-7	127 (n. 2)
10:13	42	17:1b-2	43
10:13αא	75 (n. 129)	17:1b-2b	43
10:14a	42	17:1b-7	43
10:14aα	75 (n. 129)	17:2	43
10:15b	42	17:2c	76 (n. 146)
10:21-23	42, 75 (n. 129)	17:3	42, 43, 76 (n. 147)
10:22	42	17:3-4	76 (n. 148)
10:24αβ	75 (n. 129)	17:4-6	42
10:25	75 (n. 129)	17:4-7	43, 68
10:27	75 (n. 129)	17:5-6	76 (n. 147)
11:1-3	42, 75 (n. 129)	17:6	25 (n. 114), 128 (n. 26)

Index of Biblical Passages

17:7 .... 63, 128 (n. 26), 129 (n. 56)
17:7a .... 76 (n. 146)
17:8-16 .... 42, 43, 50, 52, 53, 59, 62, 68, 128 (n. 26)
17:9 43
17:9-10 52
17:11-12 43
18 .... 44-45, 76 (n. 156), 77 (n. 159)
18:1-12 44
18:1-27 68
18:1a 44
18:1b 44
18:2-4 42
18:2b .... 64, 76 (n. 154)
18:3b-4 44
18:5 44
18:6 44-45
18:8 44
18:8-11 44
18:9 44
18:10 44
18:11 44
18:12 .... 44, 45, 76 (n. 156), 78 (n. 193)
18:13-28 44
18:15 44
18:16 44
18:19 44
18:21 .... 44, 58, 128 (n. 26)
18:21-26 54
18:22 .... 128 (n. 26)
18:23 44
18:25 .... 128 (n. 26)
18:26 .... 128 (n. 26)
19 95
19—20 48-49
19—34 45-54
19:1-2a .... 47, 48, 77 (n. 160)
19:2b 47
19:2b-3a .... 47, 49, 68, 77 (n. 165)
19:3 .... 47, 78 (n. 178), 109 (n. 60)
19:3-6 .... 124, 128 (n. 26)
19:3-8 .... 47, 78 (nn. 170, 184)
19:3a 48, 49
19:3b-8 47-48
19:3b-9 47
19:4 .... 107 (n. 25)
19:4-6 .... 48, 49, 68, 77 (n. 165)
19:5 122
19:7-11a 47
19:8 47
19:9 .... 47, 48, 128 (n. 26)
19:10-11a 47
19:11 48
19:11b-13 47
19:12 47
19:12-13 .... 48, 82 (n. 284)
19:12-15 48
19:14-17 47
19:16 49
19:16-17 .... 49, 68, 77 (n. 165)
19:17 .... 47, 48-49
19:17b .... 128 (n. 26)
19:18 .... 47, 48, 49
19:19 .... 47, 48, 49, 68, 77 (n. 165)
19:20 .... 48, 78 (n. 177)
19:20-24 48
19:20-25 47
19:23 47
19:24 47
19:25 .... 46, 78 (n. 176)
19:29 47
20:1 45
20:1-17 .... 45, 77 (n. 165), 114, 127 (n. 2)
20:2 .... 107 (n. 25)
20:3-17 .... 107 (n. 27)
20:7 114
20:14 114
20:15 114
20:16 114
20:18 .... 46, 48, 49, 128 (n. 26)
20:18-19 49
20:18-20 49
20:18-21 .... 46, 49, 53, 68, 77 (n. 165), 109 (n. 60)
20:19 .... 48, 128 (n. 26)
20:20 .... 25, 48, 49, 128 (n. 26)
20:21 .... 48, 49
20:21b .... 128 (n. 26)
20:22 46
20:22—23:33 .... 46, 118-19
21:6 46
21:13 46
22:8 (EV 22:9) .... 46, 196 (n. 197)
22:11 46
22:28 46
23:20-33 .... 78 (n. 170), 124
23:21 62
23:21-22 122
23:28 62
24 .... 45, 49-50
24:1 .... 45, 50, 54
24:1-2 .... 49, 50, 77 (n. 165)
24:1-2, 9-11 .... 49, 50, 68

24:3	46, 77 (n. 165)
24:3-8	46, 49, 77 (nn. 165, 167)
24:4	46, 62, 77 (n. 165)
24:5	46
24:7	46, 77 (n. 165)
24:8	46, 77 (n. 165)
24:9	50
24:9-11	45, 49, 50, 54
24:9-15a	77 (n. 165)
24:10	49
24:11	49, 55
24:12	128 (n. 26)
24:12-13	128 (n. 26)
24:12-15a	50, 68
24:13	50, 52, 59, 129 (n. 55)
24:13-14	50
24:13-16	50
24:14	50
24:15b-18a	50, 77 (n. 160)
24:16-18a	78 (n. 192)
24:18b	50, 68, 77 (n. 165), 128 (n. 26)
25—31	50
25:1—31:17	77 (n. 160)
31:18	77 (n. 160), 127 (n. 2)
32	50-52, 53, 79 (nn. 196, 198, 199, 202), 100, 102-5, 110 (n. 93), 115, 116, 124, 127 (n. 2)
32—33	50, 53
32—34	50
32:1-6	50, 51, 52, 68
32:7	50
32:7-8	50
32:7-8a	128 (n. 26)
32:7-14	50, 51
32:9	128 (n. 26)
32:10	53
32:10b	128 (n. 26)
32:11-14	50
32:11b	128 (n. 26)
32:12	128 (n. 26)
32:13	128 (n. 26)
32:14	50
32:15	128 (n. 26)
32:15-16	127 (n. 2)
32:15-20	50, 52, 68, 114
32:16	50
32:17	50, 52, 59
32:17-18	50
32:17-19	50
32:18	51
32:19a, 19b	128 (n. 26)
32:20	50, 51-52, 128 (n. 26)
32:21-24	50, 51
32:25-29	50, 51
32:30-34	50, 51
32:31-33	50
32:35	50, 51
33	52-54
33—34	95
33:1	52, 128 (n. 26)
33:1-3a	52
33:1-6	52
33:1-7	80 (n. 221)
33:2	52
33:3a	52
33:3-4	52
33:3b-4	52, 53
33:3b-6	52, 53, 68
33:5-6	52, 53
33:5a	52
33:5b	52
33:5c-6	52
33:6	75 (n. 114)
33:7	53
33:7-11	52, 53, 54, 59, 68
33:9	59
33:11	50, 52, 53, 54, 59, 81 (n. 252), 129 (n. 55)
33:12-17	52
33:13-23	52
33:18-23	52
33:20	53
34	39
34:1	127 (n. 2)
34:1-4	114
34:7	62
34:15	58
34:27-29	114
34:28	127 (n. 2)
34:29-35	77 (n. 160)
35—40	77 (n. 160)
35:1—Num 10:28	54

Leviticus

15:20	37

Numbers

3:6	129 (n. 53)
3:31	129 (n. 53)
3:36	129 (n. 53)
10—Deut 34	54-60
10:29	54
11	115
11—12	54-55, 80 (n. 221), 113-14

Index of Biblical Passages

Reference	Pages
11:1-3	54, 55, 68, 128 (n. 26)
11:2	69 (n. 5), 90, 124
11:4-6	127 (n. 2)
11:16-17	54, 68
11:17	53, 54, 128 (n. 26)
11:24-25	54
11:24-30	53, 54, 68
11:25	54
11:26	54
11:28	54, 129 (n. 55)
11:29	55
11:30	54
12	55, 59, 68, 127 (n. 2)
12:1-15	54
12:3	69 (n. 5)
12:4	54
12:4-8	53
12:4-10	59
12:5	54
12:6	54, 70
12:6-8	109 (n. 60)
12:7-8	55
12:8	81 (n. 252), 114
12:10	128 (n. 26)
12:13	54
13—21	55
13:5	59
13:29	129 (n. 52)
14:22	122
14:28	70 (n. 20)
20:1-3	43
20:14-18	80 (n. 222)
21:5	55
21:7	54, 69 (n. 5)
21:20	81 (n. 237)
21:21-31	80 (n. 222)
22—24	55-57
22:1	81 (n. 237)
22:2-3a	55
22:2-21	56, 57, 68
22:3	56
22:3-21	55, 56
22:3b-7	55
22:5	57
22:6	80 (n. 232)
22:7	57, 80 (n. 232)
22:8	57
22:8-9	55
22:8-10	55
22:11	55, 80 (n. 232)
22:12-16	55
22:13	57
22:14	57
22:15	57
22:17-18	55, 80 (n. 235)
22:18	57
22:18b	56
22:19-20	56
22:19-21	55
22:21	57
22:21-35	56
22:22-34	55
22:22-35	56, 80 (n. 232)
22:36a	55
22:36b	55
22:36-40	57, 68, 86
22:36-41	55, 56
22:37	80 (n. 232)
22:38	55, 56, 57
22:39	55
22:40-41	55
22:41—23:26	57, 68
23:1-26	55
23:5	57
23:6	57
23:7	80 (n. 223)
23:7-10	80 (n. 223)
23:8	80 (n. 223)
23:12	57
23:14	80 (n. 237)
23:16	57
23:17	57
23:18-24	80 (n. 223)
23:19	80 (n. 223)
23:21	80 (n. 223)
23:22	80 (n. 223)
23:23	80 (n. 223)
23:27	55, 57
23:27—24:25	57
23:28	55, 80 (n. 237)
23:29	55
24:1-3a	55
24:3-9	80 (n. 223)
24:3b-9	55
24:4	78 (n. 190), 80 (n. 223)
24:5	80 (n. 223)
24:8	80 (n. 223)
24:10-15a	55
24:15-19	80 (n. 223)
24:15b-19	55
24:16	78 (n. 190), 80 (n. 223)
24:17	80 (n. 223)
24:25	55
25	58-59, 60, 61
25:1	58, 80 (n. 237)
25:1a	58

25:1-5	58, 61, 109 (n. 81), 115, 127 (n. 2)
25:2	58, 81 (n. 238)
25:3	58
25:3a, 3b	58
25:4	58
25:5	58
25:6-18	58
27:18-23	60
31:16	109 (n. 81), 115
32	58-59, 60, 61
32:1-17	61
32:1a	58
32:3	58
32:16-17	58-59
32:17	76 (n. 136)
32:20b	59
32:34-38	59
32:39-42	58
32:40	59

Deuteronomy

1—4	80 (n. 235)
1:1—4:43	60, 153
1:6—3:9	118
1:8	128 (n. 26)
1:12	128 (n. 26)
1:13	128 (n. 26)
1:15	128 (n. 26)
1:17	128 (n. 26)
1:21	76 (n. 144)
1:31	76 (n. 144)
1:38	62
1:45	76 (n. 144)
3:28	62
4:3	109 (n. 81), 115
4:10-12	128 (n. 26)
4:12	129 (n. 48)
4:15	129 (n. 48)
4:30	129 (n. 48)
4:33	129 (n. 48)
4:36	129 (n. 48)
4:40	76 (n. 144)
5:2-4	128 (n. 144)
6:5	122
6:16	43, 128 (n. 26), 129 (n. 56)
6:17	76 (n. 144)
6:18	76 (n. 144)
6:20-24	12
7:6	78 (n. 181)
8:2	123
8:3	123
8:15	128 (n. 26)
8:16	43, 123
9	118
9:8—10:11	118
9:9	128 (n. 26)
9:12	128 (n. 26)
9:13	128 (n. 26)
9:14	128 (n. 26)
9:15	128 (n. 26)
9:16	128 (n. 26)
9:17	128 (n. 26)
9:20	69 (n. 5), 124
9:21	128 (n. 26)
9:22	43, 128 (n. 26)
9:26	69 (n. 5), 124
9:27	128 (n. 26)
9:28	128 (n. 26)
10:8	123
10:11	128 (n. 26)
10:13	76 (n. 144)
11:13	78 (n. 181)
12—26	118-19
13:2 (EV 13:1)	70 (n. 11)
13:4 (EV 13:3)	70 (n. 11), 223 (n. 56)
13:6 (EV 13:5)	70 (n. 11)
14:2	78 (n. 181)
14:21	78 (n. 181)
15:5	76 (n. 144), 78 (n. 181)
17:4	120
17:12	123
17:14-20	120
18:5	123
18:7	123
18:15-18	109 (n. 60), 114, 119
18:16	119, 128 (n. 26)
21—24	80 (n. 235)
21:5	123
22:25	76 (n. 144)
22:28	76 (n. 144)
24:9	128 (n. 26)
25:17-19	128 (n. 26)
25:18	121
26:5b-9	12, 14
26:6-8	128 (n. 26)
26:10	78 (n. 181)
26:18	78 (n. 181)
27	107 (n. 28)
27:10	129 (n. 48)
27:15-26	15
28:1	76 (n. 144), 78 (n. 181), 129 (n. 48)
28:2	129 (n. 48)
28:15	129 (n. 48)

Index of Biblical Passages

31	58, 59-60, 62, 114
31:1-6	59
31:7-8	59
31:9-11	127 (n. 2)
31:9-13	59
31:14	95
31:14-15, 23	59, 60, 68
31:16-22	59
31:23	59-60, 68
31:24-30	59
32	59, 60, 81 (nn. 244, 245), 100, 114
32:10	78 (n. 181)
33	59, 60, 81 (nn. 244, 245)
33:8	25
34	58, 59-60, 81 (n. 251)
34:1-4	60
34:1-6	60
34:1-8	95
34:7-9	60
34:9	95
34:10	81 (n. 252), 127 (n. 2)
34:10-12	60, 68, 81 (n. 252)

Joshua

1	61
1—11	19, 61-62
1—12	61
1—24	60-63
1:1	62
1:1-2, 10-11	61
1:10-11	61
1:10-18	61
1:14	76 (n. 136)
2—11	61
2:1	61, 62
3—4	95
3:5-7	62
4:5	62
4:12	76 (n. 136)
6	62
6:6	62
8:18, 26	62
8:30-34	15
10:5-6	62
11:21—12:24	61
13—22	61
22:18	109 (n. 81), 115
23	61
23—24	84
24	13, 15, 61, 62, 98, 101, 107 (n. 25)
24:1	62
24:2-13	12, 107 (n. 25)
24:8	62, 129 (n. 52)
24:12	62
24:14	53, 107 (n. 27)
24:14-15	109 (n. 74)
24:15	129 (n. 52)
24:18	129 (n. 52)
24:19	62, 79 (n. 197)
24:19-20	107 (n. 28)
24:23	38, 62, 107 (n. 27)
24:27	62
24:29	62
24:32	62, 74 (n. 100), 75 (n. 135)

Judges

2:8	62
3:20	73 (n. 81)
7:11	76 (n. 136)
7:13	70 (n. 11)
7:15	70 (n. 11)
8:23	85
19—21	128 (n. 19)

1 Samuel

1—3	86, 106 (n. 7)
1:1—4:1a	84
1:10	69 (n. 5)
1:27	69 (n. 5)
2:1	69 (n. 5)
3	113
3:1	89
3:1—4:1a	88-89
3:3	89
3:4	25
3:4b	89
3:5	25
3:6	25
3:8	25
3:10	56
3:10-14	89
3:11-14	89
3:15	89
3:16	25
3:19—4:1a	88-89
3:20	109 (n. 60)
7	84, 86, 101
7—12	88
7:2—8:22	84
7:3	38
7:5	69 (n. 5), 90
7:6	84
7:13-14	108 (n. 33)
7:15-17	84, 87

8	84, 86, 120
8:4-17	85
8:6	69 (n. 5), 90, 116
9:1—10:16	84, 86
9:16	84
10:5	98
10:17-27	84, 86
11:12-15	86-87
12	84, 87, 107 (n. 25), 125
12:1-25	84
12:8-13	88
12:12	84
12:14-15	88
12:19	69 (n. 5), 84
12:19-23	69 (n. 5)
12:20-21	112
12:23	69 (n. 5)
12:25	88
13	99
13:8-15	84, 87, 106 (n. 7)
15	84, 87, 88, 91-92, 97, 99, 107 (n. 32)
15:1	108 (n. 42)
15:2-3	92
15:10	73 (n. 81), 89
15:16	89
15:18	92
15:22	26, 91-92
16:1-13	84
19:19	90
19:23	90
22:12	25
28:6	70 (n. 11)

2 Samuel

1:7	25
8:1	108 (n. 33)
20:1	102

1 Kings

3:5	70 (n. 11)
3:15	70 (n. 11), 72 (n. 51)
11	99
11:16—12:33	102
11:29	102
11:29-31	110 (n. 84)
12	51, 79 (nn. 196, 198, 199) 102-4
12—13	52, 127 (n. 12)
12—14	115, 116
12:1-20	102, 110 (n. 84)
12:8	103-4
12:16	102
12:19	110 (n. 84)
12:20	102
12:25-33	127 (n. 2)
12:26-31	110 (n. 84)
12:28	79 (n. 197)
12:31	110 (n. 93)
12:31-33	103
13	127 (n. 2)
13:33	25
14	111 (n. 97)
14:1-18	110 (n. 84)
16:1	73 (n. 81)
16:8	95
16:31	95
16:32-33	95
17—19	94
17:2	109 (n. 71)
17:6 (LXX)	95
17:8	109 (n. 71)
17:12	25
17:17-24	99
18	94, 114
18:1	109 (n. 71)
18:3	96
18:15	96
18:19, 20	98
18:20-40	95
18:21	109 (n. 74)
18:25-29	37
18:31	109 (nn. 60, 71)
18:31-32a	98
19	95, 97-98
19:1-3	96
19:8-10	109 (n. 60)
19:9	73 (n. 81), 109 (n. 71)
19:9-15	97-98
19:9-18	97
19:9b-11a	109 (n. 65)
19:9b-14	109 (n. 69)
19:10	99
19:11b-12a	97
19:14	99
19:15-18	95
19:16-21	95
19:19	94
20—22	93, 94, 95, 97
21:1	25
21:7	96
21:17	109 (n. 71)
21:17-24	94
21:25	96
21:28	109 (n. 71)
22:17-22	99

Index of Biblical Passages

2 Kings

1—2	94
1:3	98
1:1-17	96
2	95
2:12	97
3:9-27	97
3:15	98
4:18-37	99
4:33	69 (n. 5)
6:17	69 (n. 5)
6:18	69 (n. 5)
7	97
8:12-13	99
9	94
9:3	96
9:6	96
9:7-13	97
9:12	96
13:3-6	99
13:14	97
13:14-21	94
19:15	69 (n. 5)
19:20	69 (n. 5)
20:2	69 (n. 5)

1 Chronicles

7:27	62

2 Chronicles

6:20	69 (n. 5)

Nehemiah

1:4	69 (n. 5)
1:6	69 (n. 5)
2:4	69 (n. 5)
4:3	69 (n. 5)
9:18	79, (n. 197), 103

Job

33:15	70 (n. 11)
42:8	69 (n. 5)
42:20	69 (n. 5)

Psalms

80:2 (EV 80:1)	110 (n. 88)
99:1	110 (n. 88)
105:28	115
106:19-20	110 (n. 87)
106:28	109 (n. 81)

Isaiah

1:1	78 (n. 190)
2:1	78 (n. 190)
6:8	25
37—38	69 (n. 5)
37:16	110 (n. 88)

Jeremiah

1:2	73 (n. 81)
1:4	73 (n. 81)
1:11	73 (n. 81)
1:13	73 (n. 81)
2:2	73 (n. 81)
13:3	73 (n. 81)
13:8	73 (n. 81)
16:1	73 (n. 81)
23:25	70 (n. 11)
23:27	70 (n. 11)
23:28	70 (n. 11)
23:32	70 (n. 11)
27:9	70 (n. 11)
29:8	70 (n. 11)
37:3	69 (n. 5)
38:3	69 (n. 5)
42:2	69 (n. 5)
42:4	69 (n. 5)
42:20	69 (n. 5)

Daniel

1:17	70 (n. 11)
2:1	70 (n. 11)
2:2	70 (n. 11)
2:3	70 (n. 11)
9:2	73 (n. 81)

Hosea

1—3	126 (n. 1)
1:1	73 (n. 81)
3:4	116-17
4	127 (n. 10)
4:2	114-15, 127 (n. 2)
7:3-7	116-17
8:4	116-17, 127 (n. 15)
8:4-5	127 (n. 2)
8:4-10	116
8:5-6	115
8:10	116-17
8:12	114-15, 127 (n. 2)
8:13	127 (n. 2)
8:15	115
9:3	113-14, 127 (n. 2)
9:10	109 (n. 81), 115-16, 127 (n. 2)
10:1-15	116
10:5	115
10:5-6	115, 127 (n. 2)

10:7	116-17, 127 (n. 15)
10:9	116
10:15	116-17
11:1-4	115-16, 127 (n. 2)
11:2-3	115
11:5	113-14, 127 (n. 2)
12:3-7 (EV 12:2-6)	113, 127 (n. 2)
12:4*a* (EV 12:3*a*)	113
12:5*b* (EV 12:4*b*)	113
12:7 (EV 12:6)	113
12:13 (EV 12:12)	113, 127 (n. 2)
12:14 (EV 12:13)	113-14, 127 (n. 2)
13:4-6	115-16. 127 (n. 2)
13:10-11	116-17, 127 (n. 15)

Joel

3:1 (EV 2:28)	70 (n. 11)

Amos

1:1	78 (n. 190)
3:7	32
7:13	104

Jonah

2:2	69 (n. 5)
4:2	69 (n. 5)

Micah

1:1	73 (n. 81), 78 (n. 190)

Zephaniah

1:1	73 (n. 81)

Zechariah

1:1	73 (n. 81)
1:7	73 (n. 81)
10:2	70 (n. 11)

Index of Modern Authors

Aberbach, M. 79 (n. 198)
Albright, W. F. 8, 17, 66, 76 (n. 150), 77 (n. 163), 79 (n. 196), 80 (nn. 223, 227), 82 (n. 282), 86, 87, 88, 94, 107 (nn. 18, 19, 22, 23, 24), 108 (nn. 43, 46), 109 (nn. 61, 62), 110 (nn. 87, 93)
Alt, A. 38, 74 (n. 104), 77 (nn. 163, 169), 81 (n. 257), 107 (n. 17), 109 (n. 80), 110 (n. 86), 116, 117, 120, 125, 126 (n. 1), 127 (n. 15), 128 (nn. 20, 22, 23)
Anderson, B. W. 72 (nn. 54, 62)
Anderson, G. W. 18 (n. 59)
Andrew, M. E. 77 (n. 163)
Astruc, J. 19
Baltzer, K. 13, 18 (nn. 55, 60), 77 (n. 162), 88, 107 (nn. 26, 27, 29)
Barthélemy, D. 17 (n. 30)
Beer, G. 76 (n. 143), 78 (n. 192), 79 (n. 207)
Bentzen, A. 7, 17 (nn. 22, 24, 27), 69 (n. 2), 71 (n. 48), 72 (n. 49), 77 (nn. 161, 163), 111 (n. 102)
Beyerlin, W. 18 (nn. 55, 60), 52, 53, 77 (nn. 160, 165), 78 (nn. 170, 177, 182, 188, 191), 79 (nn. 200, 213, 214, 215), 80 (n. 221)
Boling, R. G. 8, 17 (n. 34)
Botterweck, G. J. 17 (n. 36)
Breckelmans, C. 77 (n. 159), 78 (nn. 184, 185)
Briggs, C. A. 76 (n. 136)
Bright, J. 16 (n. 1), 61, 62, 81 (nn. 254, 255), 107 (n. 18), 108 (n. 33), 109 (n. 61), 110 (nn. 82, 83, 86, 94), 111 (n. 97)
Brown, F. 76 (n. 136)
Budde, K. 64, 106 (n. 3)
Buss, M. 16 (n. 8)
Campbell, E. F. 18 (n. 55)
Carmichael, C. M. 128 (nn. 29, 31)
Carpenter, G. E., and Harford-Battersby, G. 16 (nn. 1, 3), 25, 27, 28, 39, 46, 47, 55, 56, 58, 59, 62, 69 (nn. 3, 10), 70 (nn. 13, 15), 71 (n. 24), 72 (nn. 50, 60), 73 (nn. 75, 80), 74 (nn. 100, 105, 108, 110), 75 (nn. 114, 118, 129), 76 (nn. 141, 145), 77 (nn. 160, 161), 78 (nn. 170, 187), 79 (nn. 194, 195, 219), 80 (nn. 222, 223, 232), 81 (nn. 244, 251, 264); 111 (n. 99)
Carroll, R. P. 108 (nn. 58, 59), 109 (n. 60), 128 (n. 35)
Cassuto, U. 7, 8, 17 (n. 36)
Clements, R. 73 (n. 83)
Coats, G. W. 76 (n. 148)
Coggins, R. J. 16 (n. 1)
Coppens, J. 16 (n. 1)
Cornill, C. 106 (n. 3)
Cross, F. M. 17 (nn. 30, 38, 39), 18 (nn. 58, 60), 76 (nn. 138, 140), 79 (nn. 196, 201, 204, 212, 216), 80 (n. 221), 81 (nn. 245, 253, 255), 90, 104, 106 (n. 7), 107 (nn. 13, 16, 17, 18, 38, 58), 109 (nn. 64, 66, 67, 69, 70), 110 (nn. 83, 86, 90, 91, 92), 111 (n. 98), 128 (n. 28), 129 (n. 57)
Dahse, J. 7, 17 (n. 29)
Driver, S. R. 16 (n. 1), 42, 47, 52, 69 (n. 3), 74 (n. 110), 76 (nn. 136, 141, 144, 145, 147), 77 (nn. 160, 170, 172, 181, 183), 78 (n. 192), 80 (n. 222), 81 (n. 248), 118, 121, 126 (n. 26), 128 (nn. 29, 31), 129 (n. 44)
Dussaud, R. 79 (n. 200)
Ehrlich, E. L. 70 (n. 11), 72 (n. 51)
Eichhorn, J. G. 106 (n. 1)
Eichrodt, W. 79 (n. 196)
Eissfeldt, O. 56, 61, 64, 71 (nn. 22, 39), 73 (n. 75), 77 (nn. 160, 161, 165), 78 (n. 188), 79 (n. 200), 80 (nn. 226, 228), 81 (n. 244), 85, 106 (nn. 1, 3), 107 (n. 13), 110 (nn. 83, 89), 111 (n. 99)
Engnell, I. 4, 6, 7, 8, 9, 10, 12, 15, 17 (nn. 23, 25, 26, 28, 36), 33, 44, 67, 81 (n. 255), 126
Fensham, F. C. 77 (n. 159), 127 (n. 16)
Fohrer, G. 94, 106 (n. 1), 108 (nn. 47,

51, 53, 58), 109 (n. 71), 127 (n. 1), 128 (nn. 21, 30)
Frank, H. T. 18 (n. 59)
Freedman, D. N. 17 (n. 35), 18 (n. 55), 76 (nn. 138, 140), 81 (n. 245)
Fuss, W. 63, 82 (n. 284)
Goedicke, N. 127 (n. 16)
Good, E. M. 81 (n. 263)
Gordon, C. H. 110 (nn. 87, 91)
Gray, G. B. 54, 55, 58, 79 (nn. 218, 220), 80 (nn. 222, 225, 232, 236)
Gray, J. 108 (n. 46)
Gressmann, H. 4, 9, 16 (n. 12), 17 (n. 13), 71 (n. 39)
Gunkel, H. 2, 3, 4, 7, 9, 15, 16 (nn. 5, 7, 8, 9, 10, 14), 23, 27, 34, 64, 69 (n. 5), 70 (nn. 12, 13, 15, 16, 21), 71 (nn. 38, 39), 72 (nn. 49, 63), 73 (nn. 84, 85, 87, 89), 74 (nn. 96, 100), 82 (n. 276)
Habel, N. 74 (n. 113), 75 (nn. 119, 122)
Halpern, B. 110 (nn. 86, 95)
Harford-Battersby, G. See Carpenter, G. E., and Harford-Battersby, G.
Harrelson, W. 110 (n. 89)
Harvey, J. 109 (n. 60)
Hays, J. 16 (n. 8)
Hertzberg, H. W. 69 (n. 5)
Hillers, D. R. 18 (n. 60), 192 (n. 162)
Hölscher, G. 82 (n. 274), 106 (n. 3)
Holzinger, H. 42, 75 (n. 129), 76 (nn. 147, 149), 79 (n. 194)
Humbert, P. 69 (n. 2)
Hupfeld, H. 2, 8, 16 (n. 1)
Hyatt, J. P. 18 (n. 59)
Kierkegaard, S. 71 (n. 30)
Kilian, R. 23, 25, 34, 70 (n. 19), 71 (nn. 28, 33), 73 (n. 82)
Kraus, H.-J. 16 (nn. 1, 6), 108 (n. 60), 110 (n. 96), 127 (n. 11), 128 (n. 35)
Kuenen, A. 16 (n. 1)
McCarthy, D. 18 (n. 55)
Marsh, J. 81 (n. 239)
Marti, K. 106 (n. 3)
Mauchline, J. 127 (n. 15)
May, H. G. 72 (n. 62)
Mays, J. L. 114, 127 (nn. 1, 3, 4, 7, 10, 11, 12, 17, 18), 128 (n. 19)
Mazar, B. 109 (n. 61)
Mendelsohn, I. 85, 107 (n. 14)
Mendenhall, G. 13, 18 (nn. 55, 60), 46, 77 (nn. 162, 164), 82 (n. 283), 111 (n. 100)
Metzger, B. 72 (n. 62)

Mihelich, J. L. 75 (n. 130)
Miller, P. D. 15, 18 (n. 61), 76 (n. 138)
Montgomery, J. A. 108 (nn. 46, 55), 109 (nn. 65, 75), 110 (n. 85)
Mowinckel, S. 10, 12, 18 (nn. 41, 42), 63-66, 82 (nn. 274, 277, 281, 282, 284)
Muilenburg, J. 78 (nn. 180, 183, 185), 107 (nn. 25, 27, 30)
Newman, M. 76 (n. 156), 77 (n. 167), 78 (n. 187), 80 (n. 221), 107 (n. 31), 108 (n. 35), 109 (n. 73)
Nicholson, E. W. 18 (nn. 54, 55), 45, 76 (n. 137), 78 (n. 191), 120, 128 (nn. 20, 21, 33, 34), 129 (n. 40)
Nielsen, E. 93, 108 (n. 48)
North, C. 16 (n. 1), 17 (n. 23)
Noth, M. 12, 13, 14, 15, 18 (nn. 62, 63, 64), 27, 28, 31, 33, 34, 40, 41, 42, 44, 52, 55, 59, 60, 62, 65, 70 (nn. 21, 22), 71 (n. 24), 72 (nn. 50, 54, 58, 63, 65, 66), 73 (nn. 80, 86, 87, 90, 91), 74 (nn. 95, 101, 107, 108), 75 (nn. 112, 114, 118, 119, 128, 130, 131), 76 (nn. 137, 142, 145, 153, 154), 77 (nn. 160, 165, 166, 167), 78 (nn. 172, 176, 179, 182, 184, 188, 189), 79 (nn. 195, 199, 202, 205, 207), 80 (nn. 222, 225, 235), 81 (nn. 252, 253, 255, 256, 257), 84, 94, 106 (nn. 10, 11), 107 (nn. 12, 13, 15, 25), 108 (nn. 33, 46), 110 (nn. 82, 84), 111 (n. 97), 128 (n. 28)
Nyberg, H. S. 127 (n. 15)
Obbink, H. T. 79 (n. 196)
Oestreicher, T. 117, 128 (n. 22)
Oppenheim, A. L. 70 (n. 11), 72 (n. 51), 111 (n. 101)
Pákozdy, L. M. 80 (n. 231)
Pedersen, J. 4, 5, 9, 10, 12, 17 (nn. 17, 19, 20, 21)
Pfeiffer, R. 27, 64, 69 (n. 3), 77 (nn. 160, 161, 169), 84, 106 (nn. 4, 9), 108 (nn. 46, 49)
Pope, M. H. 110 (n. 91)
Prochsch, O. 1 (n. 1), 58, 70 (nn. 15, 22), 73 (n. 75), 74 (nn. 96, 110), 77 (n. 161), 79 (n. 219), 81 (nn. 244, 251), 113, 114, 127 (nn. 5, 6, 8), 128 (n. 30)
Rad, G. von 12, 13, 14, 15, 18 (nn. 50, 51, 52, 53), 27, 28, 31, 36, 69 (nn. 4, 5, 6, 7), 70 (nn. 14, 15, 20), 71 (n. 49), 72 (nn. 50, 53), 73 (nn. 68, 72, 73, 86, 88), 74 (nn. 94, 98, 101, 102), 90, 107 (n. 25), 108 (nn. 36, 39, 41, 56, 57),

109 (nn. 63, 66, 76, 79), 110 (nn. 82, 83, 96), 117, 120, 127 (n. 18), 128 (nn. 22, 24, 25, 31, 36)
Redford, D. 28, 71 (n. 44)
Reed, W. L. 18 (n. 59)
Richter, W. 41, 74 (n. 113), 75 (nn. 119, 121, 122, 127)
Ringgren, H. 17 (nn. 36, 38)
Rowley, H. H. 16 (n. 1), 77 (n. 163), 126 (n. 1)
Rudolph, W. 1 (n. 1), 6, 9, 10, 11, 12, 15, 18 (nn. 44, 45, 46, 47, 48), 26, 27, 28, 33, 44, 48, 52, 55, 56, 67, 69 (n. 2), 71 (nn. 40, 41, 42, 47), 72 (n. 60), 74 (n. 109), 78 (nn. 171, 177 189, 192), 79 (n. 207), 80 (nn. 228, 233, 237), 81 (nn. 238, 250, 251, 252), 126
Ruppert, L. 28, 32, 71 (n. 43), 73 (n. 69)
Schmidt, H. 71 (n. 39)
Schmidt, J. M. 45, 77 (n. 157)
Skinner, J. 17 (nn. 29, 31, 32), 30, 69 (n. 9), 70 (nn. 12, 13, 21), 71 (nn. 46, 49), 72 (nn. 50, 52, 59, 64), 74 (nn. 95, 96, 97, 100, 101)
Smart, J. D. 126 (n. 1)
Smend, R. 70 (n. 15)
Smith, H. P. 84, 106 (nn. 2, 6, 8)
Smolar, L. 79 (n. 198)
Snaith, N. 106 (n. 2), 108 (n. 34)
Speiser, E. A. 69 (n. 5)
Spiegel, S. 127 (n. 8)
Stamm, J. J. 77 (n. 163)
Thenius, O. 106 (n. 2)
Vaux, R. de 79 (n. 196), 204 (n. 89)
Volz, P. 1 (n. 1), 6, 9, 10, 11, 12, 15, 18 (nn. 44, 45, 46, 47, 48), 21, 26, 28, 33, 34, 44, 67, 69 (nn. 7, 8), 70 (nn. 12, 15, 16, 22), 71 (nn. 40, 41, 42, 47), 126
Ward, J. M. 114, 115, 126 (n. 1), 127 (nn. 9, 12, 13, 14), 128 (n. 19)
Weinfeld, M. 120, 121, 122, 129 (nn. 38, 44, 45, 46, 47, 49)
Weiser, A. 61, 62, 63, 76 (n. 139), 81 (n. 244), 86, 87, 88, 89, 90, 92, 106 (nn. 5, 7), 107 (nn. 13, 32), 108 (nn. 33, 37, 43, 45, 46), 110 (n. 82), 129 (n. 43)
Welch, A. 117, 128 (n. 22)
Wellhausen, J. 1 (n. 1), 2, 27, 64, 70 (nn. 15, 21, 22), 72 (nn. 49, 50), 73 (nn. 75, 76, 86), 79 (n. 194), 81 (n. 251), 84, 106 (nn. 2, 10), 111 (n. 99)
Westermann, C. 108 (n. 42)
Whybray, R. N. 71 (n. 45)
Wiener, H. M 7
Wilcoxen, J. A. 16 (n. 8)
Willis, J. T. 17 (n. 23)
Wolff, H. W. 1 (n. 2), 18 (n. 49), 23, 25, 31, 33, 69 (n. 6), 70 (nn. 17, 18), 71 (nn. 29, 31, 33), 73 (nn. 67, 70, 74), 74 (n. 111), 76 (n. 155), 80 (nn. 234, 235), 92, 108 (n. 44), 109 (n. 81), 110 (n. 96), 123, 126 (n. 1), 128 (nn. 20, 34), 129 (n. 47)
Wright, G. E. 16 (n. 1), 18 (n. 54), 74 (nn. 106, 107), 75 (nn. 130, 131), 78 (nn. 184, 185), 81 (nn. 245, 246, 247, 252), 85, 99, 107 (n. 18), 109 (n. 68), 110 (nn. 82, 89, 96), 111 (n. 98), 114, 117, 128 (nn. 21, 25, 28, 32), 129 (nn. 40, 44, 50, 56, 58)

www.ingramcontent.com/pod-product-compliance
Lightning Source LLC
Chambersburg PA
CBHW031712230426
43668CB00006B/184